D0030371

Frantic Woman's Guide to
Feeding Family and Friends

Frantic Woman's Guide to Feeding Family and Friends

Shopping Lists, Recipes, and Tips for Every Dinner of the Year

Mary Jo Rulnick

WARNER BOOKS

NEW YORK   BOSTON

Warner Books

Time Warner Book Group
1271 Avenue of the Americas, New York, NY 10020
Visit our Web site at www.twbookmark.com.

Printed in the United States of America

First Edition: September 2006
10 9 8 7 6 5 4 3 2 1

Library of Congress Cataloging-in-Publication Data

To my husband Stu, for always responding to my "I've been thinking " statements with a smile, regardless of how crazy my creativity gets. Hugs and kisses for being my number-one fan and promoting my *Frantic Books* at hockey rinks, construction sites and softball fields.

To Deanna and Josh, who have heard "just try one bite" too many times to count, yet tasted the new concoctions to make me happy. You've taken the 600-page manuscript, the computer that's booted up and a pantry full of ingredients as a part of our lives.

Stu, Deanna and Josh, you will always bring sunny days to this frantic woman's life. I love you!

Acknowledgments

To Stacey Glick of Dystel & Goderich Literary Management: Your calmness during the frantic moments will always be appreciated. Here's to many more projects together.

To my editor, Adrienne Avila, for making this project so enjoyable and believing that I was more than a one-book wonder. To Elly Weisenberg, for cheerfully hearing another promotional inspiration and another and another and always offering such sound advice. To Beth de Guzman, vice president and director of trade paperbacks, for your tremendous enthusiasm and stirring the excitement on the editorial floor. To Kristen Azzara for your keen eye to detail and that little red pencil.

To Rachel Elinsky, Anna Maria Piluso, Kallie Shimek, Sharon Weiss, Bob Castillo, and Manuel Munoz and the wonderful Warner Staff for your expertise in taking my idea from manuscript to production, to bookstores and to the media. I love being a Warner author!

To Beverly Breton Carroll, my untraditional friend who has offered her invaluable insight for a traditional book. Thank you for your steadfast friendship and for keeping this impulsive gal grounded. To Sandra Miller-

Louden and Linda Tomsho: here's to exploring creative minds and reaching goals. The best is yet to come. To Mia Cronan, for helping this technical ditz get her Web site launched. To Amanda Lynch, for that kick in the right direction. To Sue Kolton, Barb Pisone, Linda Rumbaugh and Tawnya Senchur, for always being my cheerleaders. To Leah Merola: I know you're beside me in spirit as the frantic journey continues.

To the sassy gals of the National Subaru Women's Winter Tour: you rock when it comes to promoting. To allmy CCAC and Writer College students: your feedback takes me the next level. To the girls of the Big Dogs Softball Team: get out the shoes, it's time to party. To my parent, Jim and Carol Pick and my brother-in-law and sister-in-law, Barry and Carol Rulnick, for your unwavering love and support and always asking about the next chapter in the world of publishing.

A huge thank you to my contributors for sharing a piece of your frantic life with me and my readers: Jill Allan, Sue Ault, Greg Bacasa, Donna Benzenhoefer, Pat Benzing, Rita Bergstein, Marlene Bowser, Beverly Breton Carroll, Desiree Brusco, Linda Cannon, Jan Capasso, Flo Carroll, Michelle Cautela, Dawn Check, Chefs at University of Pittsburgh Medical Center Senior Living Division, Mia Cronan, Gloria Czesnakowski, Jan Devine, Diane Disk, Lucy Elder, Diane Etherington, Kim Farrar, Norma Farrell, Katharine Gaspari, Barb, Hawk, Loriann Hoff Oberlin, Teresa Isadora, mary Joyce, Celine Jurkiewicz, Eleanor Kane, Renee Knight, Sue Kolton, Janice Kucczler, Eve Laboon, Rosalie Lesser, Renee Lloyd, connie Lovus, Ruth Lundquist, Anne Marchesani, Christy Marr, Jeanette McGrath, Alrue McNiff Daniels, Sandra Miller-Louden, Kathy Nicoletti, Karen Novak, Darcy Olson, Carol Pick, Mark Pisone, Lindsey Rankin, Dale Reable, Joann Reid, Monica Resinger, Laurie Rizzo, Johanna Roediger, Michael Roediger, Deanna Rulnick, Stu Rulnick, Tawnya Senchur, Mercy Sergi, Arla Seybert, Loretta Shelapinsky, Tony Sparber, Ann Stankiewicz, Alice Stinemetz, Karla Strite, Deanne Thomas, Linda Tomsho, Andrea Verona, Ginnette Vinski of Pennsylvania Resources Council, Inc., and Debbie Williams.

And a special thank you to my faithful kitchen tester: Jan Bronder, Katharine Gaspari, Edna Hopkins, Dorothy Jones, Eve Laboon, Anne Marchesani, Deanna Rulnick, Josh Rulnick and Stu Rulnick.

Contents

Introduction

I t was while working on the first frantic book, *The Frantic Woman's Guide to Life,* that I realized I needed a better plan for feeding my family, a plan with meals tasty enough to work during calm times (few and far between) and fast enough to work during frantic times (never-ending, it seems)—a way to know that there was always something in the pantry for dinner, ready to go. Writing this book, I got a chance to really put that system to work during one of the most hectic six months of my life, which included the beginning of my son's senior year of high school, his nine college visits, his last basketball season for which I managed to be elected booster club president, my daughter's engagement, my twelve out-of-town speaking engagements, and a new puppy—and that's after I finished my day job as a regional events planner for a senior living facility. I had plenty of firsthand experience with what the system needed to encompass.

The grocery purchasing and cooking system had to be one that would make the dinner mealtime easier for busy women with too much to do and not enough time to do it. The recipes had to be doable ones, utilizing ingredients any frantic woman could find at her local grocery store. And the meals had to be ones that anyone, from novice to experienced chef, could make in about 30 minutes or so.

And so *The Frantic Woman's Guide to Feeding Family and Friends* came to life. I discovered I enjoyed this new frantic challenge, discussing family mealtime with other frantic women and creating easy meals that fit into our lives. Through trial and error, I was able to find ways to restructure my own kitchen to make it more efficient and discover tips to minimize the cleanup process, as I'm a messy cook. This system turned what was the mealtime blues into family dinnertime again.

As frantic women, we never know what life has planned for us. However, with *The Frantic Woman's Guide to Feeding Family and Friends*, you'll always know there's something planned for dinner. I hope you enjoy your new approach to dishing up meals for your family. Bon appétit!

Frantically,
Mary Jo

What's in This Book

I realize your days are full and you don't have time to waste, but don't panic—you'll find the help you need within the pages of this book.

The book is divided into five parts, each of which represents a different piece of the overall picture of evening meal preparation.

Part One, Prep Work, offers concrete tips for making your kitchen more efficient for meal preparation. You'll discover doable solutions for maintaining an organized kitchen, the minimal pieces of cookware you should have, marathon shopping tips, freezing food know-how and additional suggestions to simplify the crazy mealtime panic that occurs after the 5:00 whistle.

Part Two, Seasonal Menus, is the main section of the book. Here's where you'll find the two-week system that was designed with you, the busy woman, in mind. The system is structured around the seasons (though all our seasons may not be exactly alike) so that you can take advantage of the fresh produce available and items that are traditionally on sale. You'll be able to make more nutritious meals while saving money at the same time. And since people tend to eat differently in the summertime than they do in the cold days of winter, the menus will reflect that, too.

With this two-week system, you'll shop on Day 1 and stock up on the necessary ingredients to make fourteen days of family-friendly meals. You'll instantly eliminate the "What should we eat tonight?" problem that plagues most households. You will make a brief stop, known as a Pit Stop, toward the end of the first week to pick up a few fresh produce items and/or a gallon of milk. You will learn other time-saving and cost-efficient strategies, such as cooking an ingredient in advance for an upcoming meal.

You'll spot Potful of Knowledge sidebars that supply informational facts connected to specific foods that could help improve your overall health, and Basketful of Tips sidebars that explain tricks of the trade that will make your life a little bit easier.

Because time is so valuable, most dishes can be completed in about 30 minutes. A complete shopping list with the required ingredients to make the 14 dinners is included with each menu plan. The necessary items are separated into two categories as follows:

- **The Frantic Woman's Cupboard:** Staples you should have on hand. For your convenience, a detailed list of these items is given in Part One, Prep Work.
- **The Frantic Woman Goes Shopping:** Things you'll need to buy. Beside each listed ingredient, there will be a number in parentheses that designates the corresponding day. So if there's a particular product a family member can't eat, you'll know immediately the dinner that requires it, and you can decide whether you want to substitute a different food or mark all the appropriate-numbered ingredients off your list.

Along with the ingredient list, you'll find a sidebar called Pit Stop, which I mentioned previously. You'll also find a section called Unloading the Load.

In Unloading the Load, you'll discover what purchases need to be stored in the refrigerator and which ones should go directly into the freezer.

In the 14-day cycle, each recipe has a particular title, so you'll know right off what type of meal you will be serving your family. This will give you a heads-up on what the cooking process will be.

- Soup's On: Presents recipes linking the seasons and ingredients together.
- No-Cook Night: Gives you a break from using the oven, stove or microwave.
- Kids' Meal: Favorite foods that a typical kid would eat, so you know what to serve when young friends come visiting.
- Sandwich Board: Offers an easy-to-prepare meal and will usually be listed for Day 1, shopping day. After all, you've just shopped for two weeks' worth of food, so you deserve a break.
- Everyday dinner: Meals that can be served any day of the year.
- Retro Meal: Throwback to comfort meals that satisfy your hungry family.
- Seafood Fest: entrees that take advantage of the wonderful fish and more found in the sea.
- Light Cooking: Dinners requiring minimal cooking time.
- Slow Cook Tonight: Meals that are made in the slow cooker that can be made on any day that you'll be late coming home from the office or the kids might have an after-school game. (Be sure to read over the recipe the night before so you can easily prepare it in the morning. Naturally, you can prepare it the night before, too.)
- Old Tradition: A classic menu idea that is still as popular today as it was when it was first created.
- Backwards Meal: A breakfast selection served as the evening choice.
- I Can with a Can: Quick meals that use canned goods and/or boxed conveniences.
- Must-Go: A dish utilizing leftovers that must go so that they don't end up in the trash.
- Company's Coming: A dinner that would be fit for relatives, friends or the boss. And even if company isn't coming, aren't you worthy of a meal suitable for guests?

Life has a way of throwing roadblocks and emergencies in your path. And because you're a frantic woman, you never know what life has in store for you. As such, most of the time you can interchange these menus throughout the two-week cycle. For example, on Day 3, the kids have friends over, so insert the Kids' Meal into the evening you need it, and bump back the rest of the meals. You might need to defrost something in the microwave, but that's okay. The good news is you have something kid-friendly to serve Austin's buddies, and you're not calling 1-800-TAKEOUT.

Additionally, there are symbols that will advise you of a particular type of meal or preparation process.

🐾 Signifies meatless meals.

🍶 Double It tells you to double an ingredient in the slicing and/or cooking process in preparation for an upcoming meal.

🍶+🍶 This represents We Go Good Together suggestions, pairing up entrees with side dishes for which recipes are located in Part Four.

The recipes propose ways to vary the dishes, too. If you'd like more or less of a variety, you can

- Jazz It Up: Suggests ways to spice up the recipe.
- Dress It Down: Gives you the chance to delete an ingredient or two to save preparation time.
- Change It Up: Recommends options for changing the cooking method or main ingredient.
- Look Ahead: Gives planning tips, from pulling stored items out of the freezer to mixing together ingredients for a slow-cooker recipe for the next night's dinner.
- Simplify It: Offers shortcuts or additional information to make your life a little bit easier in the kitchen.

In Part Three, Weekly and Daily Specials, you'll find menus designed for specific events, such as birthdays, holidays and vacations.

Part Four, Side Dishes, is divided into two sections that contain supplementary recipes.

- **We Go Good Together Recipes:** Gives recipes for designated side dishes listed in the menu plan.
- **A Dish We Must Bring:** Provides a selection of recipes from appetizers to desserts that you can bring with you to a dinner party.

In Part Five, Extra Helpings, you'll find a quick reference for cooking terms, herbs, wine, stain removal and much more.

The Resources section offers a listing of all the books, movies, Web sites and other tidbits mentioned throughout the book so your fingers don't have to do the walking through the frantic pages.

Sure, there will still be days when you feel like you're swimming against the tide. But there's one thing you can count on: *The Frantic Woman's Guide to Feeding Family and Friends* has an easy-to-follow route mapped out for you. Although the two-week system might seem a little different at first, you'll find it will become second nature to shop once every 14 days and to "Double It" on certain ingredients when cooking. And best of all, once you adopt this two-week system, you'll have more time to spend with your family.

Your days might be chaotic, and life may not always go according to plan, but one thing you can count on is that your family dinners will always be planned. So let's get started!

Part One

Prep Work

[blank]

KITCHEN SURVIVAL

Before you run off to the store with your first grocery list, you need to do a little prep work to make sure your dinner hour will be as smooth and efficient as can be. This will make meal preparation easier. However, more importantly, it will give you that much-needed time for relaxing that you and your family crave.

Whether you like it or not, kitchen survival depends on how you arrange everything in this area, from your refrigerator to your cabinets. It's time to whip that kitchen into a manageable space that will have you whistling while you work.

The Frantic Woman's Work Stations

Meal preparation goes a lot smoother when your kitchen is organized. Now, it doesn't have to look like a Tupperware commercial, with containers lined up according to size and shape. However, if you spend a little time organizing now, you'll eliminate wasted time looking for utensils, ingredients and cookware later. An organized kitchen will reward you night after night.

Your first step is to create work stations like chefs set up in the restaurant industry; every kitchen should have separate stations for prepping, mixing and cooking. Each station should have the related items you'll need to perform certain tasks nearby suggests Karen Novak, events planner for a specialty foods store and creator of a children's cooking program called Cooking With Kids. This designated space doesn't have to consist of a customized island in the center of the room. A countertop can be divided into different work stations, with the cabinets and drawers above or below housing the necessary supplies. Novak suggests that the prep area include your cutting board, knife block, vegetable peeler, kitchen shears and scrap bags within arm's reach.

The mixing area should house mixing bowls, spoons, measuring cups, the electric mixer, food processor and a blender. This area needs an outlet within close proximity.

Put the cooking station near the stove. Place pots, pans, spoon rest, nonstick cooking spray, spices and foil nearby so they are handy.

Spices should be organized together in a rack and near the stove, if possible. However, if that isn't an option and you have to store them in a cupboard, keep them in a clear storage container the size of a shoe box. Using a single container allows you to pull out all your spices in one motion. To make this container even more efficient, write with a permanent marker the herb or spice on the top of the jar lid for easy reading. This way you're not pulling jar after jar out to see what is in it. For those cooks who like to use a lot of seasonings, separate the spices into two containers. One could hold the jars you use most often, and the other could hold the seasonings you seldom use.

Ruth Lundquist of Let's Dish: Make and Take Family Meals, one of the first retail meal preparation stores in the country where customers make 8 to 12 meals in just two hours, warns, "Don't hide commonly used utensils in a drawer. When they're hard to find, you won't use them." Linquist suggests you keep cooking spoons, spatulas and whisks in a canister next to your stove-top.

If space is limited, try using a wall rack that utilizes the vertical space in the kitchen. However, a canister or basket can easily be moved to and from the cooking area if space is limited.

Repeat this process for baking, too, if you like to make cookies, cakes and pies on a regular basis. A shelf with baking supplies near the area where you'll carry out the mixing, kneading or rolling will be most practical.

Basketful of Tips: To Cut or Not to Cut

Studies concerning what type of cutting board should be used in the kitchen have been contradicting, to say the least. Some say wood cutting boards shouldn't be used, because they're not bacteria-resistant. Other studies say wood boards should be used, as bacteria thrive on plastic cutting boards not on wooden ones. And some say glass boards are dangerous due to breakage. (I know many people who have glass boards, myself included, and they love them.) To stay on the safe side, keep two cutting boards: one for raw products, like meat and poultry, and one for fruits and veggies.

Use a permanent marker to label each board for its designated use. You can mark the board around the handle or on the back of it. This way, when other people want to use the cutting board, they will know which board to use. Be sure to sanitize the boards after each use. First, scrub the board thoroughly with hot water and soap. Then, sanitize by using 1 teaspoon of liquid chlorine bleach to 1 quart of water. Or use one part vinegar to five parts water. Allow the solution to sit for a few minutes, then rinse and air dry or pat dry with paper towels. Be sure to allow the board to dry completely before you store it. Bacteria cannot survive more than a few hours without moisture. To store, prop your board on one end, if possible.

The Frantic Woman's Cookware

Have you walked down the aisles in a kitchen store lately? Well, there's a gadget for everything. And you know what? That's just what they are—gadgets. They are in today and gone tomorrow; all those doodads take up valuable kitchen space, not to mention the time you spend moving them back and forth from one place to another, searching for something else.

With *The Frantic Woman's Guide to Feeding Family and Friends*, you don't need a lot of gadgets or cookware to make the suggested menus. In fact, you probably already have most of the necessary equipment. Additionally, you probably have a whole lot of stuff you don't need that's taking up precious space.

The chefs at University of Pittsburgh Medical Center's Senior Living Division run a busy kitchen, feeding more than 1,000 people three times a day at 8:00 A.M., 12:30 P.M. and 5:30 P.M. In order to have the meals served hot and on time, the kitchen needs to be well organized. The chefs suggest what to look for when purchasing your kitchen's bare necessities:

- 2 quart and 3 quart saucepans: Perfect for cooking sauces, rice, macaroni and canned soups and vegetables. You'll need at least two. Look for a flat-bottom pan that will sit evenly on the burner with straight sides and a lid. Purchase a heavyweight stainless steel one with an aluminum base. The heavier pots will hold the heat more consistently than lightweight ones.
- Roasting pan: Great for roasting beef, chicken, ham and turkey. Before buying a pan, consider the size of the meat you usually cook and buy a pan that is 2 inches larger. If it does not come with a rack, buy one to fit. By inserting the rack, the meat will stay out of the drippings.
- 12 inch skillet: Buy one with high, slightly sloping sides for versatility. You'll be able to make everything from eggs to stir-fries in it. For the frantic lifestyle, buy one that is heavyweight, heat conducting, and nonstick. Make sure you select one that comes with a fitted lid. A second skillet that is made of cast iron will be a perfect addition for the days when you need another skillet or when you'd like to make desserts, such as pineapple upside-down cake and Irish soda cake, which turn out moister when baked in a cast-iron skillet.
- Stockpot: Look for one with an 8- to 12-quart capacity with sturdy handles and a lid. An 8-quart one is a nice size for the frantic recipes. A tall, narrow pot eliminates excess evaporation and can be used to cook everything from corn on the cob to soups. For easier cleanup, the chefs recommend a stainless steel one with a heavy aluminum base.
- Dutch oven: A 5-quart pot with a vented lid will allow steam to escape when necessary. This pot is perfect for cooking stews and pasta, too. The original Dutch ovens were made of cast iron and used for campfire cooking. Be sure to buy an aluminum nonstick one in the housewares department rather than in the sporting

goods department unless, of course, you will be cooking on a campfire.

- 9 by 13-inch baking dish: Ceramic, metal or both. Having both is recommended. The ceramic baking dish will go from oven to table and still look great, especially for company meals. Additionally, it is perfect for stickier dishes that could ruin the finish on nonstick metal pans. Ceramic baking dishes come in oval and rectangular shapes; the one you choose is a matter of preference. An aluminum pan would be a better choice for making baked goods. It can be used for macaroni and cheese and baked apple slices, too. Purchase one that has a nonstick finish.

- Baking sheet: A nonstick Teflon finish will not only guarantee a faster cleanup, but will also allow cookies and biscuits to slide right off the sheet.

- Slow cooker: Look for a 5- or 6-quart cooker with a removable crock liner. The removable liner is a must for the frantic lifestyle. Cookers without this liner are harder to clean, as you can't submerge them in water. Also, you can prepare the slow-cooker meal the night before and refrigerate it in the removable liner, as it can go from counter to refrigerator to cooker. An oval-shaped cooker is a better shape for cooking roasts and whole chickens. A 5-quart cooker will hold a meal for four to five people, and a 6-quart one will hold a meal for five to six people. You should opt for the larger of the two if you have a family of four. This way, you will be able to use it for company meals and parties.

The following cooking equipment is *optional*. Part Two, Seasonal Menus, offers some grilling recipes. (Of course, such recipes can be done in the oven as well.) Part Four, Side Dishes, has recipes that recommend the other supplies.

- Grill: Choose one that uses a propane tank or natural gas. The grill will be hot and ready to cook meals within minutes. Choose a grill that has a dual burner to keep cooked foods warm while others are still cooking.

- Grill basket: A metal basket keeps veggies from falling through the grates.
- Pie plate: A 9-inch, round, glass, ovenproof plate will go from oven to microwave to table. This is an ideal piece for making dips, appetizers and baked goods.
- 2 quart casserole: Another piece that will go from oven to microwave to table. This is perfect for side dishes and desserts. Make sure the glass is ovenproof.

FRANTIC WOMAN FUN: The Kitchen Witch

If you think you have trouble in the kitchen, *you* ain't seen nothing yet. Grab a cup of coffee and kick up your feet as you read the mapcap story of culinarily-challenged Melody Seabright after she lands a job as the host of her own cooking show in *The Kitchen Witch* by Annette Blair.

The Frantic Woman's Kitchen Tools

There are certain tools you'll need while cooking. The good news is that you probably already have most of them stored in one of the kitchen drawers. Here's a list:

- Kitchen shears: These are an absolute necessity. Shears will cut meat and chicken into bite-size cubes in half the time it would take using a knife. And there's no chance for the chicken to squiggle all over the cutting board with kitchen shears. One snip is all it takes. And if your pizza cutter is missing, kitchen shears can cut pizza, too.
- An 8-inch chef's knife and a 3-inch paring knife are musts. Knives should be sharpened twice a year. Check your local fabric and notions store to see if they provide this service. If these stores offer sewing machine repair, they usually offer knife sharpening. Strange but true.
- Grater

- Manual can opener (a necessity when the power is out)
- Dry and liquid measuring cups
- Mixing spoons
- Rolling pin
- Strainer
- Vegetable peeler
- Whisk
- Basting brush
- Tongs
- Corkscrew
- Spatulas, also called pancake turners (should be plastic, not metal, so you do not scratch the Teflon finish on your nonstick cookware).
- Instant-read thermometer. Toss out the old one. The new thermometer is pencil-thin and makes a smaller hole in the meat. Additionally, it registers the temperature more quickly than the old ones.

In this book, the only small appliances you will need are the blender, electric mixer, microwave (though oven cooking methods are given as an alternative for you non-zappers), slow cooker (a must) and toaster.

> **(TIPS) BASKETFUL OF TIPS: Bag it!**
> Keep grocery-store bags handy. When you're slicing and dicing, opening cans and packages, and cleaning up the kitchen, pull out a plastic grocery store bag (one you'd get at checkout) and put it on the counter for anything that can't be pushed down the garbage disposal. You'll save yourself plenty of steps walking back and forth to the rubbish bin.

The Frantic Woman's Cabinets

After creating work stations, you might need to do some reorganizing of your cabinets. Keep dinnerware and silverware in close proximity to the dishwasher or sink for quicker cleanup.

Think upside down when it comes to bowls, pots and pans. Invert everything when storing. Put the smallest size bowl on the bottom, working up to the largest one. For deeper cabinets (ones that seem to fit your whole body before you actually reach the back of it) that usually hold pots and pans, consider buying a lid rack that screws onto the inside of the cabinet to make use of that dead space, recommends Debbie Williams, owner of Organizedtimes.com and author of *Common Sense Organizing*. Additionally, purchase wire shelves to double the space in cabinets with only one or two shelves.

Williams says not to forget the door-mounted holders that enable you to quickly grab your plastic wrap, aluminum foil and sandwich bags.

And finally, you can donate all those cookbooks that are taking up coveted space. After all, you have *The Frantic Woman's Guide to Feeding Family and Friends*. Just kidding!

FRANTIC WOMAN FAMILY FUN: Customized Place Mats

As you're whipping your kitchen into shape, have the kids create their own place mats. But, there's one condition. Each place mat has to have the layout for the tableware. The kids will have fun creating the place mats, and you won't have to explain the proper way to set the table ever again. And the next time you ask them to set the table, they can't say they don't know how.

Cut an 11- by 15-inch rectangle out of a piece of poster board or heavy cardboard. Have the kids draw a plate in the middle, a napkin with a fork in the center of it to the left of the plate, a knife next to the plate with the ridged edge facing the plate on the right and a spoon next to the knife. (One way to have the kids remember the fork is on the left is by reminding them that *fork* is spelled with four letters, and so is *left*.) A circle for the glass can be centered or slightly to the right of the plate. Allow the kids to color it any way they want. Once the artists have finished their masterpieces, cover them with thin, clear adhesive paper (found in the housewares department at most stores) or have it laminated at a copy store. PS: If you feel the kids could use some help in the manners department, check out *Elbows Off the Table, Napkin in the Lap, No Video Games During Dinner*, by Carol McD. Wallace; *365 Manners Kids Should Know* by Sheryl Eberly; or visit www.themannerslady.com.

The Frantic Woman's Pantry

An organized pantry will save you precious minutes of needless searching and rooting around for a specific item. Put frequently used items on lower shelves. Earmark one or two shelves for dinnertime ingredients. Line them up, with labels facing forward, according to the day they will be used, allowing you to move the stock forward. For boxed items, line them up library style, with spines facing forward. In the first weeks of using the system, post a sign stating "Dinner ingredients! Hands off or else." Announce a penalty for not following the rule, and enforce it. This could save you much aggravation in the days to come. There's nothing worse than reaching for the dinner ingredients only to discover that the bread crumbs and pineapples have disappeared.

For other pantry supplies, assign a designated spot for each category. For example, make a home on the bottom shelf, where the kids can easily reach, for breakfast makings. Designate another place for snacks and so forth. Once you give an item a home, don't switch it to another place. This will keep you from losing your extra stock, and it will become habit to reach for the box of pasta on the third shelf.

Put lighter items, such as noodles, pasta, and such, on higher shelves and save the middle ones for heavier items, like flour and sugar. This way, you're not pulling a 5-pound bag of flour off a top shelf and taking the chance of dropping it on the floor and having white stuff flying from one end of the pantry to the other.

Keep whatever you can in clear canisters or containers. At a glance, you'll be able to see how much sugar or flour you have remaining and when you need to write it on your Frantic Woman Goes Shopping list. You don't have to spend a lot of money on these clear containers. Check out your dollar, discount and thrift stores for bargains.

Monica Resinger, founder of Homemakersjournal.com and author of *Handy Kitchen Cleaning Tips*, offers this tip for a clean and organized cupboard: To avoid bottles and jars holding stickier ingredients, such as honey, syrup or oil, from adhering to your cupboard or refrigerator shelf, place these things on a lid from an old plastic container on the shelf.

Also, be sure to get rid of dead cabinet space. Adjust the shelving to make sure you are utilizing all of the space in the cupboard, or purchase a few under-the-shelf baskets to make use of the wasted space. These can be found at most superstores for a reasonable price.

An over-the-door vinyl shoe holder helps you sort smaller items, like Kool-Aid, ramen noodles and dry soup mixes, that can easily get lost amongst the crowd. This is great if shelf space is limited.

For a kitchen with limited pantry space but plenty of wall space, think about using a storage unit with doors, or be creative and use a small chest of drawers. In a country kitchen, you could paint the furniture white, then stencil it with a motif that would complement your decor. Canned goods, pasta, rice and more can be stored in the drawers.

Now that your pantry is organized, check out the detailed list of ingredients you will need to have stocked in your cupboards for various recipes in this book.

The Frantic Woman's Cupboard

Items that you should have on hand. If you don't, put them on your grocery list now!

Seasonings

Bacon bits
Basil (dry)
Bouillon granules (beef, chicken)
Chili powder
Chives
Cinnamon
Cloves
Cumin
Dill
French-fried onion rings (cheddar and/or original)
Garlic (fresh, minced, powder)
Ginger
Italian seasoning
McCormick Salad Supreme
Mustard (dry, ground)
Nutmeg
Onion (minced, powdered)
Oregano
Paprika
Parsley
Pepper (black, crushed red, lemon)
Poultry seasoning
Sage (ground)
Salt (seasoned, Season-All)
Thyme

Condiments

Ketchup

Mayonnaise

Mustard (prepared)

Dressings, Oils and Sauces

Honey

Maple syrup

Oil (canola, olive, peanut, sesame, vegetable)

Peanut butter

Salad dressings, bottled (Italian, ranch)

Soy sauce

Strawberry preserves

Tabasco sauce

Teriyaki sauce

Vinegar (balsamic, cider, white)

Worcestershire sauce

Wine (cooking: red, white)

Baking Needs

Cornstarch

Flour (all-purpose, or your preference)

Sugar (brown, cane)

Vanilla extract

Frantic Necessities

Aluminum foil

Nonstick cooking spray

Plastic wrap or wax paper

Bread, Chips and More

Bread

Italian-seasoned bread crumbs

The Frantic Woman's Refrigerator

The refrigerator is vital to the frantic woman's kitchen survival. Here are a few tips to keep that icebox chilled to perfection:

- Store condiments, bottled water, soda and other items that won't spoil easily on the inside of the refrigerator door. The door temperature fluctuates because of the constant opening and closing, and perishables can quickly spoil if placed there.
- Eggs should be kept inside the refrigerator in their original carton, not in the egg slots on the door created by the manufacturer. If you want to know whether your eggs are fresh, look for the three-digit number on the carton. According to the U.S. Department of Agriculture (USDA), number 001 represents January 1, and number 365 represents December 31.
- The coldest part of the refrigerator is the lowest shelf. When you are defrosting ingredients for upcoming meals, *do not* store items in this area or they probably will not be thawed in time.

- The produce crisper drawer has a slightly higher humidity level and will keep your produce fresher longer if stored there. Deli purchases should go in the drawer designed specifically for meats and cheeses.

(TiPS) BASKETFUL OF TIPS: Kitchen Mistakes

Ruth Lundquist and Darcy Olson, founders of Let's Dish, offer this list of eight common mistakes women make in the kitchen:

- Don't forget the primary purpose of your kitchen . . . to feed your family. Don't worry if it doesn't look like a made-for-TV kitchen. Better to be organized and have everything handy (recipes, reminders, grocery lists).
- Don't stock the cabinets with things that are unfamiliar. Coconut milk may look appealing on the Food Network and in the grocery store, but if you don't normally cook with it, it's just going to take up space and ultimately end up being donated in a food drive.
- Don't put the junk food at eye level in the pantry. Keep some healthy alternatives in easy reach for the kids. Real fruit looks great in a basket on the counter and even better in the hand of a hungry four-year-old instead of the fruit-shaped character of the day.
- Don't forget to rotate. Bulk buys are great as long as you actually use the food. "A friend once told me she found a pound of hamburger that was five years old buried in her freezer," says Darcy. "Oops . . . not such a great deal."
- Don't be afraid of convenience food. "Jarred sauces can be added to cooked noodles or veggies for a quick and elegant half-scratch dish," says Ruth.
- Don't buy things that are too nice to use. Pots and pans are meant to get dirty and "seasoned." If you're afraid to tarnish a copper pot, don't buy it.
- Don't go at it alone. If organization or cooking isn't quite your thing, invite a friend over to help you get started. It seems there's always someone who has it together. Most people are flattered to be asked to help and love the company as well.
- Don't forget to treat yourself. There's nothing better than a few fresh flowers to brighten your day, even if you spring for them yourself.

Thanks, Darcy and Ruth! You've captured the frantic way of cooking.

- Store leftovers and Double It ingredients in clear, airtight containers. You'll be able to see the contents at a glance without having to open the lid.
- As with the pantry, designate a home for your different refrigerated items. Have an assigned spot for milk, juice, eggs, leftovers and such.

The following items are sometimes listed under The Frantic Woman's Cupboard, so they should be kept on hand. You'll need them to prepare various meals.

The Frantic Woman's Cold Cupboard

Items you should have on hand:

Dairy
Butter
Eggs
Milk
Orange juice

BASKETFUL OF TIPS: Replacement Products

This system has been designed to make mealtimes easier for you. So don't get yourself into a tizzy over specific products. If you or others in your family are watching your diet, go ahead and use the product that fits your needs.

- Don't change your milk product because of a recipe. Buy and use what you prefer. If a recipe calls for a particular type of milk, it will state so.
- Don't get frazzled over the nonstick cooking spray versus butter dilemma. Nonstick cooking spray is on the staples list, but if you prefer to coat your skillet with butter or margarine, do so. Just be sure to use something to give you a smoother cooking session.
- Substitute low-fat or low-sodium canned goods and dairy products if family members need you to do so for health reasons.

THE FRANTIC WOMAN GOES SHOPPING

Your shopping attitude is going to change. Forget thinking that the trip to the grocery store is a dreaded task. From here on out, think of it this way:

- First, you're going to have an hour or so to yourself. Don't take the kids. Tell your spouse this will drive up the cost of your grocery bill by at least 10 percent, as surveys show. That alone should have the kids staying home. If you're a single parent, work out a system with another mom or dad to exchange babysitting time with each other on shopping days, or pay a teenager for the hour or two. You'll save more money than you would probably spend on babysitting fees.
- Try to do your grocery shopping in one location (or two if the stores are in close proximity to each other and you want to buy the loss leaders (sale items) at both stores).
- Don't forget to take the two-week Frantic Woman Goes Shopping list with you.
- Add any staples from The Frantic Woman's Cupboard that you might be running low on to your two-week grocery list.
- Make a continuous list of supplies needed for making breakfast and lunch. Also, don't forget any household supplies you might need. Psst! A dry-erase board situated in a prominent place in the kitchen will entice family members to jot down "milk" when they've gulped down the last of it.
- Pull out your coupons and match them to your grocery list before you leave home.
- Shop during off-peak hours. Tuesdays are great days to shop. Saturday, Sunday and Monday are usually the worst days to hit the grocery store.
- Mornings, before bankers' hours, are slow, because everyone else is getting kids off to school or going to work. If you have flex hours, it is well worth it to shop before work, take the bags home

to unload, and then go off to work. Or, if you have access to a refrigerator at your workplace, you can store any perishables in there until quitting time. Over the years, bank manager Donna Benzenhoefer has frequently used this shopping method. After 8:00 in the evening is slow, too. Most parents are on their way home with their kids from extracurricular activities.

- Shop when stores are stocked. Ask the store manager which day(s) the store gets its shipments. Shop the following day, and you'll find full shelves rather than bare ones.
- Unloading the bags is much easier when like items are grouped together—all pantry items in one bag, refrigerated items in another and so forth. Placing these like items together on the cashier's conveyor belt helps ensure the products will be bagged together. Or you can offer to do the bagging yourself.
- Keep poultry, fish and meat bagged separately when shopping. These items should not touch other food purchases.
- You'll probably need to stop at the store for milk, bread and produce at the end of the first week. Plan to do this during off hours to save time. (For more tips on purchasing produce midplan, see the Basketful of Tips in the Fall One Menus section.)

(TiPS) BASKETFUL OF TIPS: Online Coupons

Before you print out pages of online coupons, ask your grocery store manager if he or she accepts them. Some stores will no longer take online coupons because they've been stung by creative counterfeits.

(TiPS) BASKETFUL OF TIPS: Size Doesn't Matter

Size doesn't matter when it comes to buying various packaged items and canned goods. At one time, 16 ounces was the standard size for most canned items. Now, you might find the same kind of product in a 14-ounce or 15-ounce can as manufacturers downsize.

The Frantic Woman Returns from Shopping

You might think unloading two weeks' worth of groceries is time-consuming. But, remember the old cliché: *Kill two birds with one stone.* Well, girlfriend, you're knocking off two grocery trips at once. Though you have more groceries, to unpack, you're efforts are cut in half. You won't spend much more time putting away twelve pantry items than you would seven. Create a system that works for you when unloading the bags from the car. Would you rather your spouse and/or kids help you carry the bags into the house? Or would you rather do it yourself, because then you have total control over unpacking the supplies and putting them where you want them?

And whatever you do, make sure the kids keep their mitts off of your dinnertime ingredients. (See the tip under The Frantic Woman's Pantry.)

The Frantic Woman's Freezer

Freezing your bread, cheese, chicken, fish, meat and poultry will be a standard biweekly task. Some days, you'll freeze Double It items, too. Plan to take a few extra minutes during unpacking so you'll be organized for two weeks.

Be sure to mark all freezer packages for upcoming meals. For example, on a piece of masking tape, write "ground beef for Day 4" or "chopped broccoli for Day 7" and tape it to the product. If you're using freezer bags, write on the bag itself with a permanent marker. Again, don't forget to warn your family that these containers and packages, especially the ones that might contain favorite foods like cheese, are not fair game for snack time.

To keep your mealtime ingredients tasting fresh when they come out of the freezer, follow these tips:

- Keep freezer temperature at 0 degrees Fahrenheit or colder.
- Freeze foods immediately after purchasing.
- Let just-cooked food cool before freezing so it does not raise the temperature of the freezer. You can cool food quickly by setting

it outside in frigid weather or by placing it in a pan of cold or ice water. Stir the food occasionally to be sure all contents are cooled before freezing.

- Packaging the items properly is extremely important to keep foods from drying out. Make sure the container or wrap you use is sealed tightly and will not leak.
- Glass and hard plastic containers, plastic bags meant for freezer use and aluminum foil should be airtight, moisture-proof and vapor-proof. Be sure to press out the air, and wrap the packaging tightly around the food. A double layer of wrap will provide an extra layer of insulation against moisture.
- Food expands when it is frozen. Allow ½-inch headspace in all containers.
- Label all containers with the contents and the designated day it will be served. Add the recipe name, too, if you want to know what meal it represents, for example, boneless chicken, Day 4, "Finger Lickin' Fried Chicken."
- Foods that need to be frozen should be placed in separate areas of the freezer or along the bottom shelf or side walls. Do not stack packages until their contents are frozen.
- Do not refreeze foods that have been thawed.
- Thaw frozen foods in the refrigerator the day/night before. You will be reminded of this in the Look Ahead tips at the end of the recipes.

TiPS BASKETFUL OF TIPS: Freezer Power
In case of a power outage, do not open the freezer door. A fully loaded freezer will hold its temperature for two days

---

THE FRANTIC WOMAN COOKS

The time has come. You're ready to prepare your first frantic meal. Before you race off, keep these tips in mind:

- Fill the sink with hot,s sudsy water before you start cooking. Drop utensils, dishes and pots into the water as you are finished using them. Cleanup will be a lot easier.
- Keep a larger spoon rest or coffee mug on your stove (or close to it). This eliminates the chance of having sauce caked on your stove top. If the dinner you're stirring is gooey, a mug will contain the goo better than a flat spoon rest.
- Read the recipes from beginning to end before you start slicing and dicing. Think about it—you wouldn't pull out of your garage to drive to a new destination without looking over the map first.

The Frantic Woman's Cheat Sheet

After a hectic day, you might be really distracted and drawing a blank about a specific measurement. Or maybe you need to find a quick substitution for a forgotten item. In that case, use the following charts to help you get through a kitchen emergency or two:

AVERAGE SERVING

Most of the recipes in this book will serve four to six people, depending on the size of the serving. Here are the average single servings.

TITLE TK	
FOOD	AMOUNT
Fish, meat and poultry	4 ounces; 1/4 pound
Fruits and vegetables	1/2 cup
Desserts	1/2 cup

STANDARD WEIGHTS AND MEASURES	
A dash	8 drops
1 teaspoon	60 drops
1 tablespoon	3 teaspoons
1 ounce	2 tablespoons
¼ cup	4 tablespoons; 2 ounces
⅓ cup	5⅓ tablespoons
½ cup	8 tablespoons; 4 ounces
1 cup	16 tablespoons; 8 fluid ounces, ½ pint
1 pint	2 cups; 16 fluid ounces
1 pound	16 ounces
1 quart	2 pints; 32 fluid ounces
½ gallon	8 cups; 64 fluid ounces; 2 quarts
1 gallon	16 cups; 4 quarts; 128 fluid ounces
1 peck	8 quarts
1 bushel	4 pecks
1 dram	$\frac{1}{16}$ ounce
1 gram	$\frac{1}{30}$ ounce
1 kilo	2⅕ pounds
1 liter	1 quart (approximate)

SIMPLE EQUIVALENTS		
INGREDIENT	AMOUNT	EQUIVALENT
Almonds	1 pound	3 cups, chopped
Apples, raw	1 pound	6 cups, cooked
Beans, dried	1 pound	6 cups, cooked
Bread	1 slice	¾ cup soft bread cubes
Butter	1 stick	½ cup; ¼ pound; 8 tablespoons
Cabbage, raw	1 pound	4 cups, shredded
Celery, fresh	1 bunch	4 cups, diced
Chicken, cooked	2½ to 3 pounds	2½ cups, diced
Corn on the cob	4 ears	1 cup kernels
Cream, heavy	1 cup	2 cups, whipped

SIMPLE EQUIVALENTS (CONTINUED)		
INGREDIENT	AMOUNT	EQUIVALENT
Garlic	1 clove	⅛ teaspoon garlic powder
Ground beef, uncooked	1 pound	2 cups, cooked
Herbs, fresh	1 tablespoon	½ teaspoon, dried
Lemon	1 whole	2½ to 3½ tablespoons juice
Macaroni	1 pound	9 cups, cooked
Mushrooms, fresh	1 pound	6 to 8 ounces, jarred
Mustard, dry	1 teaspoon	1 tablespoon, prepared
Noodles, uncooked	3 cups	4 cups, cooked
Onion, fresh	¼ cup chopped	1 tablespoon dry minced onion
Parmesan cheese	4 ounces	1 cup, grated
Pineapple, fresh	1 large	4 cups, cubed
Sour cream	8 ounces	1 cup
Spaghetti, uncooked	1 pound	8 cups, cooked
Sugar, brown	1 pound	2¼ cups, packed
Sugar, cane	1 pound	2¼ cups
Walnuts	1 pound	3¾ cups, chopped

THE FRANTIC WOMAN'S EMERGENCY SUBSTITUTIONS

You know you had that ingredient, but for some odd reason you can't locate it. Maybe one of the family members forgot to put it back or used it for something else. Remember the old cliché, *When life gives you lemons, make lemonade*. Use this list of substitutions to replace a missing ingredient. For a comprehensive list of substitutions, go to www.foodsubs.com.

INGREDIENT	AMOUNT	SUBSTITUTION
Baking powder	1 teaspoon	½ teaspoon cream of tartar and ¼ teaspoo baking soda
Buttermilk	1 cup	Add 1 tablespoon vinegar to 1 cup milk, stir and let stand for 5 minutes to thicken
Cornstarch	1 tablespoon	2 tablespoons flour
Cream sauce	1½ cups	10.75-ounce can cream-style soup plus ¼ cup liquid
Chili sauce	1 cup	8 ounces tomato sauce plus ½ cup sugar and 2 tablespoons vinegar
Mayonnaise	1 cup	1 cup sour cream; 1 cup yogurt; or 1 cup cottage cheese

Ingredient	Amount	Substitution
Tomato juice	1 cup	1/2 cup tomato sauce plus 1/2 cup water
Wine, red	any amount	replace with same amount of grape or cranberry juice
Wine, white	any amount	replace with same amount of apple or white grape juice

THE FRANTIC WOMAN'S HEALTHY SUBSTITUTIONS

Replace the standard ingredient with the substitution if you're trying to eat healthier.

Standard Ingredient	Healthier Ingredient
1 pound ground beef	1 pound ground turkey
1 egg	2 egg whites; 1/4 cup egg substitute
1 cup cream	1 cup evaporated skim milk
1 cup sour cream	1 cup plain nonfat yogurt; 1 cup low-fat cottage cheese plus 1 teaspoon lemon juice, blended smooth
1 ounce cream cheese	1 ounce Neufchâtel cheese
1 cup shortening	7 ounces vegetable oil

THE FRANTIC WOMAN'S OVEN TEMPERATURE GUIDE

Oven Temperatures	
250 degrees	very low
300 degrees	low
325 degrees	moderately low
350 degrees	moderate
375 degrees	moderately hot
400 degrees	hot
425 degrees	very hot
500 degrees	extremely hot

THE FRANTIC WOMAN WITHOUT A SLOW COOKER

Having a slow cooker can save you lots of cooking and preparation time, as most ingredients are dumped into the cooker, and then you can forget about them all day long. Most oven recipes can easily be converted into slow-cooker recipes. It take a little bit of knowledge to convert slow-cooker recipes to the oven. If, for some reason, you are without a slow cooker, here are some tips to help you make the conversion from slow cooker to oven:

- Low on a slow cooker is about 180 degrees.
- High on a slow cooker is about 300 degrees.
- Liquids in slow cookers do not evaporate as they do in oven cooking, so you might need to add more liquids (sometimes double) to a recipe you converted from slow cooking to oven cooking. Add a little extra liquid at a time.
- When converting a recipe from slow cook to oven that includes raw vegetables, sautée the vegetables beforehand to ensure tenderness.
- For casseroles, convert a 4- to 5-hour slow-cook recipe into an oven recipe by cooking at 350 degrees for about 30 minutes.
- For roasts, cook in a 350-degree oven for about 30 to 40 minutes per pound as a general rule.

THE FRANTIC WOMAN CLEANS

I realize this is a cookbook, but everyone could use a few extra shortcuts to make cleanup time quicker. If you're in a hurry, skip these additional tips from Monica Resinger. But, you never know when one of her suggestions could really come in handy.

- Save time cleaning dinner dishes. Tell everyone to rinse their own plates. (You should already have a sink full of hot, soapy water.)
- Get a better grip when scrubbing and protect your hands at the same time. Place a sponge over the scouring pad, such as Brillo, before you start scrubbing.
- Use a paint scraper or putty knife to remove baked on or cemented goo from stove tops, countertops or floors.
- Baking soda makes an excellent scouring powder, and it deodorizes, too.

One thing to bear in mind when it comes to cleaning: The Pennsylvania Resources Council (PRC) recommends reducing the amount of toxic products you use in your house. This will keep you, your family and your environment healthy. There are many manufacturers, such as Allens Naturally, Earth Friendly Products, Ecover, Seventh Generation and Sun and Earth that offer alternative cleaning products. (See Resources section for contact information.)

To help you make your own alternative products, the Pennsylvania Resources council, Inc. (PRC), in its book *Hazardous Waste in the Home: How to Safeguard Your Health and the Environment,* offers these cleaning solutions made with ingredients that you probably have sitting in your cupboards. For frantic women, that's fewer things you need to buy at the grocery store.

- All-purpose cleaner: In a spray bottle, add 1 quart warm water, 1 teaspoon liquid soap, 1 teaspoon borax and ¼ cup undiluted white vinegar. Use for cleaning countertops, floors, walls and more.
- Disinfectant: Use ¼ cup of borax in one gallon of hot water. Leave borax solution on to prevent mold or mildew from forming.
- Drain cleaner: Pour ¼ cup baking soda down the drain, followed by 2 ounces of vinegar. Cover the drain and allow it to sit for 15 minutes. Rinse with 2 quarts of boiling water. Use this treatment regularly to prevent clogged drains and to keep them smelling fresh. Get rid of grimy drain buildup by pouring boiling water down the drain on a weekly basis.
- Glass cleaner: Mix 1 quart of warm water with ¼ cup white vinegar (or 2 tablespoons lemon juice) in a spray bottle. Squirt and wipe clean.
- Oven cleaner: In a spray bottle, add 1 quart warm water, 2 teaspoons borax and 2 tablespoons liquid soap. Spray on solution and allow it to sit for 20 minutes before cleaning it off. To clean a glass oven door, dip a wet sponge in baking soda.
- Vinyl floor cleaner: In a bucket, combine 1 gallon warm water and ½ cup white vinegar (or ¼ cup borax).
- Wood floor cleaner: For unvarnished floors, dampen mop with mild vegetable oil soap.
- No-wax floor cleaner (polyurethane or Swedish finishes): Add one part vinegar to ten parts water in a bucket.

- Chrome fixture cleaner: Shine wet chrome fixtures by rubbing with newspaper, or rub with baby oil and a soft cloth. (Test first on an inconspicuous area.)

The Frantic Woman's Kitchen Smells Good

No one wants to cook in a stinky kitchen. But once in a while, there's a lingering odor. It could be from something you cooked or perhaps from something that spoiled. Whatever causes your nose to scrunch up, get rid of it with Monica's suggestions.

- Dab essential or aroma oil onto lightbulbs. When they're turned on, the heat of the bulbs will release the aroma.
- Car fresheners aren't for cars only. Hang them from kitchen cupboard knobs or other places in which they can hang.
- Use undiluted vinegar to remove odors from just about anything. Spray it on walls, chair cushions, throw rugs (test an inconspicuous area first) and so on. Or set it out in a bowl. And don't worry about the vinegar smell—it dissipates along with the original odor.
- To rid a storage container of a persistent odor, place crumpled newspapers inside it, and seal it overnight.

ONE LAST FRANTIC THOUGHT FOR THE FRANTIC WOMAN

Okay, you've heard this many times before, but here it is again: Be sure to put everything back in its original home. You'll eliminate time spent searching for an item that was not returned to its proper place. And if you had the option, would you rather spend five minutes searching for the jar of dill or sipping a hot cup of tea? If you multiply 5 wasted minutes a day by 365 days a year, that's a little more than 30 precious hours a year you could use to do something for youself!

Part Two

Seasonal Menus

[blank]

AUTUMN LEAVES ARE FALLING

The carefree days of summertime are replaced by the chilly and hectic days of autumn. The kids are back in school, extracurricular activities are in full swing, and you need substantial meals to satisfy the appetites of your energetic family. In this next section, you'll discover meals full of flavor that you can put together and serve ASAP.

FALL FARMER'S MARKET

The fruits and vegetables below are in season during the fall months. Keep in mind that some are readily available for a shorter time than others. They are marked with an asterisk. Use this list to make healthier choices for side dishes, lunches and snacks.

Fruits		
Apples	Figs*	Papayas
Avocados	Grapefruits*	Pears
Bananas	Grapes	Persimmons*
Cranberries	Lemons	Pomegranates
Coconuts	Limes*	Tangerines*
	Oranges*	Tangelos

<u>Vegetables</u>

Beans (green, waxed*)

Beets*

Belgian endives

Broccoli

Brussels sprouts*

Cabbage

Carrots

Cauliflower

Celery

Corn*

Cucumbers*

Eggplant*

Fennel

Lettuce

Mushrooms*

Onions

Parsnips*

Peppers (chile, sweet)

Potatoes (sweet, white)

Rutabagas

Squash (winter)

Turnips

* Designates the fruits and vegetables that have a shorter peak season than the others on the list

FALL PLAN ONE MENUS

Day 1—Sandwich Board: Have-It-Your-Way Hoagies

Day 2—Slow Cook Tonight: Ginger Roast

Day 3—Everyday Dinner: Chicken Triangles

Day 4—Retro Meal: Mom's Comfort Macaroni

Day 5—Everyday Dinner: Purple Parmesan (Shh! It's eggplant!)

Day 6—Backwards Meal: Cheese Omelet

Day 7—Everyday Dinner: Savory Stew

Day 8—Seafood Fest: Boxcar Fish

Day 9—Must-Go: Beef Pot Pie

Day 10—Kids' Meal: Beef Gravy Train

Day 11—Slow Cook Tonight: Chili Billie

Day 12—I Can with a Can: Chicken à la Can

Day 13—Must-Go/No-Cook Night: Taco Salad

Day 14—Company's Coming: Shrimp and Chicken Pizzazz

THE SHOPPING LISTS

The Frantic Woman's Cupboard

The following are staples you should have on hand for Fall Menu Plan One. If not, put them on your grocery list.

FALL PLAN ONE STAPLES

Seasonings
  Bacon bits
  Basil (dried)
  Chili powder
  Garlic (minced, powder)
  Pepper*
  Salt*
  Thyme

  ### Side Dishes
  Cinnamon
  Cayenne pepper
  Chives
  Parsley

Condiments
  Ketchup

Dressings, Oil and Sauces
  Oil (olive,* vegetable)
  Wine (red, white)
  Worcestershire sauce

  ### Side Dishes
  Italian salad dressing

Baking Needs
  Flour
  Sugar (cane)

Bread, Chips and More
  Bread crumbs (Italian seasoned)

Frantic Necessities
Foil

Nonstick cooking spray

Dairy
Butter* or margarine

Eggs

Milk

* Ingredient needed for both main and side dishes

The Frantic Woman Goes Shopping

MAIN-DISH INGREDIENTS YOU'LL NEED TO BUY

Produce: Fruits
1 small lemon (Day 8)

Produce: Veggies
Toppings for hoagie and taco salad, your preference (Days 1, 13)

5 small yellow onions (Days 2, 4, 7, 8, 11)

1 green pepper (Day 4)

1 large eggplant (Day 5)

1 12-ounce carton snowcap mushrooms (Days 7, 14)

1 bunch celery (Day 8)

1 16-ounce bag ready-to-eat salad mix (Day 13)

1 tomato (Day 14)

 PIT STOP: Keep It Fresh

You might want to hold off on buying 1 bunch celery, 1 lemon, 1 carton (12 ounces) mushrooms, 1 bag (16 ounces) salad mix and 1 tomato until later in the week, as this produce will not be used until then. You'll be reminded to make a pit sstop on Day 5.

Seasonings
2 1.25-ounce envelopes brown gravy mix (Day 2)

1 1.25-ounce envelope Hidden Valley Ranch salad dressing mix (Day 3)

Dressings, Oils and Sauces
2 32-ounce jars marinara sauce (Days 4, 5)

Canned Goods and Bottles
3 14.5-ounce cans beef broth (Days 2, 7)

1 14.5-ounce can stewed tomatoes (Day 7)

1 14.5-ounce can beef gravy (Day 10)

1 16-ounce can pinto beans (Day 11)

1 16-ounce can red kidney beans (Day 11)

2 14.5-ounce cans diced tomatoes (Day 11)

1 10.5-ounce can cream of mushroom soup (Day 12)

1 8-ounce can peas (Day 12)

1 16-ounce jar salsa (Day 13)

1 2.5-ounce can black olives (Day 14)

Noodles, Pasta and Rice
1 16-ounce package elbow macaroni (Day 4)

1 13.3-ounce box instant mashed potatoes (Day 10)

1 16-ounce package linguine (Day 14)

Bread, Chips and More
5 6-inch hoagie rolls (Day 1)

1 small box gingersnap cookies (Day 2)

6 slices whole-grain bread, or your preference (Day 8)

Deli
10 thick deli meat slices (about ½ pound), your preference (Day 1)

14 thick cheese slices (about ¾ pound), your preference (Days 1, 6)

Fish, Meat and Poultry

    1 3-pound chuck roast (Day 2)
    4½ pounds skinless, boneless chicken breasts (Days 3, 12, 14)
    2 pounds ground beef (Days 4, 10)
    2 pounds tilapia or orange roughy fillets (Day 8)
    1 pound cooked shrimp, peeled and deveined (Day 14)

Dairy

    1¼ packages cream cheese (Day 3)
    3 tubes refrigerated crescent rolls (Days 3,9)
    3 cups (12 ounces) Mozzarella cheese (Days 5, 14)
    ½ cup (2 ounces) Parmesan cheese, grated (Day 5)
    1 tube refrigerated biscuits (Day 12)
    ½ cup (2 ounces) cheddar cheese, shredded (Day 13)
    1 8-ounce container sour cream (Day 13)

Frozen

    1 24-ounce bag mixed stew vegetables (Day 7)

JAZZ IT UP INGREDIENTS YOU'LL NEED TO BUY

Produce: Veggies

    1 hot pepper (Day 1)
    1 12-ounce bag baby cut carrots (Day 2)
    1 8-ounce carton snowcap mushrooms, sliced (Day 3)
    1 bunch celery (Day 4)
    1 small green pepper (Day 6)
    1 small tomato (Day 6)
    Veggies, your preference (Day 9)
    1 yellow onion (Day 10)

Canned Goods and Bottles

    1 15-ounce can stewed tomatoes (Day 4)
    1 2.5-ounce can sliced black olives (Day 6)

1 10.75-ounce can beef gravy (Day 10)
1 2.5-ounce jar diced pimentos (Day 12)
1 8-ounce can asparagus (Day 14)

Deli

4 slices mozzarella cheese (Day 8)
2 cups (8 ounces) cheddar sheese, shredded or grated (Day 11)
½ cup pepperoni (Day 13)

Fish, Meat or Poultry

1 pound stew meat or veal (Day 7)

PIT STOP: Keep It Fresh
You might want to hold off buying these Jazz It Ups ingredients until later in the plan, around Day 5: Veggies, your preference, and 1 yellow onion.

WE GO GOOD TOGETHER INGREDIENTS YOU'LL NEED TO BUY

Produce: Fruit

6 Yellow Delicious or Jonathan apples (Day 5)
1 lemon (Day 5)
Fruit, your preference (Day 12)

Produce: Veggies

1 16-ounce bag coleslaw mix (Day 1)
1 squash (Day 3)
1 red pepper (Day 8)
1 red onion (Day 8)
2 pounds green beans (Day 14)
1 bunch dill (Day 14)

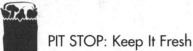

PIT STOP: Keep It Fresh
Skip buying these We Go Good Together ingredients until Day 5:
fruit of your choice, 2 pounds green beans, 1 bunch dill and
1 red onion.

Dressings, Oils and Sauces

1 12-ounce jar coleslaw dressing (Day 1)
¼ cup barbecue sauce (Day 8)

Canned Goods and Bottles

1 14-ounce can black beans (Day 8)
1 16-ounce jar applesauce (Day 9)

Noodles, Pasta and Rice

1 16-ounce bag wide egg noodles (Days 2, 11)
2 cups (4 servings) white or brown rice (Day 7)

Baking Needs

1 package fruit-flavored gelatin (Day 13)

Bread, Chips and More

White bread (Days 4, 6)
Italian bread (Days 5, 10)
Rolls, your preference (Day 11)

Fish, Meat and Poultry

1 pound ham or bacon (Day 6)
Dairy
¼ cup (1 ounce) feta cheese (Day 14)

Frozen

1 20-ounce package frozen corn (Day 8)

Unloading the Load

To make the unloading and cooking process a lot easier, store your ingredients as directed below. Be sure to mark each package with the designated day so you will know which package to defrost and cook when the time comes.

- Store the chuck roast in the refrigerator for Day 2, Ginger Roast.
- If you're feeling energetic, use kitchen shears to cut 2 pounds of chicken into bite-size pieces for Day 14, Shrimp and Chicken Pizzazz, and freeze.
- Freeze the remaining chicken for Day 3, Chicken Triangles.
- Freeze the ground beef for Day 4, Mom's Comfort Macaroni.
- Freeze 4 slices of cheese for Day 6, Cheese Omelet, if your kids will eat it beforehand.
- Freeze the fish fillets for Day 8, Boxcar Fish. Freeze the shrimp for Day 14, Shrimp and Chicken Pizzazz.
- Freeze the 4 slices of mozzarella cheese for Day 8, Jazz It Up.
- Freeze the 1 pound of stew meat or veal for Day 7, Jazz It Up.
- Freeze the grated or shredded cheddar cheese for Day 11, Jazz It Up.
- Freeze the ½ cup pepperoni for Day 13, Jazz It Up.
- Freeze the white bread for Days 4 and 6, We Go Good Together.
- Cut the Italian bread in half and freeze separately for Days 5 and 10, We Go Good Together.
- Freeze the pound of ham or bacon for Day 6, We Go Good Together.
- Freeze the feta cheese for Day 14, We Go Good Together.
- Be sure to read the Look Ahead section in each recipe to see when you must pull items out of the freezer to put into the refrigerator to defrost.

FALL: PLAN ONE

✦ Day 1—Sandwich Board: Have-It-Your-Way Hoagies ✦

Hoagies, aka submarine sandwiches, are usually a hit with kids. Italian deli meats, steak or veggies are the popular fillings around the Pittsburgh region. Layer everyone's rolls with their choice of ingredients, making Have-It-Your-Way Hoagies.

Dish up: 4 servings   Cooking time: 5 minutes
Construction time: 5 to 10 minutes   Paraphernalia: Baking sheet

INGREDIENTS:

5 6-inch hoagie rolls (aka torpedo rolls)
10 slices deli meat, thickly sliced (about ½ pound)
Toppings of choice (lettuce, tomato, pickles, onions, mushrooms and/or
    black olives)
10 slices cheese, thickly sliced (about 1/2 pound)

To make:

1. Slice hoagie rolls. Open rolls flat on a baking sheet, being careful
   not to split bread completely.
2. Layer 2 pieces of meat on each roll. Add toppings of choice. Lay
   2 pieces of cheese over the toppings.
3. Place under broiler in oven for about 5 minutes, or until cheese
   melts. Fold top over bottom. Enjoy.

Jazz It Up: Add hot peppers.

Dress It Down: Serve sandwich cold.

Change It Up: Exchange the deli meat for another cheese choice to make it a meatless meal.

We Go Good Together: Coleslaw

✦ Day 2—Slow Cook Tonight: Ginger Roast ✦

Sue Kolton cooks up this tasty version of chuck roast when one of her teenagers plans on bringing home a number of friends from college. Sue never knows if the kids will walk in the door at 4:00 or 7:00. Whenever the gang lands on her doorstep, though, she's ready for everyone to chow down. And if you've ever had a houseful of college kids, that's exactly what they do whenever there's a home-cooked meal being served.

Dish up: 5   Cooking time: 8 to 10 hours
Construction time: 5 to 10 minutes   Paraphernalia: Slow cooker

≈INGREDIENTS:

1 small onion, chopped

3-pound chuck roast 🥃 (Portion of the roast will be used for Day 9, Beef Pot Pie.)

¼ cup ketchup

1 teaspoon garlic powder

2 14.5-ounce cans beef broth

1 teaspoon sugar

12 gingersnap cookies

2 envelopes brown gravy mix

To make:

1. Peel and chop onion. Trim fat off roast.
2. Combine all ingredients in the slow cooker, except roast. Mix well.
3. Add roast and cook for 8 to 10 hours on low.
4. Serve two-thirds of the roast, and store the other third in the freezer (after it cools) for Day 9, Beef Pot Pie.

Jazz It Up: Add carrot slices.

Dress It Down: Skip the onions.

Change It Up: To convert this recipe to the oven, cook in a 325-degree oven for about 2 to 2½ hours. Be aware that you might need to add more broth to the pot.

Double It: Freeze the roast portion you set aside for Day 9, Beef Pot Pie.

We Go Good Together: Serve roast over noodles. Have the remaining gingersnap cookies for a bedtime snack with a glass of milk.

Look Ahead: Take the chicken for Day 3, Chicken Triangles, out of the freezer and store it in the fridge. You will be doubling the cooking process tomorrow by cooking enough chicken for Day 12, Chicken à la Can.

⇝ Day 3—Everyday Dinner: Chicken Triangles ⇜

After spending all day on her feet, hairdresser and mother of two little tykes Michelle Cautela likes to put together this easy dish. Once the triangles are popped into the oven, she can rest her weary legs.

Dish up: 4 servings   Cooking time: 20 minutes

Construction time: 15 minutes   Paraphernalia: 3-quart saucepan, mixing bowl, baking dish

POTFUL OF KNOWLEDGE: Cookie Cracker Craze

National Cookie Month falls in October. And did you know the design of animal crackers (small cookies shaped like animals, according to the *American Heritage Dictionary*) is more than a century old and originated in England? These cookies weren't a hit, however, until a marketing genius at Nabisco designed the box after P. T. Barnum's circus train, topping off the packaging with a string loop that turned the empty box into a little purse. By the way, the reason they are considered crackers rather than cookies is the dough is unsweetened.

INGREDIENTS:

4 skinless, boneless chicken breasts (1 to 1½ pounds) DI (4 additional chicken breasts for Day 12, Chicken à la Can.)

2 tubes crescent rolls

10 ounces cream cheese, softened (1¼ packages)

½ package Hidden Valley Ranch salad dressing, dry

To make:

1. Preheat oven to 350 degrees. Boil all the chicken, including 4 additional breasts, in a pan for about 10 minutes.
2. While chicken is cooking, open crescent rolls and place on baking sheet to make squares.
3. Cut cooked chicken into bite-size pieces. Set aside half of the chicken for Day 12, Chicken à la Can.
4. Mix all ingredients in a bowl.
5. Place chicken mixture in the middle of the squares, leaving room on the outside edges.
6. Fold square in half to make triangle and bake for 20 minutes.

Jazz It Up: Add diced mushrooms.

Change It Up: Use canned chicken in place of boneless chicken breasts.

Double It: Be sure to boil 4 additional chicken breasts for Chicken à la

Can. Once cooked, cut the chicken into bite-size pieces and freeze for Day 12. We Go Good Together: Squash

Look Ahead: Take the ground beef out of the freezer that is marked for Day 4, Mom's Comfort Macaroni and Day 10, Beef Gravy Train. Also, if you tucked bread in the freezer for Day 4 We Go Good Together, take that out now.

❧ *Day 4—Retro Meal: Mom's Comfort Macaroni* ❦

About once a week, Mom made this skillet macaroni dish. It's easy and will please just about everyone. Even my younger brother, who would only eat three things for dinner, would devour this meal without grumbling, though he did pick out the onions and pile them at the side of his plate.

Dish up: 6 servings
Construction time: 5 minutes

Cooking time: 15 minutes
Paraphernalia: Dutch oven, 3-quart saucepan, strainer

INGREDIENTS:

1 16-ounce package elbow macaroni
1 pound ground beef 🧊 1 additional pound ground beef for Day 10, Beef Gravy Train.)
1 small yellow onion, diced
1 green pepper, diced
1 32-ounce jar marinara sauce

To make:
1. Cook macaroni according to package directions.
2. While macaroni is cooking, brown ground beef, including the additional pound, in Dutch oven over medium heat.
3. Peel and dice onion. Wash and dice pepper. Add onions and peppers to beef.
4. Lower heat after beef has browned. Drain excess fat. Set aside half of the cooked ground beef for Day 10, Beef Gravy Train. Freeze this portion as soon as it has cooled.

5. Add marinara sauce to remaining pound of cooked beef. (Add the entire jar of sauce if you like a saucier dish, or ⅔ of the jar if you'd prefer a drier meal.)

6. When macaroni has finished cooking, drain and add to beef mixture. Mix well and serve.

Jazz It Up: Add a can of stewed tomatoes. Sauté diced celery and add to the beef mixture.

Dress It Down: Skip the onions and pepper.

Change It Up: Use ground turkey.

Double It: Cook an additional pound of ground beef for Day 10, Beef Gravy Train and store it in the freezer. Make sure this portion is marinara-free.

We Go Good Together: Mom always served buttered white bread.

Look Ahead: Take out the Italian bread for Day 5, We Go Good Together.

⇢ Day 5—Everyday Dinner: ⇠
Purple Parmesan (Shh! It's eggplant!) 🐮

Jan Devine's scrumptious vegetarian meal takes a little longer to cook, but it is worth it because you don't have to spend that time in the kitchen. Eggplant is bountiful during the early fall months, so take advantage of this dish. And if you have college kids, this is a great one to freeze in meal-size portions for them to thaw and heat. This is one of my daughter's frequently requested meals to take back to school with her.

Dish up: 6 to 8 servings
Construction time: 10 minutes

Cooking time: 30 minutes
Paraphernalia: 12-inch skillet, 2 small bowls, 9-by-13-inch baking dish

INGREDIENTS:
1 large eggplant, thinly sliced
1 egg
¼ cup milk

1 32-ounce jar marinara sauce
Vegetable oil
1 cup Italian-seasoned bread crumbs
½ cup (2 ounces) Parmesan cheese, grated
1 cup (4 ounces) mozzarella cheese, shredded
Salt and pepper, optional

To make:
1. Preheat oven to 350 degrees.
2. Peel and thinly slice eggplant.
3. Break egg into small bowl. Add milk and beat together.
4. Add a layer of sauce to the bottom of the baking dish.
5. Add oil to skillet. Pour enough in to have a layer of oil on the bottom of the skillet.
6. Place bread crumbs in a bowl or a zippered bag.
7. Dip an eggplant slice into the egg mixture, then into the bread crumbs. Be sure to cover both sides of the eggplant.
8. Place eggplant slice into skillet. Fry lightly, about 1 minute on each side. Then, put slice into baking dish. Flip slice in sauce to coat.
9. Sprinkle grated Parmesan and mozzarella on eggplant.
10. Repeat Steps 5, 6 and 7 with remaining slices to make a single layer in the baking dish. Cover cheese with sauce.
11. Make a second layer using the rest of the eggplant and repeating the process.
12. Bake for 30 minutes or until eggplant is heated through.

Change It Up: Use egg substitute in place of eggs. Instead of pan frying, place the breaded eggplant slices in a single layer on a baking sheet. Broil for 3 to 5 minutes on each side, then continue the baking process.

We Go Good Together: Italian bread and baked apple slices

Look ahead: Take the cheese for Day 6, Cheese Omelet, out of the freezer if you tucked it in there. If you purchased the pound of ham or bacon and white bread for Day 6, We Go Good Together, take that out of the freezer, too.

BASKETFUL OF TIPS: Apples Brown No More

Sprinkle cut apples with some fresh lemon juice to keep them from discoloring, or submerge apple slices in a pan of water mixed with lemon juice to keep the apples looking fresh.

BASKETFUL OF TIPS: Pit-Stop Tips

If you're wondering how the heck you're going to fit a fresh produce stop into your day, try these tips:

- Hit the store before you go to work. (If you have a refrigerator at work, you can store the items in it, as suggested in Part One, The Frantic Woman's Kitchen Survival. Or if the weather is not terribly hot, take a cooler and frozen ice packs with you and store your purchases in your car.)

- Make a quick stop at a grocery store near your workplace during your lunch hour.

- Stop at a roadside produce stand on your way home from work.

- Look for a local farmer's market to get fresh produce and more. To find one near you, check out www.ams.usda.gov/farmersmarkets.

- Join a Community supported Agriculture (CSA) program that delivers fresh produce right to your door. (If you're wondering what CSA is, turn to the note on the next page.)

- Order the necessary fresh food items at one of the warehouse clubs. You can place the order via telephone, Internet or fax the night before. You will need to pick up the order at a designated time, usually between 7:00 A.M. and 5:00 P.M. Though most items come in larger quantities, you could use the excess for lunches or side dishes. Remember, there's no standing in line.

POTFUL OF KNOWLEDGE: Farm Fresh to Your Doorstep

In addition to the appearance and taste, the nutritional value of meals is important to most of us. Beverly Breton Carroll, the coauthor of *The Confident Coach's Guide to Teaching Basketball*, the wife of an NBA coach and the mother of a high school athlete, has experienced firsthand the importance of nutrition. As a firm believer in using natural means to nourish soil and crops and in the higher nutritional value of freshly harvested produce, Beverly was thrilled to discover an old concept with a new twist.

Community supported agriculture (CSA) programs started in the mid-1980s with the idea that consumers can "buy into" local farms and receive fresh produce throughout the fall, spring and summer. Most people find out about CSAs through word of mouth. Such was the case with Beverly, when she heard from another mother about a local organic farm that delivered fresh fruits and vegetables and occasionally threw in an herb or two as a surprise bonus. What Beverly loved about her CSA was that it followed organic growing standards and listed the produce they were growing over the season, so members had an idea of what was going to be delivered each time. Check your telephone book or click on www.sare.org/csa or www.nal.usda.gov/afsic/csa to find out if there's a CSA that services your area.

PIT STOP:

You'll need to stop at the grocery store or a farmer's market in the next 24 hours to buy 1 bunch of celery, 1 lemon, 1 carton (12 ounces) snowcap mushrooms, 1 bag (16 ounces) ready-to-eat salad mix and 1 tomato or else you won't have the necessary produce to create the fabulous meals ahead.

If you're jazzing up your menus, you'll need to pick up these Jazz It Up ingredients: Veggies, your preference, and 1 yellow onion.

If you're making the We Go Good Together suggestions, pick up these items: 4 to 6 apples, fruit of your choice, 1 small green pepper and 1 small tomato.

☀ Day 6—Backwards Meal: Cheese Omelet ☀ 🍳

Tonight, you deserve a break. You can easily whip up this plate as is or customize it by adding green peppers, tomatoes, ham, bacon or any other ingredients your crew would prefer. Now, if you have some leftovers taking up space in the refrigerator, pull them out as an alternative to the omelet.

Dish up: 4 servings

Cooking time: 10 minutes

Construction time: 5 minutes

Paraphernalia: 12-inch skillet, bowl

INGREDIENTS:

6 eggs
4 slices cheese, your preference

To make:
1. Coat skillet with nonstick cooking spray. Heat skillet over low heat.
2. Break eggs into a bowl and scramble until yokes and whites are mixed together.
3. Pour eggs into skillet. Cook eggs, tilting skillet so the uncooked eggs move to the bottom. This will allow the uncooked portion to cook. (Some people like to flip the omelet over so the other side cooks.)
4. Add cheese slices to one side of the omelet.
5. Fold omelet in half. Divide into 4 portions, or 5 if need be. Serve.

Jazz It Up: When you add the cheese, add diced tomatoes, green peppers, black olives and so forth.

Change It Up: Use egg substitute for a healthier choice.

We Go Good Together: Ham, bacon and/or toast.

Look Ahead: Take the pound of stew meat or veal for Day 7, Jazz It Up, out of the freezer and put it in the refrigerator to defrost.

POTFUL OF KNOWLEDGE: Say Cheese

Feed your kids cheese, and see a healthy smile. According to the National Dairy Board, studies show cheese helps prevent tooth decay, and cheddar actually repairs tooth enamel that has begun to decay. So, if your kids can't brush while at school, pack them a piece of cheese to munch on after they've finished lunch.

→ Day 7—Everyday Dinner: Savory Stew →

Savory is the best word to describe this dish, which you can jazz up or dress down without worrying about ruining the taste. It's great over noodles, rice or bread.

Dish up: 6 to 8 servings
  (Set aside a portion for
  Day 9, Beef Pot Pie.)
Construction time: 5 to 7 minutes

Cooking time: 15 to 20 minutes
Paraphernalia: 5-quart Dutch oven

INGREDIENTS:

1 1/2 cup onions, diced
1 8-ounce carton snowcap mushrooms, sliced
1 14.5-ounce can stewed tomatoes
3 tablespoons olive oil
1 14.5-ounce can beef broth
1/2 cup red wine
1 24-ounce package mixed stew vegetables, frozen
1 tablespoon Worcestershire sauce
1 tablespoon ketchup
1/2 cup water
1/2 teaspoon salt
1 tablespoon flour
1 teaspoon minced garlic, bottled
1/2 teaspoon thyme, dried
1/2 teaspoon basil, dried
1 teaspoon bacon bits
1/2 teaspoon black pepper

To make:
1. Peel and dice onion. Wash and slice mushrooms. Cut stewed tomatoes smaller, if need be.
2. Heat oil in Dutch oven over medium heat.
3. Add onion and sauté for a few minutes.
4. Cut frozen vegetables smaller, if need be. (They will cook faster.)

5. Add the remaining ingredients to the pot. Mix well.
6. Cover. Raise the heat and allow it to boil, stirring often. Cook for about 5 to 10 minutes, or until vegetables are soft. Be sure to stir often so the stew doesn't stick to the bottom of the pot. When vegetables are cooked and stew thickens, pull out the bowls and ladle.
7. Set aside a good portion of the stew for Day 9, Beef Pot Pie.

Jazz It Up: Add bite-size pieces of cooked stew meat or veal.

Dress It Down: Substitute broth for the wine.

Change It Up: Use your favorite fresh veggies in place of the frozen kind.

Double It: Reserve the remaining stew as the base for Day 9, Beef Pot Pie. Store it in a container, being sure to mark it so no one enjoys it for lunch, leaving you empty-handed.

We Go Good Together: White or brown rice

Look Ahead: Pull the tilapia or orange roughy that is marked Day 8, Seafood Fest, from the freezer and put it in the refrigerator to thaw. If you bought mozzarella cheese to jazz up your menu, take it out of the freezer, too.

❖ Day 8—Seafood Fest: Boxcar Fish ❖ 🐟

The Boxcar Children was one of my daughter's favorite book series growing up. In the book *Surprise Island*, Jessie, one of the boxcar children, cooked fish for dinner. This recipe is similar to the one Jessie prepared. The fish is stuffed and piled high, so you'll probably want to serve those with smaller appetites half a fillet.

Dish up: 4 to 6 servings

Construction time: 10 minutes

Cooking time: 20 minutes

Paraphernalia: Baking dish, 3-quart pot

INGREDIENTS:

6 slices whole-grain bread

1/2 cup butter, melted

1/4 cup celery, chopped

1/4 cup onion, chopped

1 1/4 cups water
2 pounds tilapia fillets
2 tablespoons lemon juice
1/4 teaspoon pepper

To make:
1. Preheat oven to 350 degrees.
2. Toast bread. Cut toasted bread into small cubes.
3. Melt half of butter in pan over low heat.
4. Wash and chop celery. Peel and chop onion. Add celery and onions to melted butter.
5. Slowly add water. Add cubed bread and stir until moistened.
6. Rinse fish under cold water. Pat dry with paper towels.
7. Coat baking dish with nonstick cooking spray.
8. Place half of the fish in the bottom of the dish.
9. Spoon bread mixture over fillets. Place remaining fillets over bread mixture.
10. Melt remaining butter and pour over fish.
11. Cut lemon in half. Squeeze half of one lemon over fish. Sprinkle pepper on top.
12. Cover with foil and bake for about 20 minutes, or until the fish flakes apart.

Jazz It Up: Add a layer of mozzarella cheese on top of the cubed bread mixture.

Dress It Down: Make a single layer of fish and spread the bread mixture over it, then bake.

Change It Up: Use croutons or stuffing mix instead of cubed bread. Substitute your favorite fish for tilapia.

Double It: Slice the remaining part of the lemon for lemon water or for hot tea.

We Go Good Together: Barbecue Succotash

BASKETFUL OF TIPS: Iceberg Fillets

What's a frantic woman to do when she forgets to defrost the fish fillets? Place the frozen fish in a shallow dish and cover with milk. In less than 30 minutes, your entree will be thawed. Best of all, the milk takes away the frozen taste from the fillets.

FRANTIC WOMEN FAMILY FUN

Request one of the Boxcar Children books from your library. As the days grow shorter, read a chapter a night as an ongoing family activity.

✦ Day 9—Must-Go: Beef Pot Pie ✦

This satisfying recipe benefits from two previous cooking days, and no one will realize this meal was really made with leftovers. Shhh! Don't tell.

Dish up: 4 to 5 servings   Cooking time: 25 minutes
Construction time: 3 minutes   Paraphernalia: 9- by 13-inch baking dish

INGREDIENTS:
Savory Stew, stored from Day 7
Ginger Roast, stored from Day 2
1 tube crescent rolls

To make:
1. Preheat oven to 400 degrees.
2. Put Savory Stew in baking dish. Cut Ginger Roast into bite-size pieces. Add to stew.
3. Cook in oven for 15 minutes.
4. Remove from oven. Stir.
5. Open crescent rolls (keep flat) and arrange them over stew. Bake 10 minutes, or according to package directions. Keep your eye on the biscuits to be sure they do not burn.

Jazz It Up: Add cooked sliced vegetables of your choice. Dress It Down: Serve the crescent rolls on the side.

Change It Up: Use a pie crust instead of crescent rolls.

We Go Good Together: Applesauce with a sprinkle of cinnamon

Look Ahead: Pull the ground beef you cooked on Day 4 from the freezer and put it in the refrigerator to thaw. If you did not double the cooking process on Day 4, you will need to brown your ground beef. Also, take the bread out of the freezer if you tucked it in there for Day 10, We Go Good Together to keep it fresh.

☀ Day 10—Kids' Meal: Beef Gravy Train ☀

As I'm ready to type this recipe into the computer, fond memories of my high school days flash through my mind. I had to include this meal in the book, as I remember it being a gigantic hit in the cafeteria. On Gravy Train days, the lunch line was as long as it was for pizza days. And when the bell rang for lunch, everyone went running (even though we weren't allowed) to be in the front of the line.

Dish up: 4 to 5 servings

Construction time: 10 minutes

Cooking time 10 minutes

Paraphernalia: 12-inch skillet, 3-quart saucepan

INGREDIENTS:

1 pound ground beef, stored from Day 4

1 10.75-ounce can beef gravy

1 13.3-ounce box instant mashed potatoes (plus ingredients)

To make:

1. Heat browned ground beef and gravy in skillet over medium heat for 5 to 7 minutes, or until heated through. (If you did not Double It on Day 4, cook the ground beef now.)

2. While beef is heating, cook the number of servings of mashed potatoes needed according to the package directions. Cover with a lid when finished cooking.

3. Once everything has cooked, place one or two scoops of potatoes in a bowl. Top with beef mixture. Be sure to divide the mixture evenly between the bowls.

Jazz It Up: Add sautéed onions. Add another can of gravy if your kids like lots of gravy or gravy bread.

Change It Up: Make real mashed potatoes instead of instant ones.

We Go Good together: Bread to wipe gravy from the bowl.

Look Ahead: To make life easier, prepare the ingredients (except the meat, if you decide to add it) for Day 11, Chili Billie, in your slow cooker's liner and put it in the refrigerator until the morning. Then plug it in, and off to work you go. Also, if you bought grated cheddar cheese for Day 11, Jazz It Up, and it's in the freezer, take it out now.

Frantic Woman Family Fun: Edible Play Dough

Whip up a batch of play dough when the kids have friends over. It's easy to make, and they'll have a blast playing with it. Don't worry if they nibble a little—it's edible. Combine 2 cups powdered milk, 1 cup honey and 2 cups peanut butter in a mixing bowl. Dust your hands with powdered milk and blend the ingredients together using your hands. If the dough is a bit too sticky, add more powdered milk. Store in an airtight container at room temperature.

✦ Day 11—Slow Cook Tonight: Chili Billie ✦

Nothing warms the tummy better than a warm bowl of chili on a chilly autumn night. Though if your family is like mine, everyone likes their chili made a different way. It's enough to make a woman . . . well, frantic. My husband likes chili spicy, our daughter likes it without meat, and our son likes it without beans or onions. So take the following recipe and add or delete ingredients to make it a meal your family will enjoy.

Dish up: 6 to 8 servings
(leftovers will be used for
Day 13, Taco Salad.)
Construction time: 5 to 10 minutes

Cooking time: 8 to 10 hours
Paraphernalia: Slow cooker

INGREDIENTS:

1 16-ounce can red kidney beans
1 16-ounce can pinto or other white beans

1 medium onions, chopped
2 14.5-ounce cans diced tomatoes with seasonings
1 teaspoon garlic, minced
2 tablespoons chili powder
1 teaspoon pepper
Salt, optional

To make:
1. Drain and rinse beans.
2. Combine all ingredients in slow cooker.
3. Cover and cook on low for 8 to 10 hours.
4. Serve in bowls or mugs.

Jazz It Up: For a spicier flavor, add 1 teaspoon cayenne pepper in Step 2. Top with grated cheddar before serving.

Dress It Down: For blander palates, skip the chili powder and pepper.

Change It Up: Cube a pound of tofu and add to the slow cooker, or brown a pound of ground beef and add it to the cooker. For frantic chefs without a slow cooker, combine all the ingredients in a stockpot and simmer for 1 hour on top of the stove.

Double It: Store the leftover chili for Day 13, Taco Salad.

We Go Good Together: Warmed rolls or serve chili over noodles.

Look Ahead: Pull the 4 chicken breasts that you cooked on Day 3 from the freezer and thaw them in the refrigerator for tomorrow. If you did not cook the chicken on Day 3, allow enough time to do so.

 BASKETFUL OF TIPS: Late Dinner Tonight

It's one of those crazy days—you're picking up the kids from school and driving straight to a doctor's appointment or a sports game. The kids are hungry, and dinner is hours away. Unfortunately, here's where that drive-through window action takes place. But hold it. Instead of ordering fried burgers, pack a few cool sandwiches the kids will love. Toast mini waffles according to package directions. Spread strawberry preserves (or another favorite) on one side of the waffle. Add a thin apple slice. Top with another waffle, and wrap that sandwich to go. Now, this is a fun way to eat on the run.

⇥ Day 12—I Can with a Can: Chicken à la Can ⇤

This recipe is for those days when you can barely make it through the day, and dialling 1-800-TAKEOUT or hitting that fast-food joint sounds like bliss. You can whip up Chicken à la Can quicker than the delivery person can make it to your front door, and this is easier on the pocketbook.

Dish up: 4 servings

Construction time: 5 minutes

Cooking time: 10 minutes

Paraphernalia: Baking sheet, 3-quart saucepan

INGREDIENTS:
1 tube refrigerated biscuits
4 boneless chicken breasts, cooked and stored from Day 3
1 10.5-ounce can cream of mushroom soup
1 8-ounce can peas
1 cup milk

To make:
1. Make biscuits according to package directions.
2. If you haven't cut up the chicken into bite-size pieces, do so now.
3. Combine soup, milk, chicken and peas in pan and cook over medium-low heat until biscuits are finished.
4. Split biscuits in half and lay on a plate. Spoon chicken mixture over biscuits and serve.

Jazz It Up: Add diced pimentos.

Dress It Down: Skip the peas.

Change It Up: Use toast instead of biscuits.

Double It: Save the remaining biscuits for the morning. Heat, slather with jelly, and enjoy with tea or coffee.

We Go Good Together: Fruit

Look Ahead: If you bought pepperoni to add to your Taco Salad as suggested in Day 13, Jazz It Up, take it out of the freezer and put it in the refrigerator to thaw.

→ Day 13—Must-Go/No-Cook Night: Taco Salad ← 🚫

All you'll need to do is heat up the leftover chili, open a bag of ready-to-eat salad, and a bag of tortilla chips, dice some of your favorite Mexican toppings and you're all set for tonight's quick and easy dinner.

Dish up: 4 to 5 servings   Cooking time: 5 minutes
Construction time: 10 minutes   Paraphernalia: 3-quart saucepan

INGREDIENTS:
Chili, stored from Day 11
1 16-ounce bag ready-to-eat salad mix
½ cup (2 ounces) cheddar cheese, shredded
Toppings, your preference (black olives, green onions, green or hot
    peppers and tomatoes)
Salad dressing, your preference
1 8-ounce container sour cream
1 16-ounce jar salsa

To make:
1. Heat chili in pan.
2. Open salad bag and divide into bowls or plates.
3. Scoop heated chili onto each bed of lettuce.
4. Add cheddar and your favorite toppings.
5. Serve with salad dressing, sour cream and salsa.

Jazz It Up: Add ½ cup sliced pepperoni to the salad.

Dress It Down: Pop the chili in the microwave instead of using the stove top.

We Go Good Together: Fruit-flavored gelatin

Look Ahead: Pull the packages of chicken breasts and shrimp from the freezer that are marked for Day 14, Shrimp and Chicken Pizzazz, and put them in the refrigerator to defrost. If you're making the We Go Good Together side dish, take the feta cheese from the freezer and put it in the refrigerator to thaw.

✤ Day 14—Company's Coming: ✤
Shrimp and Chicken Pizzazz

This recipe makes my mouth water just thinking about it. Delectable. Wonderful. And it can be made earlier in the day and popped into the oven when company arrives. The long list of ingredients might put you off, but don't let it. This company meal is easy to prepare—the preparation work takes less time than reading the front section of the daily newspaper! It is definitely worth the ten minutes you'll spend preparing it. And just so you know, this recipe received the seal of approval from my "Mom, I don't like fish!" son.

Dish up: 8 servings
Construction time: 10 minutes

Cooking time: 15 minutes
Paraphernalia: Dutch oven, baking dish, plastic zippered bag, strainer

INGREDIENTS:

1 pound linguine
2 pounds skinless, boneless chicken breasts, cut into cubes
1 cup flour
2 tablespoons butter or margarine
1 pound cooked shrimp, peeled and deveined
1 tomato, diced
1 cup mushrooms, sliced
1 25-ounce can black olives, sliced
1 tablespoon minced garlic
½ cup white wine
2 cups (8 ounces) mozzarella cheese, shredded
1 teaspoon olive oil

To make:
1. Heat oven to 400 degrees.
2. Boil water for pasta. Cook according to package directions.
3. Cut chicken into bite-size pieces. Place flour in zippered bag. Add chicken to bag and shake to coat.

4. Melt butter in Dutch oven. Add chicken and cook for 5 minutes, stirring often.
5. Wash and dice tomato. Add to the pot and cook for 5 minutes.
6. Wash and slice mushrooms. Slice olives.
7. Chicken should be about three-fourths of the way cooked. Add remaining ingredients, except cheese and olive oil.
8. Cook another 5 minutes, or until chicken and shrimp are cooked through.
9. Arrange the chicken and shrimp mixture in baking dish. Top with cheese, then put dish in the oven. Heat until cheese has melted.
10. When pasta is cooked, drain and add 1 tablespoon olive oil to keep it from sticking together. Keep pasta in the pot, covering it to keep it warm.
11. Serve shrimp and chicken over pasta.

Jazz It Up: Add 1 cup of cooked asparagus, chopped.

Dress It Down: Skip the sliced veggies.

Change It Up: Exchange white wine for chicken broth. If someone is allergic to shellfish, add another vegetable and more chicken in place of the shrimp.

We Go Good Together: Green Beans, Feta and Dill

FALL PLAN TWO MENUS

Day 1—Sandwich Board: Big Ben Egg and Ham Sammies
Day 2—Everyday Dinner: Fettuccine Alfredo ASAP
Day 3—Everyday Dinner: Chef Dad's Mushroom Steak
Day 4—Everyday Dinner: Finger Lickin' Fried Chicken
Day 5—Slow Cook Tonight: Scarecrow Stew
Day 6—Kids' Meal: Pizza Rounds
Day 7—Everyday Dinner: Tuna Spud-Melts
Day 8—No-Csook Night: Crab-A-Dilly
Day 9—Backwards Meal: Scrambled Potatoes
Day 10—Kids' Meal: Hot Dog Mummy Wraps
Day 11—Slow Cook Tonight: Cranberry Pork Roast
Day 12—I Can with a Can: Canned Bawk Bawk Chicken
Day 13—Must-Go: Pork in a Pan
Day 14—Company's Coming: Andrea's Chicken Scampi

THE SHOPPING LISTS

The Frantic Woman's Cupboard

FALL PLAN TWO STAPLES

Seasonings

Basil*
Garlic (powder, minced)
Ginger
Mustard (dry)
Paprika*
Parsley
Pepper (black, lemon)
Salt*

Side Dishes
Onion (minced)
Poppy seeds
Jazz It Ups
Parmesan cheese

Condiments
Ketchup
Mustard

Dressings, Oil and Sauces
Oil (olive, vegetable*)
Vinegar (cider)*
Wine (dry red)

Side Dishes
Oil (canola)
Worcestershire sauce

Jazz It Ups
Dry sherry

Canned Goods and Bottles
Cheddar French-fried onion rings

Side Dishes
Peanut butter

Baking Needs
Flour

Side Dishes
Sugar

Bread, Chips and More
Bread crumbs (Italian-seasoned)

Frantic Necessities
Foil
Nonstick cooking spray

Dairy
Butter
Eggs*
Milk
Orange juice

* Ingredient needed for both main and side dishes

The Frantic Woman Goes Shopping

MAIN-DISH INGREDIENTS YOU'LL NEED TO BUY

Produce: Fruit
3 oranges (Day 11)
1 lemon (Day 14)

Produce: Veggies
1 tomato (Day 1)
1 head lettuce (Day 1)
1 medium green pepper (Day 3)
3 small yellow onions (Days 3, 9, 11)
1 8-ounce bag coleslaw mix (Day 5)
1 pound winter squash (Day 5)
1 large leek (Day 5)
8 large baking potatoes (Days 7, 9)
1 small bunch green onions (Day 14)
1 small bunch parsley (Day 14)

Dressing, Oils and Sauces
1 8-ounce can pizza sauce (Day 6)
1 8-ounce jar of cheese sauce (Day 10)

PIT STOP: Keep It Fresh

The lemon, oranges, green onions and parsley are all ingredients that are needed later in the plan. Put them on your list to pick up on Day 5 or 6, when you're more than likely buying milk. This way, the fruits and vegetables will be fresh when you need them. You can also wait to buy your potatoes until this trip.

Canned Goods and Bottles

2 4-ounce cans sliced mushrooms (Day 3)

1 14.5-ounce can diced tomatoes (Day 5)

2 15-ounce cans cannellini beans (Day 5)

2 14.5-ounce cans chicken broth (Day 5)

1 6-ounce can tuna packed in water (Day 7)

2 7-ounce cans crabmeat (Day 8)

1 16-ounce can cranberry sauce (Day 11)

1 6.25-ounce can chunk white chicken (Day 12)

1 14.5-ounce can cream of chicken soup (Day 12)

2 14-ounce cans stewed tomatoes (Day 13)

Noodles, Pasta and Rice

1 8-ounce package fettuccine (Day 2)

Boil-in-bag rice (Day 12)

Bread, Chips and More

4 kaiser rolls (Day 1)

4 large whole-wheat pitas, or your preference (Day 6)

8 flour tortillas, or your preference (Day 8)

Deli

4 thick slices maple honey ham (Day 1)

4 thick slices Colby cheese (Day 1)

¾ cup (3 ounces) Parmesan cheese (Day 2)

¼ pound (4 ounces) Canadian bacon (Day 6)

1 cup (4 ounces) mozzarella cheese, shredded (Day 6)

½ cup (2 ounces) cheddar cheese, shredded (Day 7)

Fish, Meat and Poultry

2 pounds cubed beef steak (Day 3)

5 pounds skinless, boneless chicken breasts (Days 4, 14)

8 hot dogs (Day 10)

3-pound pork loin roast (Day 11)

Dairy

1 8-ounce package cream cheese (Day 2)

1 small container plain yogurt (Day 7)

2 8-ounce containers soft cream cheese with strawberries (Day 8)

1 8-ounce tube crescent rolls (Day 10)

Frozen

1 10-ounce package frozen peas (Day 12)

1 10-ounce package frozen broccoli (Day 13)

1 10-ounce package frozen carrots (Day 13)

JAZZ IT UP INGREDIENTS YOU'LL NEED TO BUY

Produce: Fruit

1 papaya (Day 11)

1 small Jonathan apple (Day 13)

Produce: Veggies

Veggies, your preference (Day 2)

1 bunch celery (Days 7, 8)

1 small green pepper (Day 9)

1 8-ounce carton snowcap mushrooms, sliced (Day 9)

1 small yellow onion (Day 10)

1 small head cauliflower (Day 13)

1 clove fresh garlic (Day 14)

1 small tomato (Day 14)

Canned Goods and Bottles

1 8-ounce can pineapple chunks (Day 6)

1 4-ounce can sliced mushrooms (Day 12)

Deli

8 slices Colby cheese (Day 10)

Fish, Meat and Poultry

1 pound sausage, your preference (Day 1)

Dairy

1 cup (4 ounces) Mexican-blend cheese, shredded (Day 9)

PIT STOP: Keep It Fresh

You might want to hold off on buying these ingredients to jazz up your menus until later in the plan, around Day 5: 1 papaya, 1 small Jonathan apple, 1 small head cauliflower, 1 bunch celery, 1 clove fresh garlic, 1 8-ounce carton snowcap mushrooms, 1 small yellow onion, 1 small green pepper and 1 small tomato.

WE GO GOOD TOGETHER INGREDIENTS YOU'LL NEED TO BUY

Produce: Fruit

1 pound strawberries (Day 8)
Fruit, your preference (Day 10)
4 pears (Day 12)

Produce: Veggies

1 small bunch parsley (Days 3, 11)
1 small yellow onion (Day 3)
4 baking potatoes (Day 4)
1 16-ounce bag ready-to-eat salad (Day 6)
1 bunch celery (Day 7)
1 16-ounce bag spinach (Day 8)
1 red onion (Day 8)
4 red potatoes (Day 11)

Canned Goods and Bottles

1 8-ounce can mandarin oranges (Day 6)

1 16-ounce can applesauce (Day 7)

Noodles, Pasta and Rice

1 13-ounce box instant potato flakes (Day 3)

1 16-ounce bag wide no-yolk noodles (Day 14)

Bread, Chips and More

¼ cup plus 2 tablespoons saltine cracker crumbs (Day 3)

4 to 6 corn muffins (Day 5)

1 16-ounce bag potato chips (Day 10)

1 small package breadsticks (Day 13)

Fish, Meat and Poultry

1 pound bacon or sausage (Day 9)

Dairy

½ cup (2 ounces) cheddar cheese, shredded (Day 3)

Frozen

1 32-ounce bag French fried potatoes (Day 1)

1 loaf garlic toast (Day 2)

PIT STOP: Keep It Fresh

Consider buying these produce items recommended for We Go Good Together side dishes until Day 5 or 6 in the plan: Fruit and veggies of your choice, 1 small bunch parsley, 4 pears, 4 red potatoes, 1 red onion, 1 16-ounce bag ready-to-eat salad, 1 16-ounce bag spinach and 1 pound strawberries.

Unloading the Load

- Store the packages of cream cheese for Day 2, Fettuccine Alfredo ASAP, and Day 8, Crab-A-Dilly, in a safe place in the refrigerator so no one snacks on these items before you use them for meal preparation.
- Store the 3 pounds of boneless chicken for Day 4, Finger Lickin' Fried Chicken, in the freezer.
- Hide the yogurt in the refrigerator for Day 7, Tuna Spud-melts.
- Freeze the Canadian bacon, mozzarella cheese and pitas (separately) for Day 6, Pizza Rounds.
- Freeze the shredded cheddar cheese for Day 7, Tuna Spud-melts.
- Freeze the tortillas for Day 8, Crab-A-Dilly, to keep them fresh.
- Freeze the hot dogs for Day 10, Hot Dog Mummy Wrap, the pork roast for Day 11, Cranberry Pork Roast, and the remaining 2 pounds of chicken for Day 14, Andrea's Chicken Scampi. (You might want to cut the chicken into cubes now to save you some time later.)
- For the Jazz it up suggestions, freeze the Mexican-blend shredded cheese for Day 9, Scrambled Potatoes and the Colby cheese for Day 10, Hot Dog Mummy Wraps.
- Freeze the pound of bacon or sausage for Day 9, We Go Good Together. Be sure to mark it Day 9 🥓 (We Go Good Together) so you know it will be for the side dish.
- Freeze the corn muffins for Day 5, the chips (if the kids will munch on them) for Day 10 and the breadsticks for Day 13 We Go Good Together recommendations.
- Be sure to mark all of the packages.

FALL: PLAN TWO

❧ Day 1—Sandwich Board: Big Ben Egg and Ham Sammies ❧

During Pittsburgh Steelers quarterback Ben Roethlisberger's rookie year in 2004–2005, he helped the Steelers win 16 consecutive games. His popularity during his first football season caused "Ben Cuisine" to show up all over the 'burg. Big Ben is the frantic woman's variation of the popular sandwich offered at a Pittsburgh pub called Tailgaters.

Dish up: 4 servings

Cooking time: 10 minutes

Construction time: 5 minutes

Paraphernalia: Small bowl, 12-inch skillet

INGREDIENTS:

4 eggs

3 tablespoons milk

4 kaiser rolls

4 thick slices deli maple honey ham

4 thick slices Colby cheese

Lettuce

Tomato

To make:

1. Preheat oven to 350 degrees. Coat skillet with nonstick cooking spray.
2. Break eggs into a small bowl and add milk. Beat eggs and milk together.
3. Heat skillet on stove top. Add egg mixture. Cook over medium heat for 5 to 10 minutes, or until eggs are no longer runny.
4. While eggs are cooking, slice kaiser rolls. Layer ham and cheese on the bottom half of bun.
5. When eggs are through cooking, divide them into 4 portions. Top each piece of cheese with 1 egg portion, lettuce and tomato.
6. Top with other half of roll.
7. Wrap in foil and heat in oven for 5 minutes, or until cheese has melted slightly. Serve. (Simplify it: Use mini kaiser rolls for smaller appetites and littler hands.)

Jazz It Up: The original Big Ben calls for hot sausage. You can use the sausage of your choice.

Dress It Down: Make a plain egg sandwich.

Change It Up: Use egg substitute.

We Go Good Together: French-fried potatoes

POTFUL OF KNOWLEDGE: What Are Sammies?
Sandwiches were known as "sammies" in our house. Our youngest had severe ear infections when he was a toddler and always shorten three-syllable words into two. And it didn't matter how the second syllable was pronounced; he gave it an "ie" or "a" sound.

FRANTIC WOMAN FAMILY FUN: Cat Antics
The adjustment to chillier and shorter days can affect mom and kids alike. Sometimes being stuck inside the house can cause the kids to be more mischievous than you'd like. A good way to enjoy your time inside is with the delightful children's book *Cat Poems* by Dave Crawley about the funny antics of house pets.

❧ Day 2—Everyday Dinner: Fettuccine Alfredo ASAP 🐱 ❧

Our son, who has never been a great fan of pasta, loves fettuccine Alfredo. He'll gobble this dish down whether the sauce is made from scratch or poured from a jar. Though this recipe isn't quite homemade, it is still tasty.

Dish up: 4 servings

Construction time: 10 minutes

Cooking time: 10 minutes

Paraphernalia: 5-quart Dutch oven, 3-quart pot, strainer

INGREDIENTS:

1 8-ounce package fettuccine

1 8-ounce package cream cheese, cubed

³/₄ cup Parmesan cheese

¹/₂ cup butter

¹/₂ cup milk

To make:

1. Cook fettuccine according to package directions.
2. While fettuccine is cooking, stir together cream cheese, Parmesan, butter and milk and cook over low heat for about 10 minutes. Stir frequently. The mixture should be heated through and have a smooth consistency.
3. Once pasta has finished cooking, drain. Combine fettuccine and sauce, tossing lightly. Serve hot.

Jazz It Up: Add sautéed veggies.

We Go Good Together: Garlic toast

Look Ahead: Take cubed steaks out of the freezer and put them in the refrigerator to thaw for Day 3, Chef Dad's Mushroom Steak.

➤ Day 3—Everyday Dinner: Chef Dad's Mushroom Steak ➤

Dale Reabe, the head chef for a retirement village, cooks up two meals a day, five days a week for 130 or more senior citizens. Then he goes home to cook for his three kids as a single parent. Mushroom Steak is one of his daughter's favorite meals.

Dish up: 6 to 8 servings
Construction time: 5 minutes

Cooking time: 10 to 20 minutes
Paraphernalia: 12-inch skillet

INGREDIENTS:

1 medium green pepper, chopped
1 small yellow onion, chopped
2 pounds cubed beef steak
2 teaspoons salt
1/4 teaspoon lemon pepper
2 4-ounce cans sliced mushrooms
1/2 cup dry red wine

To make:

1. Wash and chop green pepper. Peel and chop onion.

2.   Sprinkle steaks with salt and lemon pepper. In a skillet, brown steaks over medium heat for about 5 to 10 minutes on each side.
3.   Stir in mushrooms, wine, green peppers and onions. Cook over low heat until mushrooms are hot, about 5 to 10 minutes. Serve.

Dress It Down: Skip the green peppers and onions.
We Go Good Together: Potato Cakes 🥔
Look Ahead: Pull the boneless chicken for Day 4, Finger Lickin' Fried Chicken out of the freezer and put it in the refrigerator to thaw.

❖ Day 4—Everyday Dinner: Finger Lickin' Fried Chicken ❖

Mark Pisone isn't a frantic woman, but his wife Barb qualifies as one. With a full-time job, three teens active in sports and lots of volunteer work, Barb looks forward to the weekend, when Mark cooks up this finger-licking-good dish. This fried chicken meal satisfies that craving for down-home comfort food.

Dish up: 6 to 8 servings   Cooking time: 40 minutes
Construction time: 7 to 10 minutes Paraphernalia: 3 medium bowls, 9- by 13-
                                                          inch baking dish, microwave,
                                                          small bowl

INGREDIENTS:

3 tablespoons oil
3 pounds skinless, boneless chicken breasts or chicken tenders
1 stick butter or margarine, melted
2 cups flour
1/4 teaspoon black pepper
1/2 teaspoon paprika
1 teaspoon salt
1/4 teaspoon garlic powder
2 eggs
3 tablespoons water
2 cups Italian-seasoned bread crumbs

To make:

1. Preheat oven to 400 degrees. Coat baking dish with oil.
2. Rinse chicken breasts well.
3. Melt butter in small bowl in microwave.
4. Mix together flour, pepper, paprika, salt and garlic powder.
5. In separate bowl, blend eggs and water together.
6. Pour bread crumbs in a third bowl.
7. Coat chicken in flour mixture. Next, dip chicken in egg and water mixture. Last, coat chicken with bread crumbs.
8. Place coated chicken in baking pan. Drizzle the top of the chicken with melted butter.
9. Cover the pan loosely with foil. Bake for 25 minutes. Then, uncover and bake for an additional 15 minutes, or until chicken is no longer pink in the center.

Change It Up: Use egg substitute in place of eggs.

We Go Good Together: Baked potatoes

Look Ahead: Take the corn muffins for Day 5, We Go Good Together, out of the freezer and put them on the counter to thaw.

FRANTIC WOMAN FAMILY FUN:
Plum-Dandy Classroom Treat

Whip up a batch of double purple cakes for your child's classroom party or birthday treat. Prepare a white cake mix for cupcakes according to directions, but add in 1/4 teaspoon of Wyler's or Kool-Aid grape flavor unsweetened drink mix before mixing. Add the remaining drink mix to the frosting. You'll have purple cake with purple icing, which is "pur-fect" if your school's color is purple, like ours is.

⋆ Day 5—Slow Cook Tonight: Scarecrow Stew ⋆

Without scarecrows, the birds would be nibbling away at the farmers' crops. So if it wasn't for scarecrows, we wouldn't be able to make this delicious stew using fall's bountiful harvest.

Dish up: 6 servings

Cooking time: 8 to 10 hours

Construction time: 10 minutes

Paraphernalia: Slow cooker

INGREDIENTS:

1 large leek, sliced
1 pound winter squash, cubed
2 15-ounce cans cannellini beans
2 14.5-ounce cans chicken broth
1 14.5-ounce can diced tomatoes
2 cups packaged coleslaw mix
1/2 teaspoon minced garlic
Salt and pepper

To make:

1. Thinly slice the leek (white and light green parts). Cut squash into 1/2-inch cubes.
2. Rinse and drain beans.
3. Toss all ingredients into slow cooker. Cook on low heat for 8 to 10 hours.
4. Add salt and pepper to taste and serve.

Jazz It Up: Substitute 1/2 can of chicken broth with 1/2 can red wine. Sprinkle Parmesan cheese on top.

Dress It Down: Skip the veggies the kids won't eat and replace with ones they like.

Change It Up: To use your stove top, toss ingredients in a stockpot and simmer on top of the stove for about 1 hour, or until veggies are soft.

We Go Good Together: Corn muffins

Look Ahead: Take the Canadian bacon, mozzarella cheese and pitas for Day 6, Pizza Rounds, out of the freezer and put them in the refrigerator to thaw.

PIT STOP: Pick Up Produce

Schedule a trip to the farmer's market or grocery store in the next 24 hours so you'll have the produce you need for the rest of the Fall Two Plan. You'll need to buy 1 lemon, 3 oranges, small bunch of green onions and small bunch of parsley. If you did not pick up 8 large baking potatoes, do so now.

If you're jazzing up your menus and held off buying some of the produce until now, you'll need to pick up 1 papaya, 1 small Jonathan apple, 1 small head cauliflower, 1 bunch celery, 1 clove fresh garlic, 1 carton (8 ounces) sliced mushrooms, 1 small yellow onion, 1 small green pepper and 1 small tomato.

You'll also need to add these items to your Pit Stop list for the We Go Good Together suggestions: 1 pound strawberries, fruit of your choice, 4 pears, 4 red potatoes, 1 red onion, 1 small bunch parsley, 1 16-ounce bag spinach and 1 16-ounce bag ready-to-eat salad.

⋆ Day 6—Kids' Meal: Pizza Rounds ⋆

The pace of the fall months seems especially busy after summer, with the kids going back to school and the start-up of their extracurricular activities. So satisfy your need for quick and easy and the kids' desire for one of their favorite meals with Pizza Rounds. By using whole-wheat pitas, you're adding a healthier ingredient to a typical fast-food meal. Best of all, this pizza meal can be rolled up if you need to eat it on the run.

Dish up: 4 servings
Construction time: 7 minutes

Cooking time: 10 minutes
Paraphernalia: Baking sheet

INGREDIENTS:

4 large whole-wheat pitas, or your preference
3/4 cup pizza sauce
1 cup (4 ounces) mozzarella cheese, shredded
4 ounces Canadian bacon, cut into bite-size pieces

To make:

1. Heat oven to 450 degrees. Place pitas on baking sheet.
2. Cut bacon into bite-size pieces with kitchen shears.
3. Spread sauce over top of each pita. Top with cheese and bacon.
4. Place in oven for about 7 to 10 minutes, or until soft and heated through. If you would like to roll the pitas to eat, do not overcook them, or they will become crisp.

Jazz It Up: Add sautéed pineapples.
Dress It Down: Skip the bacon to make it a meatless meal.
Change It Up: Heat in the microwave for 1 to 2 minutes.
We Go God Together: Green salad with mandarin oranges
Look Ahead: Take the cheddar cheese out of the freezer for Day 7, Tuna Spud-Melt and put it in the refrigerator to defrost.

➤ Day 7—Everyday Dinner: Tuna Spud-Melts ◄

Tuna Spud-Melts are a fun change from sandwiches. By topping each spud with a favorite ingredient, you can individualize the dish, too.

Dish up: 4 servings   Cooking time: 10 minutes
Construction time: 5 to 7 minutes   Paraphernalia: Microwave, small bowl

INGREDIENTS:

4 large potatoes 🥤 (4 extra potatoes for Day 9, Scrambled Potatoes)
Butter or margarine
1 6-ounce can tuna packed in water, drained
3 tablespoons plain yogurt
½ cup (2 ounces) cheddar cheese, shredded

To make:

1. Scrub potatoes. Rub with butter for softer skins. Prick skin with fork to allow steam to escape, or else your microwave will be wearing your potatoes. Cook in microwave for 10 minutes.
2. Set aside the 4 extra potatoes for Day 9, Scrambled Potatoes. Once cooled, store them in the refrigerator.

3. Combine tuna and yogurt.

4. After potatoes are baked, cut each potato in half lengthwise, almost through to the bottom. Using a spoon, scoop out potato. (Simplify it: You can use a fork to fluff up potatoes, skip the next step, and add the ingredients on top.)

5. Combine potatoes with tuna mixture.

6. Place scooped-out potato skins on a pie plate or dish. Fill each potato skin with tuna mixture. Be sure to divide the mixture evenly. Top potatoes with shredded cheese.

7. Microwave for about 1 minute. Serve.

Jazz It Up: Add diced celery to the tuna mixture.

Change It Up: For non-zappers, bake potatoes in the oven for 1 to 1 1/4 hours. Spuds can be wrapped in foil to keep the skins from turning crisp. Once you've mixed the tuna with potato, top with cheese and bake in the oven for about 5 minutes or until the cheese melts.

Double It: Make 4 extra potatoes for Day 9, Scrambled Potatoes.

We Go Good Together: Applesauce and celery sticks with peanut butter.

Look ahead: Take the tortillas for Day 8, Crab-A-Dilly, out of the freezer and put them in the refrigerator to thaw.

TiPS BASKETFUL OF TIPS: Cook 'em Your Way

How many ways can you bake a potato? By changing the oven temperature, you can bake potatoes in the amount of time that will fit into your schedule. Follow these guidelines:

- Bake at 350 degrees for 1 1/4 hours.
- Bake at 325 degrees for 1 1/2 hours.
- For faster baking, boil potatoes in water for 10 minutes, then bake at 350 degrees for about 30 minutes.
- Microwave on high (100 percent power) for 7 to 9 minutes, depending on size. For best results, arrange similar-size potatoes about 1 inch apart in a circle.
- And one last tip: If you want to reheat leftover baked potatoes, rinse with water and rebake at 350 degrees for 20 minutes.

BASKETFUL OF TIPS: No Shells About It

When I first heard the phrase "Pick over the crabmeat," I couldn't figure out what I was picking over the crabmeat for. And if you're wondering, wonder no more. You'll want to pick over the canned crabmeat to be sure tiny bits of shell aren't hiding out. No one wants to take a bite out of a crabbie and be surprised by a tiny shard that was missed. So pick through the crabmeat with your fingers to find any hidden surprises.

✦ Day 8—No-Cook Night: Crab-A-Dilly ✦

I tested out this recipe at a local specialty foods store when I was promoting my first book, *The Frantic Woman's Guide to Life*. One elderly gentleman loved Crab-A-Dilly so much that he bought the book, even though he didn't have a clue who he would give it to.

Dish up: 4 to 6 servings Cooking time: 0
Construction time: 5 to 7 minutes Paraphernalia: Bowl

INGREDIENTS:
8 flour tortillas, or your preference
2 7-ounce cans crabmeat
2 8-ounce containers soft cream cheese with strawberries

To make:
1. Lay tortillas on a flat surface.
2. Pick over the crabmeat and remove any tiny shells.
3. Mix together the crabmeat and cream cheese in a bowl. (Simplify it: Be sure the cream cheese has softened, and do not overmix.)
4. Evenly divide mixture between 4 tortillas. Spread crab mixture onto each tortilla.
5. Top each with another tortilla. Cut in quarters and serve.

Jazz It Up: Add diced celery to mixture.
Dress It Down: Use cream cheese with chives instead of strawberries.

We Go Good Together: Spinach Salad

Look Ahead: If you bought Mexican-blend shredded cheese and bacon or sausage for Day 9 Jazz it up and We Go Good Together and froze them, you'll need to take the packages out of the freezer to defrost. Tuck them into the refrigerator.

❧ Day 9—Backwards Meal: Scrambled Potatoes ❧

A satisfying breakfast meal that warms the tummy. You can jazz up this skillet dish any way you want, from adding hot peppers for those people who prefer spicier food to adding fresh veggies for those who prefer healthier meals.

Dish up: 4 to 5 servings

Construction time: 10 minutes

Cooking time: 15 minutes

Paraphernalia: 12-inch skillet, medium-size bowl

INGREDIENTS:

4 baked potatoes, stored from Day 7
½ small onion, diced
5 eggs
3 tablespoons milk
Salt and pepper, to taste

To make:
1. Peel and dice cooked potatoes. Peel and dice onion.
2. Break eggs into bowl. Add milk to eggs and mix together.
3. Coat skillet with nonstick cooking spray and preheat over medium heat.
4. Pan-fry potatoes for about 5 minutes, or until almost heated through, stirring often.
5. Pour eggs over potatoes. With spatula, scramble mixture for about 5 to 7 minutes, or until eggs are completely cooked and potatoes are hot. Add salt and pepper, to taste, and serve.

Jazz It Up: Sprinkle 1 cup (4 ounces) shredded Mexican-blend cheese over scrambled potatoes. Add ¼ cup diced green peppers and/or sliced mushrooms.

Dress It Down: Omit salt and pepper.

Change It Up: Use egg substitute, or stuff a flour tortilla with mixture to make a breakfast burrito.

We Go Good Together: Bacon or sausage

Look Ahead: Take hot dogs out of the freezer and put them in the refrigerator to thaw for Day 10, Hot Dog Mummy Wraps. If you have Colby cheese and chips in the freezer for Day 10 Jazz It Up and We Go Good Together, you'll need to put them in the refrigerator to thaw as well. Also, pull out the pork roast for Day 11, Cranberry Pork Roast, so it has plenty of time to thaw.

✦ *Day 10—Kids' Meal: Hot Dog Mummy Wraps* ✦

The spooky holiday of Halloween falls at the tail end of October. Celebrate by whipping up a Hot Dog Mummy Wrap for each of the monsters in your haunted house.

Dish up: 6 to 8 servings   Cooking time: 10 to 13 minutes
Construction time: 10 minutes   Paraphernalia: Baking sheet

INGREDIENTS:
1 8-ounce tube crescent rolls
8 hot dogs
Mustard, cheese sauce or ketchup

To make:
1. Preheat oven to 375 degrees.
2. Open crescent rolls and separate the dough. Lay flat on baking sheet.
3. Put one hot dog on each piece of crescent roll at the wide end. Starting at the wide end, roll the hot dog and dough toward the narrow side.
4. Bake for 10 to 13 minutes. Serve with mustard, ketchup or cheese sauce.

Jazz It Up: Add 8 slices Colby cheese by splitting the hot dogs lengthwise and folding the cheese into the middle of it. Add diced onions in the split of the hot dog.

Change It Up: Use deli meats instead of hot dogs.

We Go Good Together: Fruit and chips

Look Ahead: The pork roast for Day 11, Cranberry Pork Roast, should be thawed by now. You can toss together all the ingredients except the meat (to ensure food safety) in the liner of your slow cooker tonight, so all you have to do tomorrow is pop the meat in the liner, pop the liner in the cooker and plug it in. Be sure to put it in the refrigerator overnight.

FRANTIC WOMAN FAMILY FUN:
Yellow-Plate Special

During the shorter days of fall, brighten up your evening meals by having a Yellow-Plate Special. Buy a yellow or another brightly colored dinner plate. Celebrate a chore finished, a goal reached, a test passed, a skill learned or any other special achievement of someone in the family. Celebrate the occasion, however minor it may seem, by giving that person the yellow plate for dinner that day. Be sure the special plate makes the rounds to every family member, including you.

✦ *Day 11—Slow Cook Tonight: Cranberry Pork Roast* ✦

Take advantage of the rock-bottom price of cranberry sauce by pairing it up with a pot roast.

Dish up: 6 servings   Cooking time: 8 to 10 hours
Construction time: 10 minutes   Paraphernalia: Slow cooker

INGREDIENTS:
1 small onion, chopped
3 oranges, peeled and sectioned
1 16-ounce can cranberry sauce
¼ cup orange juice
2 teaspoons cider vinegar

1 teaspoon dry mustard

1 teaspoon ginger

Salt, to taste

3-pound pork loin roast, trimmed of fat 🍲 (Part of the roast will be used for Day 13, Pork in a Pan.)

To make:

1. Peel and slice onion. Peel and section oranges.
2. Mix cranberry sauce, oranges, juice, onions, vinegar, mustard, and ginger in slow cooker.
3. Add pork. Spoon some of the cranberry and orange mixture on top of pork to baste.
4. Cover and cook on low for 8 to 10 hours, or until pork is tender.
5. Remove pork from cooker. Allow it to rest for 10 minutes.
6. Cut off 1/3 of pork roast and set aside. This will be used for Day 13, Pork in a Pan, so be sure to refrigerate it promptly.
7. Slice the other part of the roast. With a spoon, scoop off any fat from the top of the liquid. Put cranberry/orange mixture into a gravy boat to top pork slices.

Jazz It Up: Slice and add 1 papaya.

Dress It Down: Skip the oranges and onions.

Change It Up: If you prefer to cook your roast in the oven, follow the directions as stated. Then, bake the roast in a 325-degree oven for about 30 minutes per pound.

Double It: Be sure you set aside ⅓ of the roast. Wrap and store it in the refrigerator for Day 13, Pork in a Pan.

We Go Good Together: Cube red potatoes and cook them in the cooker, too. Add parsley to garnish potatoes.

POTFUL OF KNOWLEDGE: Roast It Right

Let the roast sit for 10 or 15 minutes before you take the knife to it. The meat juices congregate in the center during the cooking process, which leaves the ends dry and the middle wet. As the meat sits, the juices venture from the center to other parts of the roast.

✦ Day 12—I Can with a Can: Canned Bawk Bawk Chicken ✦

Here's a toss-together-and-zap-it recipe for days when PMS or stress has taken control of your emotions and body. You can have dinner on the table within 15 minutes. For you non-zappers, pop this in the oven and increase the baking time.

Dish up: 4 servings

Cooking time: 10 minutes

Construction time: 7 minutes

Paraphernalia: 3-quart pot, 2-quart baking dish, microwave

INGREDIENTS:

2 cups instant rice
1 10-ounce package frozen peas
1 6.25-ounce can chunk white chicken
1 14.5-ounce can cream of chicken soup
½ cup milk
¼ cup cheddar French-fried onion rings
½ teaspoon chopped onion, bottled
½ teaspoon parsley, bottled

To make:
1. Cook rice according to package directions.
2. Thaw peas according to package directions.
3. Combine rice, peas and remaining ingredients in baking dish.
4. Microwave at full power for 10 minutes, stirring once. Serve.

Jazz It Up: Add 1 can sliced mushrooms and 1 tablespoon dry sherry. Sprinkle with Parmesan cheese.

Dress It Down: Skip the french-fried onions rings.

Change It Up: Cook in the oven at 350 degrees for 20 to 25 minutes.

We Go Good Together: Pears

Look ahead: Take the breadsticks for Day 13, We Go Good Together, out of the freezer and let them thaw on the countertop.

FRANTIC WOMAN FAMILY FUN: Bawk Bawk Dance
Usually, the only time you ever think about the chicken dance is when you're at a family wedding and Aunt Martha drags you to the dance floor. Granted, it isn't the cha cha or even the electric slide, but it's a classic dance that has lasted throughout the years. Give your kids a head start for the days when they'll be pulled to the dance floor, too, and teach them the chicken dance. After all, laughter and exercise are great prescriptions for PMS.

☀ Day 13—Must-Go: Pork in a Pan ☀

Leftover pork teams up with frozen veggies as the basis for this brainless meal. Toss in any favorite ingredients that make your kids smile when served.

Dish up: 4 servings
Construction time: 5 minutes

Cooking time: 15 minutes
Paraphernalia: 12-inch skillet

INGREDIENTS:
Pork, stored from Day 11
1 10-ounce package frozen broccoli
1 10-ounce package frozen carrots
2 14-ounce cans stewed tomatoes
1 teaspoon basil
1 teaspoon parsley

To make:
1. Cut leftover pork into bite-size pieces.
2. Slightly thaw carrots and broccoli in the microwave, according to package directions.
3. Coat skillet with nonstick cooking spray.
4. Add pork, stewed tomatoes with liquid, broccoli, carrots, and seasonings in skillet. Cook over medium-high heat to boiling. Boil for about 5 to 7 minutes.
5. Cover and simmer for 10 minutes, or until vegetables are tender. Serve hot.

Jazz It Up: Add diced apples or cauliflower.

Dress It Down: Add only 1 veggie to the pan if time is limited.

Change It Up: Serve vegetables on the side and meat separately if your kids hate mixing foods together.

We Go Good Together: Breadsticks

Look Ahead: Take chicken out of the freezer and put it in the refrigerator to thaw for Day 14, Andrea's Chicken Scampi.

❖ Day 14—Company's Company: ❖ Andrea's Chicken Scampi

As a working mom with two active teens who have lots of friends and an entrepreneurial husband who likes to continue business over dinner, Andrea Verona never knows who's coming for dinner. She needs a meal that tastes good and is easy to prepare. Not only that, it has to be something everyone likes. Andrea's Chicken Scampi fits the bill.

Dish up: 6 to 8 servings   Cooking time: 15 minutes
Construction time: 5 minutes   Paraphernalia: 12-inch skillet

INGREDIENTS:

½ cup butter
¼ cup olive oil
¼ cup green onions, finely chopped
2 pounds skinless, boneless chicken breasts, cubed
¼ cup fresh parsley, minced
1 tablespoon minced garlic
Juice of 1 lemon
1 teaspoon salt
½ teaspoon black pepper

To make:

1. In skillet, heat butter and oil.
2. Peel and chop onions. Wash and mince parsley.
3. Cube chicken if you haven't already done so.

4. Sauté onions and garlic for about 3 to 5 minutes over medium heat.
5. Add lemon juice, chicken, salt and pepper.
6. Stir mixture, then add parsley.
7. Cook for about 5 to 8 minutes, or until chicken is no longer pink in the middle. Stir constantly.

Jazz It Up: Chop 1 tomato and add during Step 5. Use fresh garlic and ground pepper.

Dress It Down: Decrease the garlic if your family prefers a blander flavor.

We Go Good Together: Wide no-yolk noodles

TiPS BASKETFUL OF TIPS: Juicier Lemon

To get the most juice out of your lemon, heat it in the microwave for 20 seconds, or roll the lemon between the palm of your hand and the countertop for about 30 seconds. Cut it in half and squeeze.

WINTER WONDERLAND

Winter welcomes the hectic holidays, a colder climate and darker days. Though the icy conditions may threaten outside, the atmosphere inside is warmed up by these appetizing home-cooked meals.

WINTER FARMER'S MARKET

Use these seasonal fruits and vegetables that are readily available in the colder months as side dishes and snacks.

Fruits	Vegetables
Apples	Belgian endive
Avocados	Broccoli
Bananas	Brussels sprouts
Coconuts	Cabbage
Cranberries*	Carrots
Grapes*	Cauliflower
Grapefruits	Celery
Lemons	Fennel
Honeydews	Lettuce
Oranges, mandarin	Mushrooms*
Papayas	Onions
Persimmons*	Parsnips
Pineapples*	Peppers
Pears	Potatoes, sweet*
Tangerines*	Potatoes, white
Tangelos*	Rutabagas
	Spinach
	Squash*
	Turnips

* Designates fruits and vegetables that have a shorter peak season than the others on the list.

WINTER PLAN ONE MENUS

Day 1—Sandwich Board: Pinto Burritos
Day 2—Retro Meal Updated: Unstuffed Cabbages
Day 3—Everyday Dinner: Veggie Tortilla Rollovers
Day 4—Everyday Dinner: Easy Beef and Mac
Day 5—Soup's On: Potato Asparagus Soup
Day 6—Everyday Dinner: Chicken Divan
Day 7—No-Cook Night: Chicken Caesar Salad
Day 8—Old Tradition: Penguin Goulash
Day 9—Backwards Meal: Eggel Bagels
Day 10—Kids' Meal: Linda's Cheesy Delights
Day 11—Slow Cook Tonight: Winter Roast
Day 12—I Can with a Can: Tuna Casserole
Day 13—Must-Go: Beef Stir-Fry
Day 14—Company's Coming: Penne with Spinach, Tomatoes and
    Feta Cheese

THE SHOPPING LISTS

The Frantic Woman's Cupboard

WINTER PLAN ONE STAPLES

Seasonings

Chicken bouillon granules
Basil (dried)
French-fried onion rings
Garlic powder
Ginger
Paprika
Parmesan cheese, grated
Pepper
Salt*

Jazz It Ups
Cajun or Italian seasoning
Red pepper, crushed

Dressings, Oil and Sauces
Mayonnaise*
Vinegar (balsamic)
Oil (canolas, olives, vegetable*)
Caesar salad dressing, bottled
Soy sauce

Side Dishes
Worcestershire sauce

Jazz It Ups
Wine (white)

Baking Needs
Flour (all-purpose)
Cornstarch

Frantic Necessities
Nonstick cooking spray
Foil

Dairy
Butter or margarine*
Eggs
Milk

Jazz It Ups
Eggs

* Ingredient needed for both main and side dishes

The Frantic Woman Goes Shopping

MAIN-DISH INGREDIENTS YOU'LL NEED TO BUY

Produce: Veggies

1 small bunch green onions (Day 1)

1 head cabbage (Day 2)

1 small green pepper (Day 3)

3 tomatoes (Days 3, 7)

2 winter squash (Days 3, 13)

½ pound fresh asparagus (Day 5)

1 bunch celery (Day 5)

5 medium potatoes (Days 5, 11)

4 yellow onions (Days 5, 8, 11, 13)

1 head broccoli (Days 6, 7, 13)

1 16-ounce bag Romaine ready-to-eat salad mix (Day 7)

1 12-ounce bag baby cut carrots (Days 11, 13)

1 8-ounce carton snowcap mushrooms, sliced (Day 13)

1 10-ounce bag fresh spinach (Day 14)

PIT STOP: Keep It Fresh

Check the "sell by" dates on the baby cut carrots, spinach, and romaine salad mix. Be sure the packages will still be fresh when you'll need to use them.

Consider stopping by your local grocery store near the end of the first week or on Day 5 to pick up 1 head broccoli, 1 carton (8 ounces) snowcap mushrooms and 1 winter squash.

Canned Goods and Bottles

1 16-ounce can enchilada sauce (Day 1)

1 16-ounce can pinto beans (Day 1)

1 16-ounce can refried beans with green chilies (Day 1)

3 10.5-ounce cans tomato soup (Days 2, 4)

1 10.5-ounce can cream of chicken soup (Day 6)

1 16-ounce can sauerkraut (Day 8)

1 28-ounce can stewed tomatoes (Day 11)

1 10.5-ounce can cream of mushroom soup (Day 12)

1 6-ounce can white tuna packed in water (Day 12)

1 14-ounce can beef broth (Day 13)

1 8-ounce can water chestnuts (Day 13)

1 4-ounce can sun-dried tomatoes (Day 14)

Noodles, Pasta and Rice

2 cups regular rice (Day 2)

4 cups instant rice (Days 2, 12)

1 7.25-ounce box macaroni and cheese (Day 4)

2 cups instant rice (Day 12)

1 16-ounce package penne pasta (Day 14)

Bread, Chips and More

1 6-ounce box croutons (Day 7)

4 bagels (Day 9)

4 to 6 English muffins (Day 10)

Deli

4 slices Colby cheese (Day 9)

Fish, Meat and Poultry

2 pounds ground beef (Days 2, 4)

14 chicken tenderloins or 8 chicken breasts (Days 6, 7)

2 pounds boneless pork loin(Day 8)

8 slices bacon (Day 9)

1 4- to 5-pound eye of round roast (Days 11, 13)

Dairy

2 cups (8 ounces) Monterey Jack cheese, shredded (Day 1)

12 whole-wheat tortillas, or your preference (Days 1, 3)

1 12-ounce container sour cream (Days 1, 8, 10)

2 cups (8 ounces) mozzarella cheese, shredded (Day 3)

1 8-ounce container heavy cream (Day 5)

2½ cups (10 ounces) cheddar cheese, shredded (Days 5, 6, 10)

½ cup feta cheese (2 ounces) (Day 14)

JAZZ IT UP INGREDIENTS YOU'LL NEED TO BUY

Produce: Veggies

2 tomatoes (Days 1, 9)

2 green peppers (Days 1, 12)

2 8-ounce cartons snowcap mushrooms (Days 1, 12)

1 yellow onion (Day 2)

1 bunch broccoli (Day 4)

1 bunch green onions (Day 10)

PIT STOP: Keep It Fresh

Consider buying 1 green pepper, 1 tomato and 1 carton (8 ounces) snowcap mushrooms on Day 5 to keep your produce fresh for jazzing up your menus.

Canned Goods and Bottles

1 16-ounce can stewed tomatoes (Day 2)

2 2.5-ounce cans sliced black olives (Days 4, 10)

1 4-ounce can sliced mushrooms (Day 6)

1 16-ounce can sliced carrots (Day 8)

1 5-ounce jar green olives (Day 10)

Noodles, Pasta and Rice

1 cup ziti (Day 7)

Deli

4 to 6 slices baked ham (Day 3)

Fish, Meat and Poultry
1 pound bacon (Day 5)
1 pound cooked shrimp, peeled and deveined (Day 14)

Dairy
½ cup (2 ounces) cheddar cheese (Day 12)

WE GO GOOD TOGETHER INGREDIENTS YOU'LL NEED TO BUY

Produce: Fruit
1 lemon (Day 4)
3 pears (Day 9)
3 papayas (Day 10)

Produce: Veggies
1 16-ounce bag ready-to-eat salad (Day 1)
1 16-ounce bag baby cut carrots (Days 3, 4)
1 bunch broccoli (Day 4)
1 head cauliflower or cabbage (Day 4)
1 yellow onion (Day 4)
1 small bunch parsley (Day 4)
1 head lettuce or 16-ounce bag ready-to-eat salad mix (Days 10, 13)
2 cucumbers (Days 10, 13)
2 tomatoes (Days 10, 13)
1 16-ounce bag radishes (Days 10, 13)

PIT STOP: Keep It Fresh
You might want to hold off on buying the following We Go Good Together ingredients until Day 5: 2 cucumbers, 1 head lettuce, 3 papayas, 3 pears, 1 bag radishes and 2 tomatoes.

Dressings, Oils and Sauces
Salad dressing, your preference (Days 1, 10, 13)
Ranch salad dressing (Day 3)

Canned Goods and Bottles

1 16-ounce jar applesauce (Day 12)

Noodles, Pasta and Rice

2 cups white or brown rice (Day 6)
1 16-ounce bag wide egg noodles (Day 8)
Bread, Chips and More
Bread, your preference (Day 2)
4 to 6 breadsticks (Day 5)
4 to 6 muffins, your preference (Day 7)
1 loaf Italian or French bread (Day 11)

Dairy

2 6-ounce containers Yoplait vanilla yogurt (Day 10)
4 slices cheddar cheese (Day 11)

Frozen Foods

1 8-ounce container whipped topping (Day 9)
1 package garlic toast (Day 14)

Unloading the Load

- Put the ground beef in the refrigerator for Day 2, Unstuffed Cabbages and Day 4, Easy Beef and Mac.
- Freeze the chicken for Day 6 Chicken Divan, and Day 7, Chicken Caesar Salad, in the same package, as you will cook it all at the same time.
- Freeze the pork for Day 8, Penguin Goulash, bacon for Day 9, Eggel Bagels, and the roast for Day 11, Winter Roast. (You'll get Day 13 out of the roast, too.)
- Also, freeze the Colby cheese and the bagels for Day 9, Eggel Bagels.
- Freeze 1 cup of the cheddar cheese and the English muffins for Day 10, Linda's Cheesy Delights. (You might want to freeze all

of the cheddar if your family is known to nibble on it without asking first.)

- Freeze the feta cheese for Day 14, Penne with Spinach, Tomatoes and Feta Cheese.
- Freeze the bacon for Day 5, Jazz It Up.
- Freeze ½ cup cheddar cheese for Day 12, Jazz It Up.
- Freeze the breadsticks for Day 5, We Go Good Together.
- Freeze the muffins for Day 7, We Go Good Together.
- Be sure to mark the packages with the corresponding meal.
- Be sure to read the Look Ahead section in each recipe to see when you must pull items out of the freezer to put into the refrigerator to defrost.

 BASKETFUL OF TIPS: No More Fingers

Pick up an extra apple and store it with your potatoes to keep them from sprouting those ugly fingers.

WINTER: PLAN ONE

⟶ *Day 1—Sandwich Board: Pinto Burritos* 🚫 ⟵

Give the kids the ingredients and a bowl, and before you know it, tonight's meal will be ready for the oven. You'll be able to keep an eye on the kids' progress while unpacking the groceries. Once the burritos are popped in the oven, have the kids help unload the bags.

Dish up: 4 to 6 servings
Construction time: 5 to 10 minutes

Cooking times: 10 minutes
Paraphernalia: Baking sheet

INGREDIENTS:
1 16-ounce can pinto beans
2 green onions, chopped
1 16-ounce can refried beans with green chilies

2 cups (8 ounces) Monterey Jack cheese, shredded
6 whole-wheat tortillas, or your preference
1 16-ounce can enchilada sauce
Sour cream

To make:
1. Preheat oven to 350 degrees. Coat baking sheet with nonstick cooking spray.
2. Rinse and drain pinto beans and place in bowl.
3. Rinse and chop green onions and add to bowl.
4. Add refried beans and cheese. Mix together, mashing beans slightly.
5. Lay tortilla on flat work surface. Spoon mixture onto tortilla, slightly off center. Roll up tortilla like a jelly roll.
6. Place tortillas on a baking sheet and bake for 10 minutes, or until heated though.
7. Serve with enchilada sauce and sour cream.

Jazz It Up: Add diced tomatoes, green peppers or mushrooms. A dash of crushed red pepper will give zing to the burrito.

Change It Up: If your kids snub their noses at burritos, serve the mixture as a dip with your favorite toasted bread.

Dress It Down: Skip the green onions.

We Go Good Together: Tossed salad

BASKETFUL OF TIPS: Don't Throw It Away
If you have leftover bean mixture, don't toss it. Eve Laboon serves the remaining mixture as a dip with tortilla chips. Serve it cold, or heat it in the microwave for 1 to 2 minutes.

POTFUL OF KNOWLEDGE:
Wash That Sodium Away
By washing the beans, your washing away extra sodium that you're body could do without.

✦ *Day 2—Retro Meal Updated: Unstuffed Cabbages* ✦

Working in the church office, managing the church resource center, and coordinating weddings leaves Mercy Sergi with limited time for cooking. Here's her speed-it-up version of a favorite Lithuanian entree her family loves to eat.

Dish up: 4 to 6 servings
Construction time: 10 minutes

Cooking time: 20 minutes
Paraphernalia: 12-inch skillet,
    3-quart saucepan

INGREDIENTS:

2 cups regular rice
1 pound lean ground beef 🥤 (1 additional pound of ground beef for Day
 4, Easy Beef and Mac.)
4 cups green cabbage, chopped
2 10.5-ounce can tomato soup

To make:

1. Cook rice according to package directions.

2. While rice is cooking, brown ground beef over medium heat, stirring frequently.

3. Once ground beef has cooked through, set aside the extra pound for Day 4, Easy Beef and Mac. You can store this in the refrigerator.

4. Chop cabbage into bite-size pieces. Cook in boiling water for 5 minutes to soften.

5. Add remaining ingredients to browned beef. Bring to a boil. Reduce heat. Cover and simmer for 20 minutes.

Jazz It Up: Add ½ cup of chopped onion. Stir in 1 can of stewed tomatoes.

Double It: Brown an additional pound of ground beef. Store it in the refrigerator for Day 4, Easy Beef and Mac.

We Go Good Together: Garlic toast. Spread margarine or butter on bread. Sprinkle garlic powder on top. Broil for 3 to 5 minutes, or until golden brown. Be careful not to burn.

POTFUL OF KNOWLEDGE:
A Little Tidbit About Rice

- Polishing silver is usually a good thing, but polishing rice is not. Brown rice has greater food value than white rice, because white rice has been polished. In the polishing process, the brown coating that contains many nutrients is stripped away.
- Rice is low in fat, but if you're on one of the current diets that shies away from white rice, use brown. There's even an instant brown rice on the market that can be cooked up in just 15 minutes.
- Keep rice from becoming gummy by adding a squeeze of lemon juice as the rice boils. The lemon will keep the grains separate.

☀ Day 3—Everyday Dinner: Veggie Tortilla Rollovers ☀

Tortillas have become very popular. It's no wonder, because they're easy to work with. Today's busy women can stuff a tortilla in no time with what's sitting in the refrigerator or what's in season.

Dish it up: 4 to 6 servings   Cooking time: 20 minutes
Construction time: 5 to 7 minutes   Paraphernalia: 12-inch skillet,
                                           13- by 9-inch baking dish

INGREDIENTS:

1 winter squash, diced
1 tomato, chopped
1 small green pepper, sliced
2 teaspoons olive oil
1/4 teaspoon dried basil
1 teaspoon garlic powder
4 to 6 whole-wheat tortillas, or your preference
1 1/2 to 2 cups (6 to 8 ounces) mozzarella cheese, shredded
Salt and pepper, to taste

To make:

1. Preheat oven to 400 degrees.
2. Wash veggies. Cut squash in half lengthwise, then crosswise and then dice. Chop tomatoes. Thinly slice pepper.
3. Heat oil over medium heat in skillet. Add tomato, squash, pepper, basil and garlic. Cook about 10 minutes, or until veggies are tender and liquid has evaporated. Stir occasionally.
4. Place tortillas on a flat surface. Spread about ¼ cup (⅙ if you're making more servings) of veggie mixture on one side of each tortilla. Top with mozzarella.
5. Flip up a lip on the bottom to hold in mixture, then roll from one side to the other. Place Rollovers in baking dish with the seam sides down.
6. Bake about 6 minutes, or until cheese is melted and mixture is heated through.

Jazz It Up: Add 1 slice of baked ham to each tortilla before adding veggie mixture.

Change It Up: Cook in the microwave for about 2 minutes instead of baking.

We Go Good Together: Carrots and ranch salad dressing

FRANTIC WOMAN FAMILY FUN: Candy Hunt
Pick up some flavored candy canes if they are still in season or another favorite wrapped candy on an upcoming shopping trip. (Avoid the peppermint canes, as kids usually don't care much for them.) Then, the next time you're at your wit's end trying to keep everyone from getting cabin fever, hide the candy canes. Have the kids go on a candy cane hunt. You might want to set a limit on the number of canes each person can find so everyone has a chance to get at least one.

❖ Day 4—Everyday Dinner: Easy Beef and Mac ❖

Celine Jurkiewicz spent many years as a nanny for two active boys. This quick, easy and inexpensive meal was a favorite and one often requested by her two charges.

Dish it up: 4 to 5 servings

Construction time: 12 minutes

Cooking time: 20 to 25 minutes

Paraphernalia: 12-inch skillet,
9- by 9-inch baking dish

INGREDIENTS:

1 7.25-ounce box macaroni and cheese

1 pound cooked ground beef, stored from Day 2

1 10.5-ounce can tomato soup

1/4 to 1/2 cup milk

To make:

1. Heat oven to 350 degrees.
2. Prepare macaroni and cheese according to directions.
3. Reheat browned ground beef while macaroni is cooking.
4. Place browned meat, prepared macaroni and cheese and soup in a baking dish. Add enough milk to moisten.
5. Cover and bake for about 20 to 25 minutes, or until heated through.

Jazz It Up: Add broccoli or black olives.

Change It Up: Zap it in the microwave for 8 to 10 minutes.

We Go Good Together: Stir-Fried Veggies

Look Ahead: If you put your cheddar cheese in the freezer, take it out and place it in the refrigerator to thaw for Day 5, Potato Asparagus Soup. Also, if you bought bacon to Jazz It Up and breadsticks for We Go Good Together, take them out of the freezer. Put the bacon in the refrigerator to thaw, and allow the breadsticks to thaw on the countertop.

TIPS BASKETFUL OF TIPS: Big Girls Don't Cry . . .
When Chopping Onion

- Keep from tearing up when chopping onions by doing it underwater.
- Follow Grandma's instructions and spray a bit of vinegar on the onion before you chop.
- Chef Jeff says, "Freeze them for 5 minutes or so before you chop."

By the way, you can remove the stinky onion smell from your hands by rubbing lemon juice on them.

⟿ Day 5—Soup's On: Potato Asparagus Soup 🔏 ⟿

Elementary school teacher Lindsey Rankin enjoys making up a batch of this delicious soup. Now is also a good time to pull out any leftovers you have from previous meals. Use the must-gos as a side dish, or create a smorgasbord with the soup as a starter.

Dish it up: 6 servings

Construction time: 7 minutes

Cooking time: 20 minutes

Paraphernalia: Stockpot

INGREDIENTS:

2 medium potatoes, diced

1/2 pound fresh asparagus, chopped

1 small onion, chopped

2 celery ribs, chopped

1 tablespoon chicken bouillon granules

4 cups water

1/2 cup all-purpose flour (or whole-grain flour)

1 cup heavy cream

1/2 cup milk

1/4 cup butter (1/2 stick)

1/2 teaspoon salt

1/2 teaspoon pepper

3/4 cup (3 ounces) cheddar cheese, shredded

To make:

1. Wash veggies. Peel and chop potatoes. (Simplify it: 1 medium potato equals 1 cup diced potatoes.) Chop asparagus, onion and celery.
2. Combine potatoes, asparagus, onion, celery, bouillon and water in pot, and bring to a boil. Reduce heat, cover, and simmer for about 15 minutes, or until veggies are tender.
3. Stir in butter.
4. In a bowl, combine flour, cream, milk, salt and pepper until smooth. Add to the veggies.
5. Bring to a boil, stirring for about 2 minutes, or until thickened.
6. Ladle soup into bowls. Garnish soup with shredded cheddar cheese.

Jazz It Up: Add 12 strips of crumbled bacon.

Dress It Down: Eliminate the cheese topping.

Change It Up: Substitute whole-grain flour for white flour.

We Go Good Together: Breadsticks for dunking. (Okay, Emily Post would definitely frown on you dunking your bread. But it sure does taste good!) Serve leftovers from previous meals.

Look Ahead: Pull out the chicken marked Day 6, Chicken Divan, and Day 7, Chicken Caesar Salad, and if you tucked the cheddar cheese for Day 7 in the freezer, pull that out, too, and put it in the refrigerator to defrost.

POTFUL OF KNOWLEDGE: Not So Bad Potatoes

Take potatoes off your do-not-eat list. According to the USDA, 1 baked spud (about 11 ounces) packs as powerful punch of anti-oxidants as 2 cups cooked broccoli, 1½ cups cooked asparagus or 1 cup cooked red cabbage. So, put spuds back on your have-some-tonight list.

Frantic Woman Family Fun: Zany Vegetable Adventure

Take the kids on a zany adventure by reading the children's book *Brave Potatoes* by Toby Speed. The story is filled with delightful rhymes, making it a fun read for everyone.

PIT STOP: Pick Up Produce

If you held off buying your veggies to keep them fresh, now is the time to pick them up. You'll need 1 bag (16 ounces) romaine ready-to-eat salad mix, 1 bag (12 ounces) fresh spinach, 1 bag (10 ounces) baby cut carrots, 1 carton (8 ounces) snowcap mushrooms, 1 head broccoli and 1 winter squash.

If you held off buying your Jazz It Up produce, now is the time to buy 1 green pepper, 1 tomato and an additional carton (8 ounces) snowcap mushrooms. And if you're making the We Go Good Together side dishes, you'll need 2 cucumbers, 1 head lettuce, 3 papayas, 3 pears, 1 bag radishes and 2 tomatoes.

➤ *Day 6—Everyday Dinner: Chicken Divan* ❖

Here's an easy recipe. All you need to do is open a can, chop some broccoli, and mix a few ingredients together. The oven does the rest for you. And if you're really frazzled, skip the chopping process for the broccoli. After you've popped the baking dish in the oven, brew a cup of tea and put your feet up. Or if you'd rather get the kids' homework out of the way so you can have a free evening, you'll have 30 minutes to do so.

Dish up: 4 to 6 servings

Construction time: 5 minutes

Cooking time: 30 minutes

Paraphernalia: 2 9- by 13-inch baking dishes

INGREDIENTS:

Butter

2 cups broccoli florets 🥤 (Chop 1 additional cup of broccoli florets for Day 7, Chicken Caesar Salad.)

8 pieces of chicken tenderloin (or 4 to 5 boneless chicken breasts) 🥤 (Bake 4 to 6 extra chicken tenderloins for Day 7, Chicken Caesar Salad.)

1 tablespoon butter

½ cup (2 ounces) cheddar cheese, shredded

1 10.5-ounce can cream of chicken soup

¾ cup mayonnaise

To make:

1. Preheat oven to 375 degrees.
2. Coat baking dish with butter.
3. Cut up broccoli into smaller pieces.
4. Place 8 chicken tenderloins in the baking dish. (Simplify it: When substituting a different cut of chicken, such as breasts, be sure to cut the chicken into smaller slices for quicker cooking.) Top chicken with broccoli.
5. To Double It, place 4 to 6 chicken tenderloins in another baking dish for Day 7, Chicken Caesar Salad. For moister chicken, spread mayo over these pieces. Add ½ cup broth or water. Cover with foil, then bake.

6. Mix mayonnaise and soup in a small bowl. Cover chicken and broccoli with mixture.
7. Sprinkle cheese on top.
8. Cover dish with foil, and bake for about 30 minutes, or until chicken is no longer pink. Serve hot.
9. Cool additional pieces of chicken for Double It; then put these pieces in the refrigerator.

Jazz It Up: Add ½ cup canned sliced mushrooms.

Dress It Down: Skip the broccoli.

Change It Up: You can substitute frozen broccoli for fresh. Be sure to thaw it first. You can use cream of mushroom soup instead of chicken. Also, chicken breasts work well if you can't find tenderloins.

Double It: Bake 4 to 6 extra chicken tenderloins to use for a no-cook night on Day 7. Bake chicken in a separate baking dish. Spread chicken with mayo and add ½ cup of broth or water. Once baked, store in refrigerator. Additionally, chop 1 cup of broccoli florets and store in the refrigerator for Day 7, Chicken Caesar Salad.

We Go Good Together: Serve on a bed of rice.

Look Ahead: Take the muffins for Day 7, We Go Good Together, out of the freezer and allow them to defrost on the countertop. Take the boneless pork loin for Day 8, Penguin Goulash, out of the freezer and put it in the refrigerator to defrost.

⭢ Day 7—No-Cook Night: Chicken Caesar Salad ⭠

After a week of cooking, you need a break. And that's just what you'll have with tonight's no-cook meal. Chicken Caesar Salad will get you out of the kitchen quickly so you can spend time with the kids. And if you want to skip washing up the dinner dishes, break out the disposable plates and call it a picnic. However, if your little ones, like many kids, aren't big on mixing foods together, serve them their chicken solo, with barbecue sauce or ketchup for dipping, and their salad on the side.

Dish up: 4 servings
Construction time: 7 to 10 minutes

Cooking time: 0
Paraphernalia: Large salad or
serving bowl

INGREDIENTS:

1 cup broccoli florets, stored from Day 6

2 tomatoes, diced

Chicken tenderloins, stored from Day 6

1 16-ounce bag romaine ready-to-eat salad mix

¾ cup croutons

½ cup bottled Caesar salad dressing

2 tablespoons Parmesan cheese, grated

To make:
1. Wash veggies.
2. Slice chicken. Dice tomatoes.
3. Toss all ingredients together.

Jazz It Up: Top with sliced hard-boiled eggs. Exchange the grated Parmesan cheese for fresh. Prepare 2 servings of short-cut pasta like ziti and mix it together with the salad.

Dress It Down: Forget the tomatoes.

Change It Up: Most restaurants use romaine in Caesar salads, but any type of packaged ready-to-eat salad will work.

We Go Good Together: Serve your favorite muffins.

✦ Day 8—Old Tradition: Penguin Goulash ✦

Goulash can be made many different ways, depending on your heritage or what part of the country you live in. Penguin Goulash has been tweaked from an old-country recipe made by a former Pittsburgh hockey player.

Dish up: 4 to 6 servings   Cooking time: 20 to 25 minutes
Construction time: 10 minutes   Paraphernalia: 12-inch skillet

INGREDIENTS:

½ cup vegetable oil

1 large onion, diced

2 pounds boneless pork loin, cubed

1/2 teaspoon paprika

2 cups water

1 16-ounce can sauerkraut, drained

1 cup sour cream

To make:

1. Heat oil in skillet. Peel and diced onion. Sauté onions.
2. Add paprika and pork. Brown pork for about 5 minutes over medium heat.
3. Cover pork with water. Cook about 5 to 10 minutes, or until meat is no longer pink.
4. Drain sauerkraut. Add sauerkraut to meat and let it come to a boil.
5. Add sour cream. Mix well. Cook for 5 minutes, or until heated through.

Jazz It Up: Add 1 cup canned sliced carrots during Step 3.

Dress It Down: Skip the sauerkraut and sour cream. Make pork chops with sauerkraut on the side.

Change It Up: Use veal tenderloin instead of pork.

We Go Good Together: Serve with wide egg noodles.

Look Ahead: Take the 4 slices of Colby cheese, bagels and bacon out of the freezer and tuck them in the refrigerator to thaw for Day 9, Eggel Bagel.

FRANTIC WOMAN FAMILY FUN: Take a Spin

Read the fascinating history of the dreidel in *Four Sides, Eight Nights: A New Spin on Hanukkah* by Tova Ben-Zvi with the kids. Of course, you should end the evening by spinning this time-honored toy. If you don't have a dreidel in the house, many party and discount stores sell them at this time of year.

✦ Day 9—Backwards Meal: Eggel Bagels ✦

As a young newlywed, I remember Sunday breakfast at the local family restaurant being a special treat. This is when I discovered the egg bagel. At that time, I had never heard of it. (This was before bagel sandwiches became commonplace in restaurants and the frozen foods section in the grocery store.) I could get an egg layered with cheese and bacon on a bagel for only $1.49. (This is when you sigh and think, "Oh, those were the days.") Eggel Bagels are a favorite evening meal in our house on lazy winter days.

Dish up: 4 servings (more if needed) Cooking time: 12 to 15 minutes
Construction time: 3 minutes   Paraphernalia: Microwave, microwave-
safe plate, 12-inch skillet

INGREDIENTS:
8 slices bacon
5 eggs
3 tablespoons milk
4 bagels
4 slices Colby cheese

To make:
1. Lay bacon on a microwave-safe plate and cook for 3 to 4 minutes, depending on how crisp you like your bacon. Or cook bacon in a skillet on your stove top.
2. Spray nonstick cooking spray in skillet.
3. Beat eggs and milk until mixed. (If you like more milk in your eggs, add it.)
4. Pour egg mixture into hot skillet. Cook 3 to 5 minutes, turning once. Divide eggs into 4 sections.
5. Slice bagels. Place 1 section of egg on the bottom of each bagel. Lay 1 piece of cheese and 2 pieces of bacon on the egg. Add the top of the bagel.
6. Serve. (Simplify it: Bagels are easier to eat, especially for little ones, if you cut them in half.)

Jazz It Up: Add sliced tomatoes.

Dress It Down: Omit the bacon to make it a meatless meal.

Change It Up: Change the bacon to sausage or ham. Make miniature bagels instead of full-size ones.

We Go Good Together: Fruit Parfait

Look Ahead: Pull out the eye of round roast marked Day 11, Winter Roast, from the freezer and put it in the refrigerator. Though you're not serving it for two days, it will need additional time to defrost. Pull the English muffins and cheddar cheese for Day 10 'Linda's Cheesy Delights, from the freezer, too, if you froze them.

❧ Day 10—Kids' Meal: Linda's Cheesy Delights ❧

Linda Cannon loves this meal because the kids can make it themselves. All you'll need to do is supervise. Linda makes her Delights with the "Jazz It Up" ingredients. So if you know your kids will eat them, make sure you add these ingredients, as they add flavor to the meal.

Dish up: 4 to 6 servings   Cooking time: 15 minutes
Construction time: 5 to 10 minutes   Paraphernalia: Baking sheet

INGREDIENTS:

1 cup (4 ounces) cheddar cheese, shredded
1 cup sour cream
1 cup mayonnaise
4 to 6 English muffins
Salt and pepper to taste

To make:
1. Preheat oven to 350 degrees.
2. Mix the ingredients together, except muffins. Add salt and pepper to taste.
3. Cut muffins in half lengthwise, if needed.
4. Spread mixture on muffins.
5. Lay muffins on baking sheet. Bake for 15 minutes.

Jazz It Up: Add ½ cup chopped black olives, ½ cup chopped green olives and ½ cup chopped green onions to the mixture. Add chopped vegetables to boost the nutritional value, too.

Change It Up: Exchange the mayo for plain yogurt.

We Go Good Together: Tossed salad

Look Ahead: Be sure to defrost your roast, if it is still frozen. Also, if your slow cooker has a removable crock liner, you can prepare the Winter Roast (add the meat in the morning for food safety) while you're cleaning up the kitchen. Then, put the crock liner in the refrigerator overnight. In the morning, toss in the roast, and insert the pan into the cooker. Plug it in and turn it on.

FRANTIC WOMAN FAMILY FUN:
Tender Touch Cookies

Beverly Breton Carroll and Alrie McNiff Daniels created this yummy cookie recipe. Tender Touch Cookies are perfect for cooking with very young children because no mixers or spoons are required. Pour 1 cup brown sugar, 1 cup softened butter, 1 cup flour, 1 teaspoon baking soda and 2 cups oatmeal into a large bowl. Start squishing the ingredients together by hand. (Make sure everyone's hands are clean.) Mix until all ingredients are blended and dough is soft. Place 1-inch balls of dough on an ungreased baking sheet. Use the bottom of a glass dipped in sugar to flatten each ball. Bake for 8 to 10 minutes. Enjoy! Recipe makes 4 dozen cookies.

✧ Day 11—Slow Cook Tonight: Winter Roast ✧

This is a great meal for a late night at the office or when you're rushing off to your son's basketball game or your daughter's karate lesson after work. When the dinner hour strikes, all you'll have to do is slice the roast, scoop up the veggies, and enjoy a home-cooked meal.

Dish up: 4 to 6 servings   Cooking time: 8 hours or more
Construction time: 5 to 10 minutes   Paraphernalia: Slow cooker

INGREDIENTS:
3 potatoes, cubed
1 onion, sliced

1 4- to 5-pound eye of round roast 🐄 (Half of the roast will be set
   aside for Day 13, Beef Stir-Fry.)
1 28-ounce can stewed tomatoes
1 cup baby cut carrots
1 cup water

To make:
   1. Wash and cube potatoes. Peel and slice onion.
   2. Place roast, carrots, potatoes, onion and tomatoes in slow cooker.
   3. Add water.
   4. Cook at number 3 setting or low-medium for 8 to 10 hours. If the
      roast will be cooking longer than that, lower the temperature a bit.
   5. Allow roast to stand for 10 minutes. Slice. Reserve half of the roast
      for Day 13, Beef Stir-Fry.
   6. Serve the remaining roast.

Jazz It Up: Add 1 tablespoon of Cajun or Italian seasoning.

Dress It Down: Skip the vegetables, including stewed tomatoes. Add 1
jar spaghetti sauce or 1 can tomato soup plus 1 cup water instead.

Change It Up: You can use any type of roast your family prefers. You
can exchange the stewed tomatoes for 1 can (16 ounces) of tomato sauce
and 2 fresh tomatoes, diced.

Double It: Set aside half of the roast for Day 13, Beef Stir-Fry, and store
it in the refrigerator.

We Go Good Together: Italian or French bread. Spread mayonnaise
on bread slices, then top with cheddar cheese. Put slices under the broiler
for a few minutes, until cheese is melted.

Look Ahead: If you bought cheddar cheese for Day 12, Jazz it up, pull
it out of the freezer and put it in the refrigerator to thaw.

✷ Day 12—I Can with a Can: Tuna Casserole 🐟 ✷

Tuna Casserole is a favorite speed-dial meal in our home. It is I can easily whip together that even my teenage son loves to eat as leftovers. That

is a feat, as he tends to complain about eating the same thing two days in a row. This recipe is perfect for those days when all you can manage is opening a can, maybe even with an electric can opener.

Dish up: 4 to 5 servings

Construction time: 5 to 7 minutes

Cooking time: 8 to 10 minutes

Paraphernalia: 3-quart pot, microwave, microwave-safe baking dish, wax paper

INGREDIENTS:

2 cups instant rice (Cook 2 additional cups of rice for Day 13, Beef Stir-Fry.)

1 6-ounce can white tuna packed in water, drained

1 10.5-ounce can cream of mushroom soup

1/4 cup french-fried onion rings, crumbled

1/4 cup milk

To make:

1. Cook rice according to directions. While rice is cooking, drain tuna and crumble onion rings.
2. Put half of the cooked rice into baking dish and the other half for Day 13, Beef Stir-Fry in the refrigerator.
3. Place tuna, soup, onion rings and milk into dish. Mix thoroughly.
4. Cover with wax paper. Cook in the microwave at high power for 8 to 10 minutes, or until heated through.

Jazz It Up: Add mushrooms, peppers, or any other favorite topping. Add 1/2 cup shredded cheddar cheese.

Dress It Down: Eliminate the onion rings.

Change It Up: Any creamed soup will usually work, as long as your family likes its taste. If you prefer, you can bake the casserole in a 350-degree oven for 20 to 25 minutes.

Double It: Cook 4 additional servings of rice for Day l3, Beef Stir-Fry. Store and refrigerate.

We Go Good Together: Applesauce

☀ Day 13—Must-Go: Beef Stir-Fry ☀

Dish up: 4 to 5 servings
Construction time: 5 minutes

Cooking time: 15 minutes
Paraphernalia: 12-inch skillet, bowl

INGREDIENTS:

1 cup squash, diced
1 cup broccoli florets
½ cup baby cut carrots
½ cup snowcap mushrooms, sliced
Roast, stored from Day 11
2 teaspoons vegetable oil
1 small yellow onion
1 8-ounce can water chestnuts, sliced
1 teaspoon garlic powder
½ teaspoon ginger
1 teaspoon soy sauce
1 14-ounce can beef broth
1 tablespoon cornstarch
Rice, 4 servings stored from Day 12

To make:

1. Wash veggies. Dice squash. Cut up broccoli and carrots into bite-size pieces. Slice mushrooms.
2. Slice roast into thin strips.
3. Heat oil in 12-inch skillet over medium heat. Peel and slice onion. Cut onion slices in half. Sauté onion for 2 minutes.
4. Cut carrots in half lengthwise and toss in skillet.
5. Add mushrooms and beef strips. Stir-fry 3 to 5 minutes.
6. Drain water chestnuts. Add water chestnuts, broccoli, garlic, ginger and soy sauce. Stir-fry 3 minutes.
7. Add ½ cup broth to skillet.
8. Mix cornstarch and remaining beef broth in bowl. Whisk until lumps disappear. (Simplify it: Put cornstarch and beef broth into a container with a lid and shake well.)

9. Add liquid mixture to the skillet. Cook for about 3 minutes, or until liquid thickens slightly.
10. Heat rice in the microwave for about 3 minutes, or until heated through.
11. Serve over rice.

Jazz It Up: Add ½ cup of white wine in step 5.

Dress It Down: Eliminate the water chestnuts and onions.

Change It Up: Use whatever veggies are taking up space in your refrigerator.

We Go Good Together: Tossed salad

Look Ahead: Take the feta cheese out of the freezer and put it in the refrigerator to thaw for Day 14, Penne with Spinach, Tomatoes and Feta cheese.

✦ Day 14—Company's Coming: ✦
Penne with Spinach, Tomatoes and Feta Cheese

Mmm! This is scrumptious dish fit for any company you might entertain, including the boss. It's a recipe you might find listed on the menu of a popular restaurant.

Dish up: 4 to 6 servings
Construction time: 15 minutes

Cooking time: 5 minutes
Paraphernalia: 12-inch skillet, small bowl, 5-quart pot, strainer

INGREDIENTS:

⅔ cup water
½ cup sun-dried tomatoes, drained
1 16-ounce package penne pasta
6 cups fresh spinach, washed
2 tablespoons olive oil
1 teaspoon garlic powder
1 teaspoon dried basil
2 tablespoons balsamic vinegar
½ cup crumbled feta cheese
Salt and pepper, to taste

To make:

1. Boil water. Drain tomatoes. Combine sun-dried tomatoes and boiling water. Set aside for 10 minutes. (This will soften tomatoes.)
2. Prepare pasta according to package directions, but do not add salt and oil.
3. Wash spinach.
4. Pull tomatoes from water, reserving soaking liquid. Chop tomatoes.
5. Coat skillet with nonstick cooking spray and heat.
6. Add garlic, tomatoes, tomato liquid, spinach, basil and vinegar. Cook about 5 minutes, or until spinach has wilted.
7. Stir in cheese. Heat only until cheese begins to melt. Add salt and pepper, to taste.
8. Serve immediately over pasta.

Jazz It Up: Add 1 pound cooked shrimp, peeled and deveined.
Dress It Down: Skip the spinach.
Change It Up: Use jarred marina sauce instead of tomatoes, water, garlic, basil and vinegar.
We Go Good Together: Garlic toast.

BASKETFUL OF TIPS: Searching for "Mr. Right Pasta"
Is there a right or wrong pasta to use for a particular dish? No.
Any short pasta, such as ziti, rigatoni or mostaccioli, can be substituted for penne. So buy your favorite type or, if you're watching your pennies, buy what's on sale. By the way, 2 ounces of pasta equals 1 serving. Keep this in mind if you're watching your weight. However, if you have an athlete in the house, carbohydrates are a great source of energy.

WINTER PLAN TWO MENUS

Day 1—Sandwich Board: Lucy's Joes (Sloppy Joes)

Day 2—Everyday Dinner: Yummy Chix

Day 3—Everyday Dinner: Librarian Goulash

Day 4—Old Tradition/No-Cook Night: Muffuletta Sandwich

Day 5—Retro Meal: Classic Mac & Cheese

Day 6—Backwards Meal: Breakfast Pizza

Day 7—Soup's On: Kathy's Multi-Generation Chicken Soup with Orzo

Day 8—Everyday Dinner: Mustang Kielbasa

Day 9—Everyday Dinner: Tuna Pasta Toss

Day 10—Kids' Meal: Hot Dog Trick

Day 11—Slow Cook Tonight: Old Man Winter's Roast and Veggies

Day 12—I Can with a Can: Open, Dump, Stir Veggie Supper

Day 13—Must-Go: Easy Beef Burritos

Day 14—Company's Coming: Aunt Mary's Meat Loaf Supreme

THE SHOPPING LISTS

The Frantic Woman's Cupboard

WINTER PLAN TWO STAPLES

Seasonings

Chili powder

Garlic (minced, powder)

Mustard (dry)

Onion (powder)

Salt*

Pepper

Condiments
Ketchup

Jazz It Ups
Relish
Oregano

Dressings, Oil and Sauces
Mayonnaise
Oil (olive,* vegetable)
Vinegar (white wine)
Worcestershire sauce

Side Dishes
Oil (peanut)
Honey

Baking Needs
Sugar (brown, cane*)

Side Dishes
Baking powder
Cornstarch
Flour

Bread, Chips and More
Bread crumbs (seasoned)

Frantic Necessities
Nonstick cooking spray

Dairy
Butter
Eggs
Milk

*Ingredient needed for both main and side dishes

The Frantic Woman Goes Shopping

Main-Dish Ingredients You'll Need to Buy

Produce: Veggies

6 small onions (Days 1, 8, 11, 14)

2 green peppers (Days 1, 14)

2 small bunches parsley (Days 4, 14)

1 red pepper (Day 9)

PIT STOP: Keep It Fresh

To ensure the produce for your entrees is fresh, you might want to pick up these items near the end of the first week or on Day 5 or 6: 1 small bunch parsley, 1 green pepper, 1 red pepper and 5 small onions. Also, don't hesitate to exchange the red pepper for a green one if the red peppers are too costly.

Canned Goods and Bottles

1 10.75-ounce can tomato soup (Day 1)

3 15-ounce cans chicken broth (Days 2, 7)

2 10.75-ounce cans cream of mushroom soup (Days 3, 12)

1 10-ounce jar roasted sweet red peppers (Day 4)

1 6-ounce can pitted black olives (Day 4)

1 5-ounce bottle pitted green olives (Day 4)

1 4-ounce can tomato sauce (Day 7)

1 2.5-ounce can sliced black olives (Day 9)

2 6-ounce cans tuna packed in with oil (Day 9)

2 14.5-ounce cans stewed tomatoes (Day 11)

1 16-ounce jar salsa (Days 11, 13)

2 15-ounce cans sliced potatoes (Day 12)

1 4-ounce can sliced mushrooms (Day 12)

1 14-ounce can cheddar cheese soup (Day 12)

1 8-ounce can peas (Day 12)

Noodles, Pasta and Rice

1 16-ounce package egg noodles (Day 3)
½ 16-ounce package elbow macaroni (Day 5)
1 8-ounce package orzo (Day 7)
1 12-ounce package linguine (Day 9)

Bread, Chips and More

14 hamburger buns (Days 1, 10)
1 round loaf Italian bread or 6 torpedo rolls (Day 4)

Deli

1½ pound sliced mild cheddar cheese (Day 4)
⅓ pound sliced prosciutto (Day 4)
½ pound sliced provolone cheese (Day 4)
⅓ pound sliced salami (Day 4)

Fish, Meat and Poultry

1½ pounds lean ground beef (Day 1)
4½ pounds skinless, boneless chicken breasts (Days 2, 7)
1 pound beef, cubed (Day 3)
1 pound pork breakfast sausage (Day 6)
2 pounds kielbasa (Day 8)
1 pound hot dogs (Day 10)
1 3-pound chuck roast (Day 11)
1½ pounds ground chuck (Day 14)

Dairy

1 cup (4 ounces) mozzarella, shredded (Day 2)
¾ (3 ounces) Parmesan cheese, grated (Days 2, 6)
1 8-ounce container low-fat sour cream (Day 3)
3 cups (12 ounces) sharp American or Swiss and American cheese,
    shredded (Day 5)
1 8-ounce tube refrigerated crescent rolls (Day 6)
1 cup (4 ounces) medium or sharp cheddar cheese, shredded (Day 6)
1 8-ounce tube refrigerated biscuits (Day 12)
1 10-count package flour or whole-wheat tortillas (Day 13)

Frozen

1 16-ounce package hash brown potatoes (Days 6, 10)

JAZZ IT UP INGREDIENTS YOU'LL NEED TO BUY

Produce: Veggies

Vegetables, your preference (Day 2)
1 small head broccoli (Day 5)
1 small bunch green onions (Day 5)
3 or 4 potatoes (Day 11)
1 rib celery (Day 14)

Dressings, Oils and Sauces

1 6-ounce jar pesto sauce (Day 7)
1 16-ounce bottle barbecue sauce (Day 10)

Canned Goods and Bottles

1 4-ounce can sliced mushrooms (Day 3)
1 8-ounce can peas (Day 5)
1 10-ounce jar jalapeño peppers (Day 8)
1 8-ounce jar marinated artichoke hearts (Day 9)
1 8-ounce jar roasted Italian vegetables (Day 11)
1 5-ounce can chunk, lean ham (Day 12)

Bread, Chips and More

1 6-ounce box croutons (Day 5)

Deli

⅓ pound mortadella (Day 4)
¼ pound ham (Day 5)
8 slices cheddar cheese (Day 10)

Dairy

8 ounces sour cream (Day 13)

WE GO GOOD TOGETHER INGREDIENTS YOU'LL NEED TO BUY

Produce: Fruit

2 Red Delicious apples (Day 4)

4 bananas (Day 6)

Fruit, your preference (Day 10)

Produce: Veggies

2 pounds green beans (Day 3)

3 plum tomatoes (Day 3)

6 cloves garlic (Day 3)

1 8-ounce carton portobello mushrooms (Day 3)

1 small head cauliflower (Day 8)

1 8-ounce bag baby cut carrots (Day 8)

1 16-ounce package ready-to-eat salad (Day 9)

3 to 4 Idaho potatoes (Day 14)

Canned Goods and Bottles

1 10.75-ounce can tomato soup (Day 5)

1 16-ounce can pears (Day 12)

1 16-ounce jar nacho cheese sauce (Day 13)

Noodles, Pasta and Rice

8 ounces pasta (Day 2)

Bread, Chips and More

4 to 6 breadsticks (Day 7)

1 16-ounce bag nachos chips (Day 13)

Dairy

¾ cup (3 ounces) Parmesan cheese, grated (Day 3)

Frozen

1 32-ounce bag french fries or potato chips (Day 1)

1 loaf garlic toast (Day 11)

PIT STOP: Keep It Fresh

Consider buying these ingredients for the Jass It Up and We Go Good Together suggestions on Day 5 or 6: 4 bananas, fruit of your choice, 1 small head cauliflower, 1 bag (8 ounces) baby cut carrots, 6 to 8 Idaho potatoes, 1 package (16 ounces) ready-to-eat salad mix and 1 bunch celery.

Unloading the Load

- As you're unloading the grocery bags, store the mozzarella cheese, boneless chicken breasts and 1½ pounds of the lean ground beef in the refrigerator to use in the next few days.
- Put 3 tablespoons of Parmesan cheese in the freezer for Day 6, Breakfast Pizza, and the rest in the refrigerator for Day 2, Yummy Chix.
- Freeze the beef cubes for Day 3, Librarian Goulash.
- Freeze the sharp American or Swiss and American for Day 5, Classic Mac & Cheese.
- Freeze the pork sausage and cheddar cheese for Day 6, Breakfast Pizza.
- Freeze the kielbasa for Day 8, Mustang Kielbasa.
- Freeze the hot dogs and 8 hamburger buns for Day 10, Hot Dog Trick.
- Freeze the chuck roast for Day 11, Old Man Winter's Roast and Veggies.
- Freeze 1½ pounds ground chuck for Day 14, Aunt Mary's Meat Loaf Supreme.
- Freeze 8 cheddar cheese slices for Day 10, Jazz it up.
- Freeze the ham for Day 5, Jazz it up.
- Freeze the mortadella for Day 4, Jazz it up.
- Freeze the breadsticks for Day 7, We Go Good Together.
- Freeze the nacho chips for Day 13, We Go Good Together if you think your family will snack on them.

- Be sure to mark all packages with their contents and designated days.
- Be sure to read the Look Ahead section in each recipe to see when you must pull items out of the freezer to put into the refrigerator to defrost.

WINTER: PLAN TWO

✦ Day 1—Sandwich Board: Lucy's Joes (Sloppy Joes) ✦

Here's a retro meal from Lucy Elder, the mom of one of my dearest frantic friends. (Sorry Andrea, you really are frantic.) My and Andrea's kids think Lucy's Joes are tastier than the sandwiches made with the canned product similar to this.

Dish up: 6 servings
Construction time: 10 to 15 minutes

Cooking time: 15 minutes
Paraphernalia: 12-inch skillet

INGREDIENTS:
1 small onion, chopped
1 green pepper, cut in half
1½ pounds lean ground beef
1 tablespoon Worcestershire sauce
1 10.75-ounce can tomato soup
½ cup water
Salt and pepper, to taste
6 hamburger buns

To make:
1. Peel and chop onion. Wash pepper. Cut off top of green pepper and cut it in half.
2. In skillet over medium heat, brown ground beef with onion. Drain excess fat from beef.
3. Add Worcestershire sauce. Stir in soup and water.

4. Add green pepper on top of beef mixture. Simmer 15 minutes.
5. Remove green pepper from skillet. Salt and pepper the beef mixture, to taste.
6. Serve on buns.

Jazz It Up: Top Joes with relish.
Dress It Down: Skip the onion.
We Go Good Together: French fries or potato chips
Look Ahead: Make sure the chicken for Day 2, Yummy Chix, is in the refrigerator just in case you tucked it in the freezer by mistake.

☀ Day 2—Everyday Dinner: Yummy Chix ☀

Rita Bergstein finds herself on the go all the time. Between handling clients at her day job as an insurance agent, promoting her children's picture book *Your Own Big Bed*, and raising three teenage daughters, her dinner meals must be tasty, quick and easy. Everyone in her family prepares this dish with ease.

Dish up: 5 to 6 servings
Construction time: 12 to 15 minutes

Cooking time: 20 to 30 minutes
Paraphernalia: 12-inch skillet,
2 baking dishes, 2 bowls

INGREDIENTS:

3 pounds skinless, boneless chicken breasts 🥤 (Cook 1 1/2 pounds chicken breasts for Day 7, Kathy's Multi-Generation Chicken Soup with Orzo.)
1/2 cup mayonnaise
1/2 cup water
1 egg
2 tablespoons milk
2 cups bread crumbs, seasoned
1 cup vegetable oil
1 cup (4 ounces) mozzarella, shredded
1 15-ounce can chicken broth
1/2 (2 ounces) cup Parmesan cheese, grated

To make:

1. Preheat oven to 350 degrees.

2. Spread mayonnaise on 1½ pounds of chicken breasts for Day 7, Kathy's Multi-Generation Chicken Soup with Orzo. Put chicken in a baking dish with ½ cup water.

3. Break egg into bowl. Add milk to egg and beat together.

4. Put bread crumbs into a separate bowl.

5. Pour oil into skillet and place over medium heat.

6. Dip chicken into egg mixture, then coat with bread crumbs. (Simplify it: Pour bread crumbs into a plastic zippered bag. Toss dipped chicken into bag, seal closed, then shake bag to coat chicken.)

7. Place coated chicken into skillet. Fry for about 3 to 5 minutes on each side.

8. Put coated chicken into baking dish. Add broth. Put both baking dishes in oven and bake for about 10 to 15 minutes. Pull dish containing coated chicken out, and cover chicken with mozzarella and Parmesan. Cook both dishes another 10 to 15 minutes.

9. Freeze the mayo-basted chicken for Day 7, Kathy's Multi-Generation Chicken Soup with Orzo.

Jazz It Up: Add sliced vegetables before you pop the dish into the oven.

Dress It Down: Skip the cheeses.

Change It Up: Replace bread crumbs with whole-wheat flour.

Double It: Cook 1½ pounds chicken breasts for Day 7, Kathy's Multi-Generation Chicken Soup with Orzo.

We Go Good Together: Serve chicken over pasta.

Look ahead: Pull the beef cubes for Day 3, Librarian Goulash, from the freezer and put them in the refrigerator to thaw.

✦ Day 3—Everyday Dinner: Librarian Goulash ✦

Librarian Teresa Isadora loves when her daughter Melissa cooks up this wonderful, low-fat dish. But Melissa cooks like a lot of women and tosses in a dash of this and a pinch of that. To get the recipe, Teresa had to sit, watch and scribble the ingredients down on paper as Melissa prepared Librarian Goulash.

Dish up: 4 to 5 servings

Construction time: 15 minutes

Cooking time: 10 minutes

Paraphernalia: 12-inch skillet, 3-quart pot

INGREDIENTS:

1 tablespoon butter

2 tablespoons onion powder

1 teaspoon garlic powder

1 pound beef, cubed

1 16-ounce package egg noodles

1 10.75-ounce can cream of mushroom soup

8 ounces low-fat sour cream

To make:

1. Melt butter in skillet over medium heat.
2. Add onion and garlic powder. Add beef and stir-fry for about 10 minutes, or until slightly pink in the middle.
3. While beef is stir-frying, boil water for noodles and cook according to package directions.
4. Lower heat on beef. Stir in undiluted mushroom soup. (Do not add water or milk.) Stir in sour cream. Cook until hot, about 5 to 7 minutes.
5. Pour over cooked noodles.

Jazz It Up: Add 1 can (4 ounces) sliced mushrooms.

Dress It Down: Use ground beef instead of beef cubes.

Change It Up: Use low-fat soup.

We Go Good Together: Desi's Fresh Veggies 🌎

Look Ahead: Take your sandwich fixings, the meats and the cheeses, out of the freezer and put them in the refrigerator for Day 4, Muffuletta Sandwich. Also, take the Italian bread or torpedo rolls out and put them on the countertop to thaw.

FRANTIC WOMAN FAMILY FUN: Story Time

A family can't eat Librarian Goulash without ending the evening with a little story time. *We Eat Dinner in the Bathtub* by Angela Shelf Medearis is a whimsical chapter book that deals with accepting people's differences. Keeping with the food theme, *If You Give a Mouse a Cookie* is another delightful book about a generous boy and greedy mouse who makes a mess.

❖ Day 4—Old Tradition/No-Cook Night: ❖
Muffuletta Sandwich

Muhf-fuh-leht-tuh is a specialty of New Orleans that dates back to 1906. For the past century, the Central Grocery in New Orleans has served up the Muffuletta sandwich. And since New Orleans's famous celebration, Mardi Gras, usually falls in February, the frantic-style Muffuletta is an ideal winter menu choice.

Dish up: 6 to 8 servings   Cooking time: 0
Construction time: 10 minutes   Paraphernalia: Small bowl

INGREDIENTS:

1 round loaf Italian bread or 6 torpedo rolls
1 cup pitted green olives, chopped
1 cup pitted black olives, chopped
$1/2$ cup roasted sweet red peppers, chopped
3 teaspoons fresh parsley, chopped
1 teaspoon minced garlic
2 tablespoons white wine vinegar
1 cup olive oil
$1/3$ pound salami
$1/3$ pound prosciutto
$1/2$ pound provolone cheese
$1/2$ pound mild cheddar cheese

To make:

1. Cut the loaf in half horizontally.
2. Scoop out some of the inside bread to make a small well.
3. Chop olives and sweet peppers. Wash and chop parsley.
4. In a small bowl, combine olives, peppers, garlic, parsley and vinegar to make olive salad.
5. Drizzle some of the olive oil and some of the juice from the olive salad on the inside of both halves of the bread.
6. On the bottom half, fill the well with olive salad and layer with salami, prosciutto, cheddar and provolone cheese. Top with the other bread half. Slice into wedges.

Jazz It Up: Buy ⅓ pound mortadella (deli meat) and add to the sandwiches. You would find mortadella on a traditional Muffuletta sandwich.

Dress It Down: Skip the olive salad.

Change It Up: Use individual torpedo rolls instead of the round Italian bread. Eliminate the deli meats to make it a meatless meal.

We Go Good Together: Sliced apples with honey

Look Ahead: Take the sharp American or Swiss and American cheese you bought for Day 5, Classic Mac & Cheese, out of the freezer and put it in the refrigerator to thaw. Also, if you bought ham for Day 5 Jazz It Up, take it out of the freezer and put it in the refrigerator to thaw.

⇢ Day 5—Retro Meal: Classic Mac & Cheese 🐷 ⇠

Macaroni and cheese is a dinner staple in most American homes. Though some frantic cooks are serving those boxed packages with the dried cheese mix, this easy-to-make meal can be dished up in about the same amount of time, and it tastes a whole lot better.

Dish up: 4 servings

Construction time: 15 minutes

Cooking time: 5 minutes

Paraphernalia: 3-quart pot, strainer

INGREDIENTS:

8 ounces elbow macaroni

3 cups (12 ounces) sharp American or Swiss and American cheese, shredded or cut into ½-inch cubes

1 cup milk

To make:

1. Cook macaroni according to package directions.
2. While macaroni is cooking, cut cheese into 1/2-inch cubes if not shredded.
3. Drain macaroni when finished cooking. Combine cooked macaroni, milk and cheese in pot. Cook over medium heat until cheese has melted, stirring occasionally.
4. Serve hot.

Jazz It Up: Add cooked broccoli, green onions, peas or ham. Top with crushed croutons. (Simplify it: Put croutons in a plastic zippered bag and push a rolling pin back and forth across the croutons to crush them.)

Change It Up: Use jarred cheese sauce rather than making the one suggested.

We Go Good Together: Tomato soup

Look Ahead: Take the pork sausage, Parmesan cheese, 1 cup frozen hash brown potatoes and cheddar cheese for Day 6, Breakfast Pizza, out of the freezer and put them in the refrigerator to thaw.

BASKETFUL OF TIPS: Frozen Assets

Double the Classic Mac & Cheese recipe and freeze it for a hot lunch later. Put macaroni in individual freezer containers that can be microwaved. Make sure the lids fit tightly. You can freeze them for 2 months. To thaw, place containers in the refrigerator 24 hours prior to eating. Add a drop or two of milk, then microwave on high for 1 to 2 minutes or until heated through. Stir once, halfway through cooking time.

PIT STOP: Pick Up Produce

Schedule your trip to these supermarket for fresh produce in the next 24 hours. You will need 1 small bunch parsley, 1 green pepper, 1 red pepper and 5 small yellow onions to complete the rest of the meals for Winter Plan Two.

Also, you'll need to buy these ingredients if you're preparing the We Go Good Together suggestions: 4 bananas, fruit of your choice, 1 small head cauliflower, 1 bag (8 ounces) baby cut carrots, 3 to 4 Idaho potatoes and 1 package (16 ounces) ready-to-eat salad mix.

✦ Day 6—Backwards Meal: Breakfast Pizza ✦

Founder of Greetingcardwriting.com and mother of two Sandra Louden has one child who is a picky eater. Over the years, Sandy has tweaked Breakfast Pizza. This is one dish her daughter, Alexis, now 21 and a marine, will definitely eat when she comes home on leave.

Dish up: 6 to 8 servings

Cooking time: 20 to 25 minutes

Construction time: 5 to 10 minutes

Paraphernalia: Small bowl, round pizza pan, 12-inch skillet

INGREDIENTS:

1 cup frozen hash brown potatoes, defrosted (You will use the remaining hash brown potatoes for Day 10, Hot Dog Trick.)

1 pound pork breakfast sausage

1 8-ounce tube refrigerated crescent rolls

1 cup (4 ounces) cheddar cheese, medium to sharp, shredded

5 medium eggs

¼ cup milk

½ teaspoon salt

¼ teaspoon pepper

3 tablespoons Parmesan cheese, grated

To make:

1. Preheat oven to 350 degrees. Take the hash browns from the freezer if you have not done so already. (Simplify it: If frozen, defrost in the microwave for 2 to 3 minutes.)

2. In skillet over medium heat, sauté sausage until it is no longer pink.

3. Unroll crescent rolls and separate the dough. In a 12-inch round pizza pan, arrange crescent rolls with their points toward the center of the pan. Press rolls over the bottom and up the sides of the pan to form the pizza crust, sealing the perforations.

4. Top pizza crust with cooked sausage, cheddar cheese and potatoes.

5. In a separate bowl, combine eggs, milk, salt and pepper. Pour egg mixture very slowly over sausage and potato mixture.

6. Sprinkle Parmesan cheese over the top.

7. Bake 20 to 25 minutes.

Jazz It Up: Top with a light dusting of oregano.

Dress It Down: Skip the sausage for a meatless meal.

Double It: Be sure to close the hash brown potatoes package tightly. You will be using the rest of the package for Day 10, Hot Dog Trick.

We Go Good Together: Fried Bananas

Look Ahead: Take the cooked chicken out of the freezer, and put it in the refrigerator to thaw for Day 7, Kathy's Multi-Generation Chicken Soup with Orzo. Take the breadsticks for Day 7, We Go Good Together out of the freezer and put them on the countertop to thaw.

✤ Day 7—Soup's On: ✦
Kathy's Multi-Generation Chicken Soup with Orzo

Kathy Nicoletti writes a weekly newspaper feature called "Kathy's Cooks" about local people at the beaches near Jacksonville, Florida. Like many women, Kathy learned about cooking from both her mother and mother-in-law. Chicken Soup with Orzo combines ideas from both women. Her mother always added a little tomato soup to her homemade chicken soup for extra flavor. Meanwhile, her Greek mother-in-law often served orzo, a small variety of pasta, with roasted chicken. This recipe is a nice change of pace from traditional chicken noodle soup, and the orzo is very easy for young children to eat.

Dish up: 4 servings   Cooking time: 15 minutes
Construction time: 10 minutes   Paraphernalia: Dutch oven

INGREDIENTS:
2 14.5-ounce cans chicken broth
1 3-ounce can tomato sauce
$\frac{1}{2}$ cup orzo
2 cups cooked chicken, stored from Day 2

To make:
1. In pot, combine broth and tomato sauce and bring to boil over medium heat.
2. Add orzo pasta to broth/sauce mixture and bring to a boil again.
3. Cover pot and turn off heat.
4. Do not open for 9 to 10 minutes, or according to the orzo package directions.

5. Uncover and check to see if orzo is tender. If not, recover pot for a few more minutes.
6. Add chicken, turning heat to low and cooking for a few minutes to heat chicken.
7. Add salt and pepper, to taste. Serve hot.

Jazz It Up: Top with a little pesto sauce.

Dress It Down: Skip the chicken and use vegetable broth for a meatless meal.

Change It Up: Add cooked meatballs to the broth for an easy wedding soup variation. Substitute 1 quart of homemade broth for canned.

We Go Good Together: Pull out any leftovers that might be hanging out in your refrigerator, serve breadsticks on the side.

Look Ahead: Take the kielbasa out of the freezer and put it in the refrigerator to defrost for Day 8, Mustang Kielbasa.

❖ Day 8—Everyday Dinner: Mustang Kielbasa ❖

Marlene Bowser is the kind of grandmother everyone should be lucky enough to have. Fortunately, our basketball boosters' organization is privileged to have her. Marlene is team parent for her grandson's basketball team. She cooks up a roaster full of haluski, an ethnic dish also known as cabbage and noodles, whenever we ask. And she not only bakes cookies for the concession stand, she volunteers to work the stand, too. Well, I could go on, but I'd never get to her recipe. This dish is one she brought to the Senior Night celebration we had for our graduating players. And within five minutes of uncovering the Mustang Kielbasa, the serving platter was empty. Thanks, Marlene!

Dish up: 8 servings
Construction time: 10 to 15 minutes

Cooking time: 25 to 30 minutes
Paraphernalia: Dutch oven,
9- by 13-inch baking dish

INGREDIENTS:
2 pounds kielbasa
¼ cup onion, chopped

1 cup ketchup
1/4 cup sugar
1/8 cup Worcestershire sauce
1/2 teaspoon vinegar

To make:
1. Preheat oven to 350 degrees.
2. In Dutch oven, boil kielbasa for 10 minutes over medium heat. (By boiling the kielbasa, you're removing some of the grease.)
3. Peel and chop onion.
4. Mix together the rest of the ingredients while kielbasa is cooking.
5. After kielbasa has cooked, allow it to cool for 5 minutes. Slice kielbasa into bite-size pieces.
6. Mix sauce with kielbasa in baking dish and cook for 25 to 30 minutes, or until heated through.

Jazz It Up: Add sliced jalapeño peppers.
Dress It Down: Skip the chopped onions.
Change It Up: Use smoked sausage instead of kielbasa.
We Go Good Together: Carrots and cauliflower

[TiPS] Basketful of Tips: Wintry Home Brew

Cook up a wintry brew for your home. That's right, this one is for the house. A wonderful seasonal scent will pervade your home, making it cozier than ever. It's great when there are guests in the house. In a pot, combine 2 cups water, 1 cup pineapple juice, 1 cup orange juice, 2 cinnamon sticks, a handful of cloves, the juice of 1 lemon and the squeezed lemon rind (cut in half). Simmer to fill the room with a unique blend of scents. You can refrigerate it and use it again, but do *not* drink it.

✤ Day 9—Everyday Dinner: Tuna Pasta Toss 🐟 ✤

Combining tuna and pasta creates a filling meal perfect for the colder months of winter. Best of all, this dish is easy to make and easy on the budget.

Dish up: 4 to 6 servings

Construction time: 15 minutes

Cooking time: 5 minutes

Paraphernalia: 12-inch skillet, Dutch oven, strainer

INGREDIENTS:

1 12-ounce package linguine

2 6-ounce cans tuna packed in oil

1 teaspoon minced garlic

1 red pepper, cut into strips

1 2.5-ounce can pitted black olives, sliced

To make:

1. Cook pasta according to package directions.
2. While pasta is cooking, drain oil from tuna into skillet. Add garlic and sauté.
3. While that is cooking, slice olives and cut peppers into strips. Add olives, peppers and tuna to skillet and cook over low heat.
4. Drain pasta when finished cooking. Add tuna mixture to pasta. Toss, thoroughly mixing the ingredients. Serve hot.

Jazz It Up: Add 1 small jar marinated artichoke hearts to the skillet.

Dress It Down: Use seasoned diced tomatoes instead of tuna, garlic and peppers.

Change It Up: Substitute jarred roasted peppers for fresh peppers.

We Go Good Together: Green salad

Look Ahead: Pull the hot dogs and buns from the freezer and put them in the refrigerator to thaw for Day 10, Hot Dog Trick. Pull out the roast for the slow-cooker meal on Day 11, Old Man Winter's Roast and Veggies, and put it in the refrigerator to thaw. Pullout the cheddar cheese slices if you bought them for Day 10, Jazz It Up.

FRANTIC WOMAN FAMILY FUN: Kids' Kitchen Gifts
Stir up a batch of this easy café au lait mix for the kids to give as gifts for upcoming holidays or celebrations. While you're at it, double or triple the recipe so you can keep some for yourself. Combine 1 cup nondairy creamer, 1 cup sugar and ⅔ cup instant coffee powder in a bowl. Blend ingredients well. Put café au lait mix into small, airtight containers or jars. Write the directions on an unruled index card, or type them into a computer file using a fancy font. To make: Place 2 tablespoons café au lait mix in a cup. Add 1 cup boiling water. Stir. Enjoy! Attach the directions to the jar with a piece of ribbon or raffia.

❧ Day 10—Kids' Meal: Hot Dog Trick ❧

The kids will love eating these as much as they'll love watching the straight dogs curve into round dogs . . . that is, if you have a window on your oven door so the kids can watch as the transformation takes place.

Dish up: 6 to 8 servings
Construction time: 2 minutes

Cooking time: 10 minutes
Paraphernalia: Baking sheet, 9- by 13-inch baking dish

INGREDIENTS:
1 pound hot dogs (8–10 per pound)
1 8-count package hamburger buns
1 package hash brown potatoes, stored from Day 6
Condiments: Kids' preference

To make:
1. Preheat oven according to directions on the hash brown potatoes package. Make hash browns according to directions.
2. Place hot dogs on baking sheet. Make 5 vertical slices at ½-inch intervals, from the top of each hot dog almost down to the bottom of it. Be careful not to split the entire way through the dogs, but slice down far enough for the hot dogs to curl. Leave space between the dogs, because they will form a circle as they cook.

3. 10 minutes before the hash browns are finished baking, cook hot dogs for 5 minutes on each side, or until they curl.

4. Place dogs on the bottom of a hamburger bun and put potatoes in the middle. Top with condiments of choice and then the other half of the bun.

Jazz It Up: Baste hot dogs with barbecue sauce. Add cheddar cheese slices on top of the dogs and spuds.

Dress It Down: Skip the hash browns.

Change It Up: Exchange the hash browns for coleslaw or baked beans.

We Go Good Together: Fruit

Look Ahead: If you haven't taken out your 3-pound roast for Day 11, Old Man Winter's Roast and Veggies, from the freezer to thaw, do so immediately. You will be preparing your slow-cooker meal tonight or tomorrow morning. The decision is yours. (Be sure not to put the roast in until right before cooking.)

 FRANTIC WOMAN FAMILY FUN:
Summer in the Wintertime

Reverse the seasons and throw a "Summer in the Wintertime" night. Wear your summer gear, serve dinner on a picnic blanket, make smoothies, or dole out Popsicles for dessert, and finish the theme with a family favorite movie, like *The Sandlot* or *Because of Winn-Dixie*. Or make plans to swim at an indoor pool in your area. Check with your school district to see if they offer open swim nights for a minimal cost.

✦ Day 11—Slow Cook Tonight: ✦ Old Man Winter's Roast and Veggies

Opening the door to a cozy home with a hot meal waiting for you is a warm welcome after Old Man Winter has you shivering in your boots. All you have to do is scoop out the veggies and slice the roast, and you'll have dinner on the table.

Dish up: 5 to 6 servings   Cooking time: 8 to 10 hours
Construction time: 5 to 10 minutes   Paraphernalia: Slow cooker

INGREDIENTS:

1 tablespoon oil

1 teaspoon minced garlic

3 yellow onions, sliced

1 3-pound chuck roast 🥤 (Set aside ⅓ of the roast for Day 13, Easy Beef Burritos.)

1 16-ounce jar salsa 🥤 (Save ⅓ of the salsa for Day 13.)

2 14.5-ounce cans stewed tomatoes

To make:

1. Put oil and garlic on the bottom of the slow cooker.

2. Peel and slice onions. Place onions on the bottom of the slow cooker.

3. Put roast in next. Pour ⅔ of the jar of salsa and all of the tomatoes over onions and roast. Save the remaining salsa for Day 13, Easy Beef Burritos.

4. Cover and cook on low for 8 to 10 hours.

5. Remove meat. Allow it to stand for 10 minutes, then slice.

6. Top roast slices with onions, tomatoes and a bit of the sauce.

7. Set aside a portion of the onions and tomatoes for Day 13. Save all of the leftover sauce for Day 13, too. Store onions, tomatoes and sauce in the refrigerator.

Jazz It Up: Add a jar of roasted Italian vegetables. Add 3 or 4 potatoes at the beginning of the cooking process. Be sure to cut them into cubes first.

Dress It Down: Skip the veggies.

Change It Up: If you need to cook the roast in the oven, bake at 325 degrees for about 30 minutes per pound.

Double It: Set aside ⅓ of roast for Day 13, Easy Beef Burritos. Set aside a portion of the onions and tomatoes, and save the remaining sauce for Day 13. And don't forget to mark the salsa so no one eats it.

We Go Good Together: Garlic toast

BASKETFUL OF TIPS: Keep 'em Moist

Do you prefer your veggies moist? If so, use this trick when cooking meats and vegetables together in a slow cooker. Place the veggies on the bottom of the cooker, then put the meat on top. The meat and juices protect the veggies and keep them from drying out.

⇝ Day 12—I Can with a Can: ✦ Open, Dump, Stir Veggie Supper 🐄

Here's one meal that takes full advantage of the invention of cans and is so simple, the kids could prepare it.

Dish up: 4 to 5 servings   Cooking time: 10 minutes
Construction time: 3 minutes   Paraphernalia: 12-inch skillet, baking sheet

INGREDIENTS:

2 15-ounce cans sliced potatoes, drained
1 10.75-ounce can cream of mushroom soup
1 14-ounce can cheddar cheese soup
1 4-ounce can sliced mushrooms
1 8-ounce can peas, drained
1 8-ounce tube refrigerated biscuits

To make:
1. Bake biscuits according to package directions.
2. Coat skillet with nonstick cooking spray and heat it over medium heat.
3. Open all cans and dump ingredients into the skillet, mixing well.
4. Cover and cook until the potatoes are hot and the rest of the ingredients are heated through, stirring occasionally.
5. Serve over biscuits or with biscuits on the side.

Jazz It Up: For heartier appetites, add 1 can (5 ounces) of chunk, lean ham. Be sure to drain and chop the ham before adding it to the skillet.

Change It Up: Use canned asparagus, corn or beans instead of peas.

We Go Good Together: Canned pears

Look Ahead: Take the nacho chips for Day 13, We Go Good Together, out of the freezer, and hide them from the family until tomorrow.

✦ Day 13—Must-Go: Easy Beef Burritos ✦

With the leftovers from the slow cooker meal, you can whip this dinner together in no time at all. Of course, if you like spending extra time in the kitchen, by all means, do so.

Dish up: 4 servings

Construction time: 5 minutes

Cooking time: 10 minutes

Paraphernalia: 12-inch skillet, baking sheet

INGREDIENTS:

4 to 6 tortillas

Beef, stored from Day 11

Onions, stored from Day 11

Tomatoes, stored from Day 11

½ cup sauce, stored from Day 11

1 teaspoon chili powder

Salt and pepper, to taste

Salsa, stored from Day 11

To make:

1. Preheat oven to 300 degrees. Lay tortillas on a baking sheet, and place in the oven to warm.
2. Shred beef.
3. Coat skillet with nonstick cooking spray. Heat beef, onions, tomatoes and sauce in a skillet over low-medium heat.
4. Add in seasoning and heat thoroughly.
5. Fill warmed tortillas with beef mixture.
6. Serve hot with salsa.

Jazz It Up: Serve with sour cream.

Dress It Down: Skip the seasonings for those who prefer blander foods.

Change It Up: Use whole-wheat tortillas to boost the nutritional value.

We Go Good Together: Nacho chips and cheese sauce

Look Ahead: Pull the ground chuck out of the freezer and put it in the refrigerator for Day 14, Aunt Mary's Meat Loaf Supreme.

BASKETFUL OF TIPS: Sorbet Cocktail
Replace shrimp cocktail with sorbet cocktail. Uncover those white wine glasses that are gathering dust. Put 2 small scoops of raspberry sorbet or frozen berries whirled first in the blender into each glass (after you rinse the glasses first, of course). Add about ½ glass of nonalcoholic sparkling wine to each glass. (If this is an adults-only feast, you can put in the real stuff. Be sure to get the A-okay from your dinner companions first. If you need help selecting a wine to complement the food, refer to Part Five, Extra Helpings.) Serve before the meal as a cocktail or after the meal as dessert.

Day 14—Company's Coming: *Aunt Mary's Meat Loaf Supreme*

My uncle Tom says his sister Mary's meat loaf is the best he's ever tasted. And that's saying a lot because Uncle Tom, a man of the cloth who has had his own parish for more than 40 years, has attended more potluck suppers than anyone I know. This recipe was handed down to Aunt Mary from Uncle Tom when he was in his seminary days at Josephinum Seminary in Worthington, Ohio, many, many years ago. Although this has a longer cooking time than most of the entrees in this book, you'll have time to prepare the side dishes or mingle with your family or guests. Double the recipe if you're serving a crowd. Psst! If you need a quicker cooking time, see Change It Up.

Dish up: 6 servings

Construction time: 5 to 7 minutes

Cooking time: 50 minutes

Paraphernalia: 12-inch skillet, large mixing bowl, small mixing bowl, baking dish

MEAT LOAF INGREDIENTS:

1/2 cup onion, minced

1/2 cup green pepper, diced

2 tablespoons fresh parsley, minced

3 tablespoons butter

1 cup bread crumbs

1 1/2 pounds ground chuck

1 tablespoon Worcestershire sauce

1 teaspoon dry mustard

2 teaspoons salt

1/8 teaspoon pepper

3/4 cup milk

2 eggs

SAUCE INGREDIENTS:

1/2 cup ketchup

2 tablespoons brown sugar

2 tablespoons vinegar

To make:

1. Preheat oven to 350 degrees.
2. Peel and mince onion. Wash and dice pepper. Wash and mince parsley.
3. Melt butter in skillet. Sauté the onion, green pepper and parsley in butter.
4. In a mixing bowl, add bread crumbs to sautéed ingredients and mix well. (Do not overmix.)
5. Add in the remaining ingredients. Work the mixture until everything is blended. Put into a baking dish and shape into a loaf.
6. Bake for 30 minutes.
7. While meat loaf is baking, mix ketchup, brown sugar and vinegar together. After 30 minutes, spread the sauce over the top of the loaf and bake for an additional 20 to 24 minutes.

Jazz It Up: Add diced celery.

Dress It Down: Skip the onions and peppers.

Change It Up: If you need a shorter cooking time, make 3 miniature meat loaves. With the end of a large wooden or plastic serving spoon, push a hole in the middle of each loaf. The smaller size and the hole in the middle of each mini loaf will shorten the cooking time by 20 minutes or so.

We Go Good Together: Baked potatoes (For tips on baking potatoes, see Basketful of Tips in Fall Two Plan under Day 7, Tuna Spud-melts.

BASKETFUL OF TIPS: Aunt Mary's Secret

If you tend to overmix your ingredients, admit it, and then stop doing so. Aunt Mary's secret for making Supreme Meat Loaf is to use 2 knives to cut in the ingredients with one another. The warning she gives to the compulsive cook: Do not overblend. Overmixing the meat toughens it.

SPRING IS IN THE AIR

Spring brings breezy days spent with the windows open in the house and the kids playing outside. The crisp air entices you to search for lighter fare after weeks of preparing winter's comfort foods. With these easy-to-follow menus mapped out and a detailed grocery list, you'll have more time to sit outside and breathe in the fresh, fragrant air of spring.

SPRING FARMER'S MARKET

The following fruits and vegetables are ripe for the picking during the spring months, according to the USDA. (This might differ in some regions.) Some produce will be available throughout spring, while others will be in season for a limited time. Now is the time to buy these tasty fruits and vegetables, because they are so much tastier and cheaper when in season. Also, use this list to help you incorporate healthier choices for side dishes, lunches and snacks.

<u>Fruits</u>
Apples
Avocados
Bananas
Cantaloupes*
Cherries*
Coconuts*
Cranberries
Grapefruits
Honeydews
Lemons
Limes*
Mangoes*
Oranges
Papayas
Pears
Pineapples
Tangerines*
Tangelos*
Watermelons

<u>Vegetables</u>
Artichokes
Asparagus
Avocados
Beans (green, lima, wax)*
Belgian endives
Broccoli
Cabbage
Carrots
Celery
Corn*
Cucumbers*
Lettuce
Mushrooms*
Okra*
Onions
Parsnips*
Peas
Peppers
Potatoes (white)
Radishes*
Rhubarb
Rutabagas*
Shallots
Spinach
Squash
Tomatoes*
Turnips*

* Designates fruits and vegetables that have a shorter peak season than the others on the list.

SPRING PLAN ONE MENUS

Day 1—Retro Meal Updated: Classic Cheese Sammies
Day 2—Everyday Dinner: Baked Ziti
Day 3—Backwards Meal: Hollywood Eggs
Day 4—Everyday Dinner: All-for-One Pierogi Skillet
Day 5—Everyday Dinner: Mr. Pepper
Day 6—Soup's On: Smoccoli Broccoli Soup
Day 7—Sandwich Board: Easy Mexican Calzones
Day 8—Everyday Dinner: Traffic Light Chicken
Day 9—Old Tradition: Kentucky Hot Browns
Day 10—Kids' Meal: Chicken Quesadillas
Day 11—Slow Cook Tonight: Dump and Forget Beef Tips Dinner
Day 12—I Can with a Can: Hobo Pasta and Beans Supper
Day 13—No-Cook Night: Waldorf Tuna Roll-ups
Day 14—Company's Coming: Glazed Chicken, Apples and Onions

THE SHOPPING LISTS

The Frantic Woman's Cupboard

SPRING PLAN ONE STAPLES

Seasonings
Chili powder
Garlic (minced, powder*)
Parmesan cheese
Pepper*
Salt*
Thyme

Jazz It Ups
Cinnamon

Condiments
Mayonnaise
Mustard (honey or prepared)

Dressings, Oil and Sauces
Oil (olive, vegetable)
Ranch salad dressing
Wine (white)

Baking Needs
Flour (all purpose)

Frantic Necesssities
Nonstick cooking spray
Foil

Dairy
Butter* or margarine
Eggs
Milk

*Ingredients you'll need for both main and side dishes

The Frantic Woman Goes Shopping

MAIN-DISH INGREDIENTS YOU'LL NEED TO BUY

Produce: Fruit
1 Granny Smith apple and 2 Jonathan apples (Days 1, 13, 14)
¼ pound cherries (Day 8)

Produce: Veggies
6 large green peppers (Day 5)
1 bunch celery (Days 6, 13)
2 small heads broccoli (Days 6, 8)
2 small yellow onions (Days 6, 14)
2 large tomatoes (Day 9)
1 small tomato (Day 10)

PIT STOP: Keep it Fresh

You might want to hold off on buying some of the produce until later in the week. With the nice weather, farmer's markets will allow you to pick up fresh produce quickly. So, consider waiting until Day 5 to buy these items for your entrees: 1 Granny Smith apple, 1 Jonathan apple, ¼ pound cherries, 2 small heads broccoli, 2 large tomatoes and 1 onion.

Seasonings

1 1.25-ounce package taco seasoning mix (Day 7)
1 1.25-ounce package dry onion soup mix (Day 11)

Dressings, Oils and Sauces

1 16-ounce jar salsa (Day 10)

Canned Goods and Bottles

1 16-ounce can tomato puree (Day 2)
1 16-ounce can diced tomatoes with seasonings (Day 2)
1 6-ounce can tomato paste (Day 5)
1 26-ounce can chicken broth (Day 6)
1 4-ounce can green chilies (Day 7)
1 8-ounce can pineapple chunks (Day 8)
1 16-ounce jar salsa (Day 10)
1 10.75-ounce can cream of celery soup (Day 11)
1 10.75-ounce can cream of mushroom soup (Day 11)
1 4-ounce can mushroom pieces (Day 11)
1 16-ounce can baked beans (Day 12)
1 16-ounce can stewed tomatoes (Day 12)
2 6-ounce cans white tuna packed in water (Day 13)

Noodles, Pasta and Rice

1 16-ounce box ziti (Day 2)

Cereal, Nuts and Such

Handful of sunflower seeds (Day 10)
Handful of raisins (Day 10)
4 ounces walnuts (Day 13)

Beverages

4 ounces apple juice (Day 14)

Bread, Chips and More

16 slices white or whole-wheat bread, or your preference (Days 1, 3, 9)

Deli

8 slices cheddar or American cheese (Day 1)
8 slices turkey breast (Day 9)

Fish, Meat and Poultry

2½ pounds ground beef (Days 5, 7)
4½ pounds skinless, boneless chicken breasts (Days 8, 10, 14)
1½ pounds stew meat (Day 11)

Dairy

1 15-ounce container ricotta cheese (Day 2)
4 cups (16 ounces) mozzarella cheese, shredded (Days 2, 7)
2 cups (8 ounces) cheddar cheese, shredded (Days 4, 9)
1 8-ounce container half and half (Day 6)
1 15-ounce package refrigerated piecrust (Day 7)
2 cups (8 ounces) Monterey Jack cheese, shredded (Day 10)
1 8-ounce container sour cream (Day 10)
16 whole-wheat or flour tortillas (Days 10, 13)

Frozen

1 10-ounce package broccoli (Day 4)
1 16-ounce package potato pierogies (Day 4)

Jazz It Up Ingredients You'll Need to Buy

Produce: Fruit

Handful seedless grapes (Day 13)

Produce: Veggies

1 8-ounce carton snowcap mushrooms, sliced (Day 2)

1 green pepper (Day 2)

2 yellow onions (Days 4, 10)

1 head lettuce (Days 7, 10)

1 ripe tomato (Day 7)

2–4 jalapeño peppers (Day 10)

2 celery ribs (Days 10, 11)

3 to 4 red potatoes (Day 11)

PIT STOP: Keep It Fresh

You might want to hold off on buying these items until Day 5 if you plan to jazz up your dinner meals: Handful seedless grapes, 1 head lettuce, 1 ripe tomato, 2–4 jalapeño peppers, 1 bunch celery, 1 yellow onion, and 3 to 4 red potatoes.

Canned Goods and Bottles

2 15-ounce cans stewed tomatoes with seasonings (Days 1, 12)

2 2.5-ounce cans sliced black olives (Days 2, 14)

1 8-ounce can chow mein noodles (Day 8)

Noodles, Pasta and Rice

1 cup instant brown rice, or your preference (Day 5)

Fish, Meat and Poultry

½ pound bacon (Day 9)

Dairy

1 8-ounce container herb-flavored cream cheese (Day 1)

½ (2 ounces) cheddar cheese, shredded (Day 6)

1 8-ounce container sour cream (Day 7)

WE GO GOOD TOGETHER INGREDIENTS YOU'LL NEED TO BUY

Produce: Fruit

2 bananas (Day 3)
1 cantaloupe (Day 3)
1 papaya (Day 3)
2 tangelos (Day 3)
Fruit, your choice (Day 7)

Produce: Veggies

4 celery ribs (Day 4)
Mixed veggies, your choice (Day 5)
1 16-ounce package ready-to-eat salad (Day 6)
1 16-ounce package ready-to-eat Caesar salad (Day 13)
1 head cauliflower (Day 14)

PIT STOP: Keep It Fresh

To keep your produce fresh for the recommended side sides, you might want to hold off on buying these items until Day 5: Fruit, your choice, 1 head cauliflower, 1 16-ounce package ready-to-eat salad and 1 16-ounce package ready-to-eat Caesar salad.

Canned Goods and Bottles

1 15-ounce can tomato soup (Day 1)

Noodles, Pasta and Rice

1 16-ounce box instant brown rice, or your preference (Day 8)
1 16-ounce bag egg noodles (Day 11)

Cereal, Nuts and Such

Handful raisins (Day 4)

Beverages

1 2-liter bottle ginger ale (Day 9)

Bread, Chips and More

4 to 6 slices Italian bread, or your preference (Day 2)
1 small roll Lifesavers mint candy (Day 9)

Dairy

1 8-ounce package cream cheese (Day 4)
1 8-ounce tube refrigerated dinner rolls (Day 12)
1 3-ounce container plain yogurt (Day 14)
¼ cup (1 ounce) Monterey Jack cheese, shredded (Day 14)

Frozen

1 loaf garlic bread (Day 6)
1 32-ounce package french fries (Day 10)

Unloading the Load

- Freeze the ground beef for Day 5, Mr. Pepper, and Day 7, Easy Mexican Calzones, in the same package.
- Freeze a little more than half of the chicken for Day 8, Traffic Light Chicken, and Day 10, Chicken Quesadilla, in the same package.
- Freeze the other half of the chicken breasts for Day 14, Glazed Chicken, Apples and Onions.
- Freeze 1 cup mozzarella cheese for Day 7, Easy Mexican Calzones.
- Freeze the turkey breast, 4 slices of bread and 1 cup of cheddar cheese for Day 9, Kentucky Hot Browns.
- Freeze the tortillas for Day 10, Chicken Quesadillas.
- Freeze the stew meat for Day 11, Dump and Forget Beef Tips Dinner.
- Be sure to mark each package with the date and contents so you

can easily pull out the necessary ingredients from the freezer when needed.

- Hide the roll of Lifesavers mint candy.
- If you're jazzing up your menus, freeze ½ cup of shredded cheddar cheese for Day 6 and the bacon for Day 9.
- Also, freeze 2 cups of Monterey Jack cheese for Day 10, Chicken Quesadillas, and ¼ cup for the Day 14 We Go Good Together suggestion.
- You might want to hide the ginger ale, too.
- Be sure to read the Look Ahead section in each recipe to see when you must pull items out of the freezer to put into the refrigerator to defrost.

SPRING: PLAN ONE

⇢ Day 1—Retro Meal Updated: Classic Cheese Sammies 🐾 ⇠

Grilled cheese sandwiches are considered old school by the younger crowd and comfort food by the older population. However you want to say it, the grilled sandwich is here to stay. Try this trendier rendition of the old classic.

Dish up: 4 servings Cooking time: 5 to 10 minutes
Construction time: 5 to 10 minutes Paraphernalia: Skillet

INGREDIENTS:
8 slices white or whole-wheat bread
Butter or margarine, softened
1 medium Jonathan apple, sliced
8 slices cheddar or American cheese

To make:
1. Butter one side of each slice of bread.
2. Wash and peel apple. Slice thinly.
3. Place 1 slice of bread in skillet, buttered side down, over medium heat. Add 2 slices of cheese to the plain side. Add 2 apple slices.

4. Top with bread, buttered side up.

5. Heat for about 3 to 5 minutes over medium heat, or until the bottom is a light golden color.

6. Flip and cook for about 5 minutes or until golden.

7. Cut in half and serve.

Jazz It Up: Spread a layer of herb-flavored cream cheese (dill or garlic) on the inside of the bread slices.

Dress It Down: Eliminate the apple slices.

Change It Up: Exchange the whole-wheat bread or white bread for marbled bread.

We Go Good Together: Tomato soup, of course

BASKETFUL OF TIPS: The Perfect Classic

Making a grilled cheese sandwich isn't science but for a really great one, follow these tips:

- Hard to semihard cheeses, such as fontina, mild or medium cheddar, Gruyère, Monterey Jack, provolone or Swiss, make the gooiest cheese-only grilled sammies.

- Sharp cheddar doesn't melt as easily as other cheddar, but it does add a flavorful bite to the sandwich.

- Sliced breads, such as rye, white and whole wheat, provide the best foundation for your classic sammies. If you have homemade bread with big air holes, use it for something else.

- Be careful not to spread too much butter on the bread, or it will become soggy.

- Hoagie rolls, long baguettes, or round buns make delectable grilled sandwiches, too.

- Add slices of fruits and veggies for something unusual and to increase the nutritional value.

✳ Day 2—Everyday Dinner: Baked Ziti ✳

There are as many ways to make Baked Ziti as there are types of pasta. Here's one version offered by Jeannette McGrath. You can whip up this simple meal and then spend some time in the fresh air while dinner is cooking in the oven. Psst! This is a great meal to serve to unexpected company when you Jazz It Up.

Dish up: 4 to 6 servings   Cooking time: 20 minutes
Construction time: 10 to 15 minutes   Paraphernalia: Dutch oven, strainer, bowl, 9-by-13-inch baking pan

INGREDIENTS:

8 ounces ziti noodles (8 additional ounces ziti noodles for Day 12,
    Hobo Pasta and Beans Supper)
1 15-ounce container ricotta cheese
3 cups (12 ounces)mozzarella cheese, shredded
1 16-ounce can tomato puree
1 16-ounce can diced tomatoes with seasonings
Parmesan cheese, to taste

To make:
1. Preheat oven to 350 degrees.
2. Cook ziti according to package directions for al dente.
3. Drain ziti and place in a large bowl. If you doubled the pasta as suggested, put half in a container to freeze for Day 12, Hobo Pasta and Beans Supper. Be sure it has cooled before doing so.
4. Mix ricotta cheese and half of the mozzarella cheese with the ziti.
5. Cover bottom of baking pan with the can of tomato puree. Spoon ziti mixture into pan. Cover with remaining can of diced tomatoes with seasonings.
6. Sprinkle with Parmesan cheese. Top with remaining mozzarella cheese.
7. Cover with foil and cook for 15 minutes. Take off foil and cook for another 5 minutes, or until cheese is melted.

Jazz It Up: Add mushrooms, peppers, stewed tomatoes or sliced black olives.
Change It Up: Use jarred spaghetti sauce instead of the puree and diced tomatoes.

Double It: Cook an additional 8 ounces of ziti for Day 12, Hobo Pasta and Beans Supper. Store pasta in the freezer.

We Go Good Together: Buttered bread

POTFUL OF KNOWLEDGE: Watching the Waist-line

Margarine users, consider replacing your margarine product with butter. The latest diet tips suggest dieters stay away from hydrogenated fats. Margarine is a hydrogenated product, containing artificially configured molecules that do not exist in nature. So, if you're watching the waistline, consider switching.

➤ Day 3—Backwards Meal: Hollywood Eggs 🐄 ⫷

I'm not sure where this one originated, maybe somewhere in Hollywood. It's a combination of a "dippy" egg and French toast. And from what I'm told, dippy eggs are a 'Burgh thing, but I don't think that's exactly true.

Dish up: 4 servings
Construction time: 5 minutes

Cooking time: 10 minutes
Paraphernalia: 12-inch skillet, wide spatula, bowl

INGREDIENTS:

4 bread slices
5 eggs
2 tablespoons milk

To make:
1. Cut a hole in the center of bread big enough to fit the egg inside it. (Simplify it: Push down on a small-mouth juice glass to easily make the hole.)
2. Coat skillet with nonstick spray and heat over medium heat.
3. Crack 1 egg into a bowl. Add milk to egg and beat.
4. Dip each bread slice into egg mixture.
5. Place 2 egg-coated slices in skillet.

6. Crack an egg into the hole.
7. Cook about 3 to 4 minutes, or until bread is toasted.
8. With wide spatula, flip carefully. Cook another 3 or 4 minutes, or until egg has cooked through.
9. When these two have finished cooking, move them to a plate and cover to keep warm until the next two are cooked.

Jazz It Up: Sprinkle cinnamon on top.
We Go Good Together: Fruit salad

FRANTIC WOMAN FAMILY FUN: Hollywood Hits
Keeping in tune with tonight's meal, settle back on the sofa with the kids and watch a family-rated box-office hit: one of the Harry Potter movies, Shrek, Scooby-Doo, or one of your own favorites from the past.

❧ Day 4—Everyday Dinner: All-for-One Pierogi Skillet ❧

Once upon a time, this was a favorite dish to cook up at our house. It's easy to prepare, and the kids loved it. Unfortunately, it was a no-think meal that I cooked up about a dozen times too often, and my family grew sick of it. After putting this recipe aside for a year or so, it's back on the menu again.

Dish up: 4 servings   Cooking time: 15 minutes
Construction time: 5 minutes   Paraphernalia: 12-inch skillet

INGREDIENTS:
1 tablespoon vegetable oil
1 16-ounce package frozen potato pierogies, thawed
1 10-ounce package frozen broccoli, thawed
½ teaspoon salt
¼ teaspoon pepper
1 cup (4 ounces) cheddar cheese, shredded

To make:

1. Heat oil in skilletover medium heat.
2. Add pierogies and cook for about 5 minutes, or until heated through.
3. Stir in broccoli, salt and pepper. Top with cheese.
4. Reduce heat to low. Cover and cook for about 5 minutes, or until cheese is melted and broccoli is heated through.

Jazz It Up: Add sliced sautéed onions.

Dress It Down: Eliminate the broccoli.

Change It Up: Add firm tofu to the pot. Be sure to cut tofu into small, cube-size chunks.

We Go Good Together: Ants on a Log, aka celery sticks with cream cheese. Wash and cut each rib into 4-inch pieces. Spread cream cheese inside; top sticks with raisins for Ants on a Log.

Look Ahead: Pull the 2 pounds of ground beef for Day 5, Mr. Pepper and Day 7, Easy Mexican Calzones from the freezer to thaw.

✤ Day 5—Everyday Dinner: Mr. Pepper ✤

Move over, Mr. Potato Head; here comes Mr. Pepper. Kids will love the new name attached to this old favorite. Allow them to stuff their own pepper. Once the stuffed peppers are cooked, let the kids decorate the top of their Mr. Pepper with cheese, olives and carrot slices.

Dish up: 4 to 6 servings
Construction time: 10 minutes

Cooking time: 20 minutes
Paraphernalia: Large pot, 12-inch skillet, baking dish

INGREDIENTS:

6 large green peppers
1½ pounds ground beef 🥤 (1 additional pound ground beef for Day 7, Easy Mexican Calzones)
1 6-ounce can tomato paste
1 teaspoon minced garlic

1 tablespoon chili powder
Parmesan cheese

To make:

1. Preheat oven to 350 degrees.
2. Boil water in pot large enough to fit the peppers. Cut the top (at stem) off the peppers. Remove seeds and white pulp. Cook peppers in boiling water for 5 minutes. Drain.
3. Coat skillet with nonstick cooking spray. Brown meat in skillet over medium heat. Be sure to break apart meat so it is in chunks. Pour off excess fat.
4. If doubling the recipe as suggested, brown an additional pound of ground meat. Once browned, store it in a container in the refrigerator.
5. Add tomato paste, garlic and chili powder. Add salt and pepper, to taste, if desired. Cook on low for 5 minutes.
6. Remove from heat. Spoon meat mixture into peppers. Sprinkle tops with Parmesan cheese.
7. Place stuffed peppers in shallow baking dish. Add ½-inch water to keep peppers from burning and sticking to the dish.
8. Bake for 20 minutes.

Jazz It Up: Add 1 cup of cooked white or brown rice (your preference) to the meat mixture.

Dress It Down: Add spaghetti sauce in place of the tomato paste and seasonings.

Double it: Brown another pound of ground beef for Day 7, Easy Mexican Calzones.

We Go Good Together: Mixed veggies

Look Ahead: Pull out the cheddar cheese for Day 6, Jazz It Up from the freezer and put it in the refrigerator to thaw.

PIT STOP: Pick Up Produce

Schedule a trip to buy fresh produce in the next 24 hours. If you haven't picked up these items because you held off as recommended at the beginning of the week, you'll need to buy these items for your entrees: 1 Granny Smith apple, 1 Jonathan apple, ¼ pound cherries, 2 small heads broccoli, 2 large tomatoes and 1 yellow onion.

Additionally, you'll need to buy these items if you plan to jazz up your dinner meals: Handful seedless grapes, 1 head lettuce, 1 ripe tomato, 2–4 jalapeño peppers, 1 bunch celery, 1 yellow onion, and 3 to 4 red potatoes.

For the recommended side dishes in the We Go Good Together section, you will need: Fruit, your choice, 1 head cauliflower, 1 package (16 ounces) ready-to-eat salad and 1 package (16 ounces) ready-to-eat Caesar salad.

✦ Day 6—Soup's On: Smoccoli Broccoli Soup ✦

Stir up a pot of creamy soup made from the season's best. As you're blending the ingredients together, see who can say the tongue twister "Smoccoli Broccoli Soup" five times without messing it up. Everyone will be giggling, and the kids won't realize you're sneaking in the veggies.

Dish up: 4 servings
Construction time: 10 minutes

Cooking time: 20 minutes
Paraphernalia: Stock pot, 12-inch skillet, whisk

INGREDIENTS:

3 tablespoons butter
½ cup white cooking wine
½ cup onions, diced
½ cup celery, diced
1 cup broccoli, diced
3 tablespoons flour
3 cups chicken broth
⅛ teaspoon salt
⅛ teaspoon pepper
⅛ teaspoon thyme
1 cup half and half

To make:

1. Melt butter in stockpot.
2. Add wine and sauté onions, celery and broccoli for about 5 minutes on low heat.
3. Blend in flour and broth. Bring mixture to a boil.
4. Add seasonings and allow to simmer for 25 to 30 minutes, or until veggies are tender.
5. Blend in half and half and heat until hot, but do not allow soup to boil.
6. Serve when heated through.

Jazz It Up: Top with shredded cheddar cheese.

Dress It Down: Eliminate the onions.

Change It Up: Replace half and half with milk, rice milk or half plain yogurt and half water.

We Go Good Together: Pull out and serve any leftovers from previous meals, or serve a nice salad and some garlic bread.

Look Ahead: Pull the cooked ground beef and 1 cup mozzarella cheese for Day 7, Easy Mexican Calzones, from the freezer, and put it in the refrigerator to thaw.

TIPS BASKETFUL OF TIPS: Thicken Soup the Healthy Way

One healthy way to thicken creamed soups is to whirl a handful of oats in a food processor or blender, then toss it into the soup, suggests the author Beverly Breton Carroll.

✦ Day 7—Sandwich Board: Easy Mexican Calzones ✦

Serve up a simple Mexican meal with these easy calzones that can be individualized according to your family's preference.

Dish up: 4 servings Cooking time: 10 to 15 minutes
Construction time: 10 minutes Paraphernalia: 12-inch skillet

INGREDIENTS:

1 pound cooked ground beef, stored from Day 5
1 4-ounce can green chilies, diced
1/4 cup water
1 1.25-ounce package taco seasoning mix
1 15-ounce package refrigerated piecrust, room temperature
1 cup (4 ounces) mozzarella cheese, shredded

To make:

1. Preheat oven to 425 degrees.
2. Placed browned ground beef in skillet over medium heat and cook until heated through. Drain any excess.
3. Add chilies, water and seasoning. Mix well.
4. Place unwrapped piecrusts on cutting board. Unfold. Cut each crust in half. You'll have 4 half-circles.
5. Place about ½ cup beef filling on half of each semi-circle crust.
6. Top with ¼ cup cheese.
7. Dampen edge of crust with water. Fold side over filling. Crimp edges with tines of fork.
8. Place on a greased baking sheet. Bake for 10 to 15 minutes or until golden brown.
9. Cool for a few minutes before eating, as the center filling will be hot.

Jazz It Up: Serve with sour cream, chopped lettuce and tomato on the side.

Dress It Down: If your kids prefer their meals a little blander, use very little of the taco seasoning mix. You might want to use a little marinara or pizza sauce instead. And definitely skip the green chilies.

We Go Good Together: Sliced fruit

Look Ahead: Pull out the chicken marked Day 8, Traffic Light Chicken, and Day 10, Chicken Quesadillas, from the freezer, and put it in the refrigerator to thaw.

❧ Day 8—Everyday Dinner: Traffic Light Chicken ❧

Sneak in some green, yellow and red fruits and veggies with this fun recipe created just for those who say, "Chicken again?!" You can line up the fruits and veggies to resemble a traffic light, too.

Dish up: 4 to 5 servings

Cooking time: 25 to 30 minutes

Construction time: 5 to 10 minutes

Paraphernalia: Skillet, baking dish, steamer

INGREDIENTS:

5 skinless and boneless chicken breasts (about 1½ pounds) 🍶

(4 additional skinless, boneless chicken breasts for Day 10, Chicken Quesadillas)

4 tablespoons mayonnaise

2 tablespoons vegetable oil

2 cups broccoli, chopped

1 8-ounce can pineapple chunks

⅓ cup cherries, pitted and chopped

To make:

1. Preheat oven to 350 degrees.
2. Coat baking dish with nonstick cooking spray. Spread mayonnaise on both sides of chicken breasts. (Do this with the extra chicken for Double It, too.)
3. Cook for about 20 minutes in oven.
4. Steam broccoli for about 5 to 7 minutes, or until soft, while chicken is cooking. (Simplify it: If you do not have a steamer pot, place broccoli in a pan with about 1 cup water and cook on low-medium heat.)
5. Once chicken is cooked, cut it into bite-size pieces.
6. Cut the extra 4 chicken breasts into bite-size pieces, and store in the refrigerator. Be sure to mark it as such.
7. Heat oil in skillet. Add chicken, broccoli, pineapples and cherries.
8. Cook for about 5 minutes, or until heated through.

Jazz It Up: Top with chow mein noodles.
Dress It Down: Skip the fruit.

Change It Up: Use two 10-ounce cans of chunk chicken breasts instead of cooking the raw chicken. Replace the pineapples with a can of sweet corn.

Double it: Cook 4 additional boneless chicken breast and store them in the refrigerator for Day 10, Chicken Quesadillas. Cut into bite-size pieces before you store it.

We Go Good Together: Brown rice

Look Ahead: Pull the turkey breast, 4 slices of bread and 1 cup cheddar cheese from the freezer and put it in the refrigerator to thaw for Day 9, Kentucky Hot Browns. If you bought the bacon to jazz up your Hot Browns, pull that package from the freezer, too, and put it in the refrigerator.

BASKETFUL OF TIPS: Tasty Brown Rice

Brown rice is replacing white rice as a side dish for many people watching their weight. The high-fiber bran coating is good for you, too. But watch out, because that coating causes brown rice to go rancid quicker.

So store the darker rice in your pantry for *6 months only*. Brown rice will last a month longer if stored in the refrigerator.

FRANTIC WOMAN FAMILY FUN: Child's Play

Grab the kids, go outside, and play a game of Green Light, Yellow Light, Red Light, Stop after the dinner dishes are washed and put away.

BASKETFUL OF TIPS: Moisten the Bird

Flo Carroll, Tawnya Senchur and several other cooks spread a bit of mayonnaise over raw chicken before they pop it in the oven. Though it sounds a little strange, adding mayo makes for a moister piece of chicken and is the perfect preparation for Traffic Light Chicken. For a healthier version, use plain yogurt in place of the mayo.

✦ Day 9—Old Tradition: Kentucky Hot Browns ✦

Kentucky Hot Browns are a favorite food in Kentucky, especially during Derby season. Hot Browns date back to 1920s, when chef Fred K.

Schmidt of Louisville's Brown Hotel created them. During the 1920s, the Brown Hotel drew over 1,200 guests each evening for its dinner dance. Around midnight, the band would quit, and hungry guests would want a bite to eat. When guests grew tired of the traditional ham and eggs, Chef Schmidt came up with a new dish called Hot Browns.

Dish up: 4 servings

Construction time: 10 minutes

Cooking time: 10 minutes

Paraphernalia: 9-by-13-inch baking dish, wide spatula, 3-quart saucepan, toaster

INGREDIENTS:

2 tablespoons butter or margarine

2 tablespoons flour

1 cup milk

1 cup (4 ounces) sharp cheddar cheese, finely shredded

4 slices white or whole-wheat bread

8 slices turkey breast

8 slices tomatoes

To make:

1. Preheat oven to 350 degrees.
2. Melt butter in pan. Stir in flour, mixing well to avoid lumps.
3. Remove from heat. Add milk and stir.
4. Replace on stove top, and stir until thick.
5. Remove from heat. Add cheese, stirring until melted.
6. Toast bread. Place toast in baking dish. Be sure not to overlap pieces. Add two slices of turkey to each piece of toast.
7. Spread cheese sauce over the turkey.
8. Lay tomato slices on top of the cheese.
9. Place dish in oven and cook for about 10 minutes, or until heated through. With a wide spatula, slide onto a dinner plate. Serve hot.

Jazz It Up: Top with cooked bacon strips.

Dress It Down: Forget about the tomatoes.

We Go Good Together: Mock Mint Juleps

Look Ahead: Pull the tortillas and Monterey Jack cheese from the freezer and put it in the refrigerator for Day 10, Chicken Quesadillas. Also, pull stew meat from the freezer and place it in the refrigerator for Day 11, Dump and Forget Beef Tips Dinner.

 FRANTIC WOMAN FAMILY FUN:
Frantic Mock Mint Juleps
Enjoy the festivities of the Kentucky Derby in your own home. Serve an imitation of the traditional beverage of the Kentucky Derby to go with your Hot Browns. Fill an 8-ounce glass with ginger ale and crushed ice. Stir in 1/4 teaspoon dried mint or 1 piece mint candy, such as Lifesavers.

✦ Day 10—Kids' Meal: Chicken Quesadillas ✦

Quesadillas have become a very popular item on restaurant menus and in the frozen food section. They are simple to make and will please choosey eaters when you supply an array of toppings and let them customized their own. This is a great menu idea when there's a bunch of kids running through the house.

Dish up: 5 to 6 servings   Cooking time: 15 minutes
Construction time: 10 minutes   Paraphernalia: Skillet, baking sheet

INGREDIENTS:
1 small tomato, diced
1 tablespoon olive oil
Chicken, stored from Day 8
Handful of sunflower seeds, shelled
Handful of raisins
12 whole-wheat or flour tortillas
2 cups (8 ounces) Monterey Jack cheese, shredded
Salsa
Sour cream

To make:

1. Wash, core and dice tomato.
2. Heat olive oil in skillet over medium heat for about 2 minutes. Add chicken, sunflower seeds and raisins. Cook until thoroughly heated, about 5 to 7 minutes. (Cook and cut 4 chicken breasts into bite-size pieces if you didn't do so on Day 8.)
3. Lay 6 tortillas on a baking sheet. Add a layer of cheese. (Be sure to save some for the final layer.) Layer the chicken mixture next. Add diced tomatoes over chicken mixture. Sprinkle with the remaining cheese. Top with the 6 remaining tortillas.
4. Pop the sheet into the oven for about 5 to 10 minutes, or until cheese is melted. You can heat these in a skillet for a few minutes or microwave them for 1 or 2 minutes.
5. Cut the quesadillas into quarters, and serve with salsa and sour cream.

Jazz It Up: If serving teenagers or adults, spice them up with chopped jalapeños. Add celery and onions to the chicken mixture. Add shredded lettuce on the side.

Dress It Down: Make a chicken-and-cheese–only quesadilla.

Change It Up: Use mild cheddar or Colby cheese if you prefer it.

We Go Good Together: French fries

Look Ahead: Think about preparing Day 11, Slow Cook Tonight, now instead of first thing in the morning. Put all of the ingredients, except meat, in your slow cooker's liner or a bowl and refrigerate. Then, all you'll need to do is put the liner in the cooker, add the meat, and plug it in.

❧ Day 11—Slow Cook Tonight: ❧
Dump and Forget Beef Tips Dinner

Dump the five ingredients into the slow cooker in the morning, then forget about it until dinnertime. What could be easier than that?

Dish up 4 to 6 servings
Construction time: 5 minutes

Cooking time: 8 to 10 hours
Paraphernalia: Slow cooker

INGREDIENTS:

1½ pounds stew meat, cubed

1 10.75-ounce can cream of mushroom soup

1 10.75-ounce can cream of celery soup

1 1.25-ounce package dry onion soup mix

1 2.5-ounce can mushroom pieces

To make:

1. Dump all ingredients into the slow cooker.
2. Cover and cook on low for 8 to 10 hours.
3. Serve hot.

Jazz It Up: Add cubed potatoes, celery or another favorite fresh veggie.

Change It Up: Instead of using a slow cooker, brown stew meat in a Dutch oven. Dump remaining ingredients in Dutch oven and cook over low heat for 1 hour, stirring occasionally.

Dress It Down: Skip the onion soup mix.

We Go Good Together: Serve over noodles.

Look Ahead: Take ziti stored from Day 2 out of the freezer and put it in the refrigerator to thaw for Day 12, Hobo Pasta and Beans Supper.

✸ Day 12—I Can with a Can: ✸ *Hobo Pasta and Beans Supper*

Hobo Pasta and Beans Supper is traditionally a little of this and a can of that thrown into a pot and cooked over a fire. Today's version uses leftovers and canned goods tossed in a skillet and cooked on the stove top. This is much easier than the old-fashioned way!

Dish up: 4 to 6 servings   Cooking time: 15 minutes

Construction time: 10 minutes   Paraphernalia: 12-inch skillet

INGREDIENTS:

8 ounces ziti, stored from Day 2

1 16-ounce can baked beans

1 16-ounce can stewed tomatoes, diced

To make:

1. Toss pasta, beans and tomatoes into skillet. Cook for about 10 minutes on low-medium heat, or until heated through.
2. Serve in large mugs. Or, if you have scouts in the family, pull out their mess kits to use.

Jazz It Up: Buy stewed tomatoes with seasonings to add an extra zip to the dish.

Dress It Down: Skip the pasta and tomatoes.

We Go Good Together: Refrigerated dinner rolls

FRANTIC WOMAN FAMILY FUN: Impromptu Campout
Pull out a blanket or two for the kids to make a tent. If weather permits, use a picnic table for the support. If rain has chased everyone inside, use a couple of kitchen chairs. And if you're really adventurous, serve the mugs of Hobo Supper under the tent.

✦ Day 13—No-Cook Night: Waldorf Tuna Roll-Ups ✦

Having a no-cook night doesn't mean you have to serve cold cereal. This is an ASAP dinner that takes only minutes to make. (By the way, there isn't anything wrong with having cereal for dinner, according to the latest survey announced in the news.)

Dish up: 4 servings   Cooking time: 0
Construction time: 5 minutes   Paraphernalia: Mixing bowl

INGREDIENTS:

1 Granny Smith apple, cored and diced
1/2 cup walnuts, chopped
1 celery rib, chopped
2 6-ounce cans white tuna packed in water, drained
1/2 cup mayonnaise
1/4 cup ranch salad dressing
4 whole-wheat tortillas
Salt and pepper, to taste

To make:
1. Wash, core and dice apple. Chop walnuts. (Simplify it: Put walnuts in a plastic zippered bag and crush with a rolling pin.) Wash and chop celery.
2. Flake tuna into a bowl. Mix tuna, apple, walnuts and celery together well.
3. Add salt and pepper, to taste.
4. Spoon 1/4 of the mixture onto one side of each tortilla. Spread it out over half of the tortilla.
5. Snugly roll up each tortilla as if you were rolling a rug. Insert two toothpicks in each one to keep it from unrolling.
6. Cut each roll-up in half.

Jazz It Up: Add chopped grapes.

Dress It Down: Skip the walnuts.

Change It Up: Use ¼ cup mayonnaise, 1 tablespoon prepared Dijon-style mustard and 1 teaspoon sweet pickle relish instead of the ranch salad dressing. Use chunk tuna in place of white tuna.

We Go Good Together: Caesar salad

Look Ahead: Pull the chicken for Day 14, Glazed Chicken, Apples and Onions, and the Monterey Jack cheese for We Go Good Together from the freezer and put them in the refrigerator to thaw.

✦ Day 14—Company's Coming: ✦
Glazed Chicken, Apples and Onions

A sweet taste combined with a bit of tang gives this chicken dish a unique flavor. Serve it with green veggies to make a colorful presentation for your company.

Dish up: 6 servings
Construction time: 5 minutes

Cooking time: 20 minutes
Paraphernalia: Skillet, small bowl

INGREDIENTS:
2 teaspoons vegetable oil

6 skinless and boneless chicken breasts (about 2 pounds)
¼ cup water
1 large Jonathan apple, sliced
1 medium onion, thinly sliced
¾ cup honey mustard
½ cup apple juice

To make:
1. Add oil to skillet. Brown both sides of chicken over medium-high heat.
2. Reduce heat to medium-low, and add ¼ cup water. Cook about 7 to 10 minutes.
3. Wash, core and slice apple (with skins still on for color). Peel and slice onion.
4. Add onion and cook for about 3 minutes, stirring occasionally.
5. Add apple. Cook for 5 minutes, or until onion and apple are tender.
6. In a small bowl, combine mustard and apple juice. Add to skillet and cook about 5 minutes, or until heated through.
7. Put in a serving dish with chicken on the bottom. Spoon the apples, onions and sauce over the chicken.

Jazz It Up: Add sliced black olives for additional color.
Dress It Down: Skip the onions.
Change It Up: Can be made with pork chops instead of chicken.
We Go Good Together: Mashed Cauliflower

POTFUL OF KNOWLEDGE: An Apple for the Family

As you polish an apple for the teacher, polish one for each family member, too, because they're a healthy snack for everyone.

- Apples are 85 percent water, which is why they quench thirst.
- Apples are reported to clean the digestive tract and teeth.
- Apple eaters have fewer headaches, intestinal disorders, colds and respiratory problems.

TiPS BASKETFUL OF TIPS: Watching the Carbs

A number of people today are watching their carbs. If you're one of them, whip up a batch of mashed cauliflower that can almost replace the taste of mashed potatoes.

TiPS BASKETFUL OF TIPS: Frantic Woman Has Company

Many frantic women want to run at the mere mention that company could be coming. At some point, everyone will deal with guests, whether it is a party or a holiday dinner. As the party expert on Mainstreet-mom.com reports, one question subscribers often ask is, "Should you clear the table while guests are talking over coffee or ask for help cleaning up?"

Miss Manners probably dictates a proper way to handle this situation, and she might not agree with my way of thinking, but here's my opinion:

First, consider the type of gathering and the guests attending. For example, when my husband and I are hosting a business dinner, I don't want to make anyone feel obligated, and that's what would happen if I started clearing dinner dishes. So, I stick whatever needs to be refrigerated inside the refrigerator and move everyone to the living room for coffee and dessert as soon as I see everyone has finished with the main course. Additionally, I bypass trying to switch the leftovers into smaller bowls, too. I open, stuff, and close the refrigerator.

Now, if the dinner guest, such as a family member, friend or neighbor, happens to be the same one holiday after holiday and never returns invitations, never offers to bring a covered dish, and you feel as if you're being taken advantage of, the floor's all yours. A gracious smile with a polite, "Would you mind handing me that empty bowl on the table?" should do the trick. Once the guest sits down, ask, "Oh, my hands are slippery. Could you pass me the dirty dishes?" He or she might get the hint. But, then again, you might have to work your way down to the silverware.

SPRING PLAN TWO MENUS

Day 1—Sandwich Board: Tuna Melts
Day 2—Everyday Dinner: Sweet with a Touch of Sour Chicken
Day 3—Sandwich Board: Hot Reubens All Around
Day 4—Retro Meal: Eddy Spaghetti
Day 5—Soup's On: Cheese Soup
Day 6—Backwards Meal: Freddie French Toast
Day 7—Kids' Meal: Chicken Fingers
Day 8—Seafood Fest: Don't Smell on Me Fish
Day 9—Everyday Dinner: Oh, Sweet Ham of Mine
Day 10—Kids' Meal: Mini Pizzas
Day 11—Slow Cook Tonight: Irish Beef Stew
Day 12—I Can with a Can: Ham It Up
Day 13—No Cook Night: Meatball Hoagies
Day 14—Company's Coming: Linguine with White Clam Sauce

THE SHOPPING LISTS

The Frantic Woman's Cupboard

SPRING PLAN TWO STAPLES

Seasonings

Caraway seeds
Cinnamon*
Crushed red pepper
Dill
Garlic (fresh, powder)
Mustard (ground)
Oregano
Salt*
Pepper

Side Dishes
French-fried onion rings
Paprika
French-fried onion rings

Condiments
Ketchup
Mayonnaise
Mustard (prepared)

Jazz It Ups
Mustard (prepared)

Dressings, Oil and Sauces
Maple syrup
Soy sauce
Vinegar
Worcestershire sauce

Side Dishes
Italian salad dressing

Canned Goods and Bottles
Grape jelly

Jazz It Ups
Peanut butter

Baking Needs
Flour (all-purpose flour* or your preference)
Sugar (cane, brown)*

Side Dishes
Baking powder

Baking soda
Cornstarch

Bread, Chips and More
Bread crumbs (Italian seasoned)

Frantic Necessities
Nonstick cooking spray
Foil

Dairy
Butter* or margarine
Eggs
Milk*

Jazz It Ups
Milk

*Ingredient you'll need for both main and side dishes

The Frantic Woman Goes Shopping

MAIN-DISH INGREDIENTS YOU'LL NEED TO BUY

Produce: Fruit
1 small Golden Delicious apple (Day 1)

Produce: Veggies
1 bunch celery (Day 1)
1 medium green pepper (Day 2)
1 medium bunch parsley (Days 3, 14)
1 bunch green onions (Day 4)
3 large baking potatoes (Day 11)
1 12-ounce package baby cut carrots (Day 11)

PIT STOP: Keep It Fresh

Check the sell-by date on the bag of carrots. You'll want to make sure they will still be fresh when you need them. Also, fresh parsley usually doesn't last for two weeks, so you might want to freeze a bit of it for later.

Seasonings

1 envelope dry onion soup mix (Day 11)

Dressings, Oils and Sauces

1 8-ounce bottle Thousand Island salad dressing (Day 3)

2 32-ounce jars marinara sauce (Day 4)

1 16-ounce bottle ranch salad dressing (Day 7)

Canned Goods and Bottles

2 6-ounce cans white tuna packed in water (Day 1)

1 16-ounce can applesauce (Day 4)

1 20-ounce can pineapple chunks (Day 2)

1 16-ounce can sauerkraut (Day 3)

1 16-ounce can chicken broth (Day 5)

2 8-ounce cans tomato sauce (Day 10)

1 15-ounce can extra-long asparagus spears (Day 12)

1 6-ounce can baby clams with juice (Day 14)

Noodles, Pasta and Rice

1 16-ounce box spaghetti (Day 4)

1 16-ounce box linguine (Day 14)

Beverages

1 large can tomato juice (Day 11)

Bread, Chips and More

4 sandwich rolls (Day 1)
4 slices rye bread (Day 3)
6 slices white or whole-wheat bread (Day 6)
6 English muffins (Day 10)
4 6-inch hoagie rolls (Day 13)

Deli

4 slices Colby cheese (Day 1)
1 pound turkey pastrami (Day 3)
5 ounces blue cheese (Day 5)
¾ cup (3 ounces) Parmesan cheese, grated (Day 14)

Fish, Meat and Poultry

3½ pounds skinless, boneless chicken breasts (Days 2, 7)
2½ pounds ground beef (Days 4, 10)
1½ pounds tilapia fillets (Day 8)
2 pounds ham (Days 9, 12)
2 pounds stew beef, cubed (Day 11)

Dairy

3 cups (12 ounces) Monterey Jack cheese, shredded (Days 3, 5)
1 small container half and half (Day 5)
3½ cups (16 ounces) mozzarella cheese, shredded (Days 10, 12, 13)
1 8-ounce can crescent rolls (Day 12)

JAZZ IT UP INGREDIENTS YOU'LL NEED TO BUY

Produce: Veggies

1 small bunch green onions (Day 5)
1 8-ounce carton snowcap mushrooms (Day 10)
1 yellow onion (Day 13)
1 green pepper (Day 13)

Canned Goods and Bottles

1 16-ounce can peas (Day 11)

Noodles, Pasta and Rice

Chow mein noodles (Day 2)
1 16-ounce box tricolor pasta (swap for linguine) (Day 14)

Cereal, Nuts and Such

⅛ cup (2 ounces) walnuts, chopped (Day 1)
⅛ cup (2 ounces) almonds, sliced (Day 9)

Bread, Chips and More

1 4- to 6-count package pita bread (Day 1)

Deli

½ (2 ounces) Parmesan cheese, grated (Day 7)
2 ounces pepperoni (Day 10)

Fish, Meat and Poultry

1 pound bulk sausage (swap for 1 pound ground beef) (Day 4)
4 ounces bacon (Day 5)
1 pound cooked baby shrimp without tails (Day 14)

 PIT STOP: Keep It Fresh

Hold off buying 1 carton (8 ounces) of snowcap mushrooms for jazzing up your dinner meal until the end of the first week, or around Day 5.

WE GO GOOD TOGETHER INGREDIENTS YOU'LL NEED TO BUY

Produce: Fruit

2 to 4 Red Delicious apples (Day 5)
1 pound strawberries (Day 6)
1 pint blueberries (Day 6)
6 Yellow Delicious or Jonathan apples (Day 13)

Produce: Veggies

2 16-ounce packages ready-to-eat salad (Days 10, 14)

1 8-ounce carton snowcap mushrooms (Day 12)

PIT STOP: Keep It Fresh

To minimize the chance of your produce spoiling before you can use it for the We Go Good Together suggestions, pick up these ingredients later in the first week: 1 pound strawberries, 1 pound blueberries, 6 yellow Delicious or Jonathan apples, 2 packages (16 ounces) ready-to-eat salad and 1 carton (8 ounces) snowcap mushrooms.

Dressings, Oils and Sauces

Barbecue, honey mustard, ranch salad dressing and/or hot sauce (Day 7)

1 16-ounce jar cheese sauce (Day 8)

Salad dressing, your preference (Days 10, 14)

Canned Goods and Bottles

2 16-ounce cans French-style green beans (Day 9)

1 14.5-ounce can cream of mushroom soup (Day 9)

Noodles, Pasta and Rice

2 cups instant rice (white, brown or fried) (Day 2)

Cereal, Nuts and Such

2 cups baking raisins (Day 11)

Bread, Chips and More

1 16-ounce bag potato chips (Day 3)

4 to 6 whole-grain rolls (Day 5)

Frozen

1 loaf garlic bread (Day 4)

1 32-ounce bag french fries (Day 8)

Dairy

1 quart buttermilk (Day 11)
1 8-ounce can dinner rolls (Day 14)

Unloading the Load

- Before you put the chicken in the freezer, divide it in half.
- Using your kitchen shears, cut one portion of the chicken into bite-size pieces and mark it for Day 2, Sweet with a Touch of Sour Chicken and put it in the refrigerator.
- Cut the other half of the chicken into 1-inch strips and mark it for Day 7, Chicken Fingers, and freeze it.
- Cut the ham almost in half (one part should be a little bigger than the other), and mark the bigger piece for Day 9, Oh, Sweet Ham of Mine, and the smaller piece for Day 12, Ham It Up. Freeze both ham packages.
- If your family might eat the turkey pastrami for Day 3, Hot Reubens All Around, put it in the freezer for safe keeping.
- Freeze 2 pounds of the ground beef for Day 4, Eddy Spaghetti. (This will make meals for Days 4 and 13.)
- Freeze the remaining ½ pound ground beef for Day 10, Mini Pizzas.
- Freeze the stew beef for Day 11, Irish Beef Stew. If you bought a larger piece of beef instead of the stew beef, cut the meat into cubes now.
- Freeze the tilapia fillets for Day 8, Don't Smell on Me Fish.
- Put the hoagie rolls for Day 13, Meatball Hoagies, and English muffins for Day 10, Mini Pizzas in the freezer, too.
- Tuck the cheese in the freezer. Divide the mozzarella: 1½ cups for Day 10, Mini Pizzas; 1 cup for Day 12, Ham It Up and 1 cup for Day 13, Meatball Hoagies.
- Tuck the other cheeses in the freezer if your family might nibble on them before you use them for cooking. Put 1 cup of Monterey Jack and blue cheese for Day 5, Cheese Soup, and Parmesan cheese for Day 14, Linguine with White Clam Sauce, in the freezer.

- Freeze the ingredients for jazzing up your entrees. This includes 2 ounces Parmesan cheese for Day 7, Chicken Fingers, and 2 ounces pepperoni for Day 10, Mini Pizzas.
- Be sure to read the Look Ahead section in each recipe to see when you must pull items out of the freezer to put into the refrigerator to defrost.

SPRING: PLAN TWO

⇢ Day 1—Sandwich Board: Tuna Melts 🐟 ⇠

After a marathon shopping day, a quick meal will be on the menu with a selection from the sandwich board. Toss together the ingredients for this simple yet delicious recipe.

Dish up: 4 servings
Construction time: 7 minutes

Cooking time: 1 minute
Paraphernalia: Microwave, microwave-safe dish, paper towels

INGREDIENTS:

1 celery rib, finely chopped
½ small Golden Delicious apple, finely chopped
2 6-ounce cans white tuna packed in water, drained
3 tablespoons mayonnaise
4 sandwich rolls
4 slices Colby cheese

To make:
1. Wash and chop celery and apples. (Simplify it: Use a vegetable peeler, aka potato peeler, rather than a paring knife to peel apples and other fruits. You'll get rid of the skin without losing as much fruit.) Drain water from tuna.
2. Combine tuna, mayonnaise, celery and apple.
3. Spread mixture on the bottom of the sandwich rolls. Lay cheese onto mixture. Add the top of the roll.

4. Wrap each roll in a paper towel or napkin.
5. Zap it in the microwave for about 30 to 60 seconds, or until the sandwich is heated through and the cheese is melted.

Jazz It Up: Swap pita bread for sandwich rolls. Add chopped walnuts.

Dress It Down: Skip the celery and apples. Serve cold.

Change It Up: Use canned chicken if your family dislikes tuna. If you'd prefer not to zap your food, individually wrap sandwiches in foil and bake in a 325-degree oven for 5 to 10 minutes, or until heated through.

We Go Good Together: Wash the remaining celery sticks and slice the remaining apple half. Spread peanut butter on apples and celery.

 **POTFUL OF KNOWLEDGE: Fish Does the Body Good**

Holy mackerel! Eating fish can help reduce harmful cholesterol in the blood and can keep your heart healthy. Fresh fish has a hefty dose of potassium that can help keep your blood pressure down. So eat up!

✤ Day 2—Everday Dinner Sweet with a ✤ Touch of Sour Chicken

This popular entree which is listed on the menu at most Chinese restaurants can easily be whipped up and popped in the oven. You'll have time to change your clothes and sift through the mail while dinner's cooking.

Dish up: 4 to 6 servings
Construction time: 5 minutes

Cooking time: 30 to 35 minutes
Paraphernalia: 9-by-13-inch baking dish, 12-inch skillet

INGREDIENTS:

4 to 6 skinless, boneless chicken breast, cut up

4 tablespoons soy sauce, divided

2 tablespoons flour

¼ cup brown sugar

¼ cup vinegar

3 tablespoons water

1 20-ounce can pineapple chunks, drained

1 medium green pepper, chopped

To make:

1. Preheat oven to 350 degrees.
2. Cut chicken into bite-size pieces if you skipped this step when unloading the grocery bags. In a skillet, add 2 tablespoons soy sauce, and brown chicken over medium heat for about 5 minutes.
3. Put flour in baking dish. Blend brown sugar, vinegar, water and 2 tablespoons soy sauce with flour.
4. Drain pineapple chunks. Wash and chop pepper.
5. Add pineapples and peppers to mixture. Stir.
6. Add chicken and stir to coat. Smooth all the ingredients into an even layer.
7. Cover the dish with foil. Cut several slits in the foil to vent. Bake 20 to 25 minutes.

Jazz It Up: Add chow mein noodles.

Dress It Down: Skip the peppers.

We Go Good Together: Hot cooked white, brown or fried rice.

Look Ahead: If you tucked the deli meat for Day 3, Hot Reubens All Around, into the freezer, pull it out.

❧ Day 3—Sandwich Board: Hot Reubens All Around ❧

Reuben sandwiches are an old standby and a favorite of Kim Farrar, the mother of two young boys and the owner of a screen printing business. On the days when she's up to her elbows in ink and t-shirts and wearing too many hats, she needs an all-in-one meal. This adaptation of Reuben sandwiches lets the microwave oven do the cookingand eliminates the need to grill the sandwiches one by one. Besides, whose sandwich is always the last one made, and who is usually eating all by herself? I'm sure I don't have to give you the answer.

Dish up: 6 servings   Cooking time: 10 minutes
Construction time: 5 to 7 minutes   Paraphernalia: 9- or 10-inch glass
microwave-safe pie pan, microwave

INGREDIENTS:
4 slices rye bread
1 pound turkey pastrami
1 16-ounce can sauerkraut
1 teaspoon caraway seeds
2 cups (8 ounces) Monterey Jack cheese, shredded
1/2 cup Thousand Island salad dressing
1/3 cup butter, melted
2 tablespoons fresh parsley, chopped

To make:
1. Cut bread into 1/2-inch cubes. Cube turkey pastrami.
2. Wash and drain sauerkraut. Layer sauerkraut on pan's bottom. Sprinkle with caraway seed, 1 cup of cheese, dressing, turkey pastrami and the remaining cheese.
3. Melt butter in microwave for about 20 seconds.
4. Toss bread with melted butter. Sprinkle over the cheese.
5. Microwave on medium for about 10 minutes, or until cheese is heated through.
6. Chop parsley while casserole is cooking. Top cooked casserole with parsley when finished.
7. Cut into six pieces and serve.

Dress It Down: Skip the sauerkraut if you think the kids won't eat it.

Change It Up: You can use turkey ham. Bake in a 325-degree oven for about 5 to 7 minutes, or until cheese has melted.

We Go Good Together: Potato chips, of course

Look Ahead: Pull the ground beef for Day 4, Eddy Spaghetti, out of the freezer and put it in the refrigerator to thaw.

⇢ Day 4—Retro Meal: Eddy Spaghetti ⇠

Growing up, good old spaghetti was a typical meal in my parents' house, and more than likely it still is for most families. This is one meal you can count on the family to eat . . . usually. Even my younger brother, who only liked hamburgers, hot dogs and boxed macaroni and cheese, would eat spaghetti. (See his pasta version below.) And the meatball recipe has a kid-friendly ingredient in it that is sure to please the youngsters in your house.

Dish up: 4 to 6 servings

Construction time: 10 minutes

Cooking time: 20 minutes

Paraphernalia: 5-quart Dutch oven, baking sheet, mixing bowl, strainer

INGREDIENTS:

2 pounds ground beef 🥤 (Half of the beef will be uesed for Day 13, Meatball Hoagies)

1 cup Italian-seasoned bread crumbs

2 eggs

2 cups applesauce

4 tablespoons green onions, chopped

2 teaspoons salt

1/4 teaspoon pepper

1 16-ounce box spaghetti

2 32-ounce jars marinara sauce 🥤 (Half will be used for Day 13, Meatball Hoagies)

To make:

1. Preheat oven to 400 degrees.
2. Boil water for pasta.
3. Mix beef, bread crumbs, eggs, applesauce, onion, salt and pepper.
4. Form into 1- to 1½-inch balls and place on a baking sheet. (Simplify it: Give the kids a smaller ice cream scoop and have them make the meatballs.)
5. Bake for about 15 to 20 minutes, or until no longer pink in center. (Simplify it: Cook in the microwave at medium-high for 7 to 9 minutes.) Drain off excess fat.

6. Cook spaghetti according to package directions while meatballs are cooking.

7. Heat jarred marinara sauce in a pan over low heat. Add meatballs to sauce when finished. (Put half of the meatballs and sauce in a container and freeze for Day 13, Meatball Hoagies.

8. Serve meatballs and sauce over cooked spaghetti.

Jazz It Up: Use 1 pound sausage and 1 pound ground beef, rather than 2 pounds ground beef.

Dress It Down: Use frozen, precooked meatballs.

Change It Up: Try my brother's favorite way to eat pasta. Melt 1/2 stick of butter in the microwave or on the stove top. Toss spaghetti with melted butter and sprinkle with grated Parmesan cheese.

Double It: Divide meatballs and sauce in half. You have a complete meal for Day 13, Meatball Hoagies. Store the meatballs and sauce in a container or freezer bag (separately), and freeze until Day 12.

We Go Good Together: Garlic bread

Look Ahead: Pull cheeses out of the freezer marked for Day 5, Cheese Soup.

✦ Day 5—Soup's On: Cheese Soup 🚫 ✦

Stir up a pot of cheese soup, and serve it with a loaf of whole-grain bread. Pull out any leftovers from previous meals to serve as side dishes.

Dish up: 4 servings
Construction time: 5 minutes

Cooking time: 20 minutes
Paraphernalia: Stockpot

INGREDIENTS:
1/2 stick butter
4 tablespoons flour
1 16-ounce can chicken broth
1 1/4 cups half and half
5 ounces blue cheese
1 cup (4 ounces) Monterey Jack cheese, shredded
Black pepper

To make:
1. Melt butter in a pot over medium-low heat.
2. Add flour, broth and half and half to melted butter. Cook and stir for 5 minutes
3. Add cheeses to broth and mix until melted. (Be sure to add slowly. Be careful not to overheat and burn the cheese.)
4. Serve hot.

Jazz It Up: Add crumbled bacon and/or chopped green onions on top.

We Go Good Together: Whole-grain rolls and sliced apples

Look Ahead: The bread slices for tomorrow's meal should be stale. When you go off to work in the morning, allow the 6 slices (more if your family loves French toast) to sit on the counter.

✦ Day 6—Backwards Meal: Freddie French Toast ✦

Eating breakfast for dinner is probably a favorite thing for many kids. Nothing beats French toast; it is a great way to use up your stale bread, because the dish cooks up so much easier when the bread is stale rather than fresh.

Dish up: 4 to 6 servings

Construction time: 5 minutes

Cooking time: 16 minutes

Paraphernalia: 12-inch skillet, baking sheet, spatula

INGREDIENTS:

2 eggs

½ cup milk

6 slices stale bread

Butter or margarine, optional

Maple syrup, optional

Cinnamon, optional

To make:
1. Preheat oven to 250 degrees.
2. Coat skillet with nonstick cooking spray. Heat skillet on medium heat.

3. Beat eggs and milk with fork until mixed.
4. Dip both sides of bread, one slice at a time, in the egg mixture.
5. Cook about 3–4 minutes, or until golden brown on each side. (Simplify it: You should be able to cook 2 to 3 pieces of bread at one time.)
6. When finished, place the cooked French toast on a baking sheet, cover with foil, and put in the oven to keep warm.
7. Repeat Steps 4 and 5 with the remaining bread. Smother with your favorite toppings: Butter, maple syrup or cinnamon.

Jazz It Up: Heat the syrup before serving.

We Go Good Together: Sliced berries

Look Ahead: Pull out the package of chicken strips and the Parmesan cheese for Day 7, Chicken Fingers from the freezer and defrost them in the refrigerator.

✦ Day 7—Kids' Meal: Chicken Fingers ✦

You'll find this favorite kids' meal on the menu at most fast food restaurants. Cook up your own crispy chicken the kids will love with this recipe.

Dish up: 6 to 8 servings
Construction time: 10 minutes

Cooking time: 20 minutes
Paraphernalia: Baking sheet, 2 bowls

INGREDIENTS:

1 16-ounce bottle ranch salad dressing
1 teaspoon Worcestershire sauce
2 cups Italian-seasoned bread crumbs
2 pounds skinless, boneless chicken breasts, cut into strips
¼ cup butter or margarine, melted

To make:
1. Preheat oven to 350 degrees. Coat baking sheet with nonstick cooking spray. (Cut chicken into 1-inch strips if you did not do so when unloading the groceries.)

2. Combine ranch salad dressing and Worcestershire sauce in a bowl.

3. Dump bread crumbs in a bowl. Dip strips into dressing mixture, then coat with bread crumbs. (Simplify it: Dump bread crumbs into a large plastic zippered bag. Add dipped chicken strips. Shake to coat.)

4. Place coated strips on baking sheet. Melt butter in a small bowl in the microwave for about 20 seconds. Drizzle melted butter over strips.

5. Bake for 20 minutes, or until chicken is no longer pink.

Jazz It Up: Add 2 or 3 teaspoons grated Parmesan cheese to bread crumb mixture.

Dress It Down: Change the bread crumbs to all-purpose flour or whole-grain flour.

Change It Up: Use sour cream instead of ranch salad dressing.

We Go Good Together: Serve with dipping sauces, such as barbecue or honey mustard. Or follow kitchen tester Eve Laboon's lead: Mix ½ cup of hot sauce with ½ ranch salad dressing to make a dipping sauce.

Look Ahead: Pull out the fish for Day 8, Don't Smell on Me Fish, and put it in the refrigerator to thaw.

> **TIPS BASKETFUL OF TIPS: Healthy Sneak Attack**
> Add 1 or 2 teaspoons wheat germ to the bread crumbs. Be sure to mix it thoroughly. The kids won't even know you're adding a healthy dash to their favorite fast-food knockoff.

→ *Day 8—Seafood Fest: Don't Smell on Me Fish* ←

You know fish is good for you and your family, but the thought of cooking fish and having your house smelling fishy all night long leaves a lot to be desired. With tilapia, you can eat your fish and cook it, too, without the lingering odor.

Dish up: 4 servings

Construction time: 15 minutes

Cooking time: 10 to 15 minutes

Paraphernalia: small bowl, 9-by-13-inch baking dish

INGREDIENTS:

4 tilapia fillets (about 1 to 1 1/2 pounds)

2 tablespoons mayonnaise

1/2 teaspoon prepared mustard

1/4 teaspoon ground mustard

1/2 teaspoon sugar

1/2 teaspoon ketchup

1/2 teaspoon garlic powder

1/4 teaspoon crushed red pepper

To make:

1. Preheat oven to 500 degrees.
2. Rinse fillets and pat dry.
3. Combine all the remaining ingredients in a small bowl.
4. Coat baking dish with nonstick cooking spray.
5. Lay fish in dish, and spread the mixture over the fillets. Allow fish to marinate for 10 minutes.
6. Bake for 10 to 15 minutes, or until fish flakes easily with a fork. Dish it up immediately.

Jazz It Up: Sprinkle paprika over fish.

Dress It Down: Skip the crushed red pepper seasoning.

Change It Up: You can use trout, catfish, orange roughy or any other mild-flavored fish.

We Go Good Together: French fries with cheese sauce. Buy jarred sauce and heat it in the microwave for about 30 to 60 seconds on medium power.

Look Ahead: Pull out the larger ham section from the freezer and place it in the refrigerator to thaw for Day 9, Oh Sweet Ham of Mine.

TiPS BASKETFUL OF TIPS: Smell No More

Keep the fish from stinking up your house with Beverly Breton Carroll's trick. Pour vinegar in a small bowl and keep it in your kitchen the evening you cook fish. For some reason, it takes the odor away. And Beverly says the vinegar doesn't smell either, because it evaporates into the air.

✦ Day 9—Everday Dinner: Oh, Sweet Ham of Mine ✦

This recipe came about as a result of my buying a large piece of ham at a great price. My dilemma was trying to find a way to serve it other than as plain, boring ham slices.

Dish up: 4 to 6 servings
Construction time: 15 minutes

Cooking time: 5 minutes
Paraphernalia: 1-quart saucepan, 12-inch skillet

INGREDIENTS:

$\frac{1}{2}$ cup grape jelly
2 tablespoons prepared mustard
$\frac{1}{4}$ teaspoon cinnamon
1 to 1$\frac{1}{2}$ pound ham, cut into 4 to 6 slices

To make:
1. Combine jelly, mustard and cinnamon in saucepan.
2. Heat until ingredients have turned into a sauce and the lumps from the jelly have disappeared.
3. Coat skillet with nonstick cooking spray. Lay ham slices in the skillet and cover with sauce. Let them marinate for 10 minutes.
4. Cook on medium heat for 5 minutes, or until ham slices are heated through.

Jazz It Up: Add sliced almonds
Dress It Down: Serve plain slices.
Change It Up: You can use deli ham.
We Go Good Together: Green Bean Casserole ✦+✦

Look Ahead: Pull out the ground beef, English muffins and 1 ½ cups of mozzarella cheese for Day 10, Mini Pizzas, from the freezer and put them in the refrigerator. Pull out the pepperoni if you are jazzing up your pizza. Also, take the stew beef for Day 11, Irish Beef Stew, out of the freezer and put it in the refrigerator to thaw.

⇒ Day 10—Kids' Meal: Mini Pizzas ⇐

Imagine twenty-some excited little girls, ages six to eight, sitting around a campfire. Actually, they were sitting around a handmade oven made out of a box, aluminum foil and charcoal, cooking pizzas as part of a scouting project. And when dinner was ready, they chowed down. Well, you don't have to build a foil-boxed oven to enjoy this quick and easy supper.

Dish up: 4 to 6 servings
Construction time: 10 minutes

Cooking time: 5 minutes
Paraphernalia: Oven broiler, toaster, skillet, baking sheet

INGREDIENTS:
½ pound ground beef
2 8-ounce cans tomato sauce
⅛ teaspoon oregano
⅛ teaspoon dill
6 English muffins
1 ½ cup (6 ounces) Mozzarella cheese, shredded

To make:
1. Preheat broiler.
2. Cook and drain fat from ground beef.
3. Add tomato sauce and seasonings, and simmer for a few minutes.
4. Split English muffins and toast in toaster. Place on baking sheet.
5. Spoon mixture onto each half. Top with cheese.
6. Put under broiler for a few minutes, until cheese is melted.

Jazz It Up: Add diced mushrooms and diced pepperoni or your favorite topping to the mixture.

Dress It Down: Skip the ground beef for a vegetarian meal.

Change It Up: Use jarred pizza sauce.

We Go Good Together: Tossed salad

Look Ahead: You might want to prep Day 11, Irish Beef Stew, tonight and refrigerate it until tomorrow. This way, all you have to do in the morning is plug in the slow cooker. Remember, don't add the beef until tomorrow for food safety.

FRANTIC WOMAN FAMILY FUN: Eggs in a Nest

With sounds of spring in the air, the kids will love this treat. Melt 1 pound of chocolate (found at craft supply stores) or chocolate baking chips in the top of a double boiler (about 5 to 10 minutes). Add in ¼ cup of flaked or shredded coconut. Stir well. Drop 1 tablespoon of mixture, aka the nest, onto a cold baking sheet. (Place baking sheet in the refrigerator for a few minutes.) Place 5 miniature jelly beans, aka the eggs, in the middle of the nest. Repeat. Put baking sheet in the refrigerator to set candy (about 5 minutes). This is a great party or classroom treat.

❧ Day 11—Slow Cook Tonight: Irish Beef Stew ❧

St. Patrick's Day is the ever-popular holiday that turns everyone Irish for a day. Be sure to serve this one on March 17 to celebrate at home. Or if you plan to be out for the evening, serve it the next day and celebrate twice. Remember, you must prepare this in the morning.

Dish up: 4 to 6 servings

Construction time: 10 minutes

Cooking time: 8 to 9 hours

Paraphernalia: Slow cooker

INGREDIENTS:

2 cups carrots, diced

2 cups potatoes, diced

2 pounds stew beef, cubed

1 cup flour

1 envelope dry onion soup mix

1 large can tomato juice

1 cup water

Pepper, to taste

To make:

1. Wash and dice veggies.
2. Cube meat if need be, and coat it with flour. (This will thicken the sauce.)
3. Place beef, onion soup mix, tomato juice (use enough to almost cover the ingredients), water, pepper, carrots and potatoes in slow cooker and cover.
4. Cook on low for 8 to 9 hours. Serve hot.

Jazz It Up: Add cooked peas before serving.

Dress It Down: Skip the fresh veggies. Heat and add canned carrots and potatoes.

Change It Up: Instead of cooking Irish Stew in a slow cooker, use a Dutch oven. Place 1 teaspoon olive oil in Dutch oven. Add and brown flour-coated beef cubes over medium heat. Add the remaining ingredients and cook over medium-low heat for 1 hour, or until beef and veggies are completely cooked.

We Go Good Together: Grandma's Irish Cake

Look Ahead: Pull out the ham and mozzarella cheese for Day 13, Ham It Up, from the freezer and tuck it into the refrigerator to defrost.

FRANTIC WOMAN FAMILY FUN: Spring Smoothies
Whip up a batch of Spring Smoothies. Combine 2 cups of honeydew melon or kiwi fruit (cut into small pieces), 1 cup milk, 2 tablespoons lemon juice and 4 tablespoons sugar in the blender. Cover and blend on high speed for about 1 minute. Add in 4 scoops of lime sherbet and blend on high for 3 to 4 minutes or until smooth. Yum. Yum.

❧ Day 12—I Can with a Can: Ham It Up ❧

Tonight's meal has a bonus. Not only is it simple, using a can of rolls and a jar of veggies, but the kids can make it themselves, with your supervision. While the little ones are doing their thing with the roll-ups, you can read the daily newspaper. And best of all, you're serving up several food groups without the fuss of making several dishes.

Dish up: 8 roll-ups

Construction time: 10 minutes

Cooking time: 16 to 20 minutes

Paraphernalia: Baking sheet, 2-quart saucepan

INGREDIENTS:

1 8-ounce can crescent rolls

8 thin slices ham

1 15-ounce jar extra long asparagus spears

2 tablespoons butter or margarine

2 tablespoons flour

1 cup milk

1 cup (4 ounces) mozzarella cheese, shredded

1/4 teaspoon pepper

To make:

1. Heat oven to 375 degrees. Coat baking sheet with nonstick cooking spray.
2. Separate dough into 4 rectangles.
3. Cut each rectangle into 2 triangles. Top each triangle with 1 ham slice.
4. Drain asparagus spears. Lay 1 asparagus spear on the wide end of each triangle.
5. Roll up dough starting at wide side of triangle, and roll toward opposite end.
6. Bake at 375 degrees for 16 to 20 minutes.
7. Melt butter in a small saucepan.
8. Stir in flour until smooth. Cook over medium heat for 1 minute, stirring constantly.
9. Gradually stir in milk and cook until thick and bubbly, stirring constantly.
10. Add cheese and pepper, and stir until cheese melts.
11. Pour cheese sauce over warm roll-ups.

Jazz It Up: Add a squirt of mustard to each roll-up during Step 4.

Dress It Down: Serve warm roll-ups without the cheese sauce.

Change It Up: Heat already-prepared jarred cheese sauce in the microwave for a few minutes, or until cheese is warm and can be poured over the roll-ups.

We Go Good Together: Mushrooms marinated in Italian salad dressing.

Look Ahead: Pull out the Applesauce Meatballs, sauce, hoagie rolls and mozzarella cheese from the freezer, and store them in the refrigerator to thaw for Day 13.

→ Day 13—No-Cook Night: Meatball Hoagies ←

Today all you'll need to do is heat up the Applesauce Meatballs with some sauce for a home-cooked meal without the fuss.

Dish up: 4 servings
Construction time: 5 minutes

Cooking time: 10 minutes
Paraphernalia: Saucepan

INGREDIENTS:

Meatballs and sauce, stored from Day 4
4 6-inch hoagie (torpedo) rolls
1 cup (4 ounces) mozzarella cheese, shredded

To make:
1. Preheat oven to 325 degrees.
2. Heat meatballs and sauce in a saucepan over medium heat for about 10 minutes.
3. Slice rolls, if need be.
4. Put 3 meatballs on the bottom half of each roll.
5. Top with cheese.
6. Wrap sandwiches in foil. (Or you can bake them open face for a crunchier sandwich.) Place in oven on rack. Bake 7 to 10 minutes, or until cheese is melted.

Jazz It Up: Add sautéed sliced onions and green peppers. If you like your hoagie crunchy, toast the buns under the broiler on both sides first.

Dress It Down: Skip the oven-baking step.

Change It Up: Heat meatballs and sauce in the microwave for about 3 to 4 minutes. Make sandwiches, and wrap each in a napkin or paper towel. Microwave for 1 minute.

We Go Good Together: Baked Apple Slices 🥮

Look Ahead: Pull out the Parmesan cheese, and put it in the refrigerator to thaw for Day 14, Linguine with White Clam Sauce.

⇸ *Day 14—Company's Coming:* ⇷ *Linguine with White Clam Sauce* 🐾

Sue Kolton, a working mother of three, whips up this simple recipe when it's her turn to host the family birthday celebration dinner. Double the recipe if you're serving a crowd.

Dish up: 6 to 8 servings
Construction time: 10 minutes

Cooking time: 20 minutes
Paraphernalia: 12-inch skillet, pot, strainer

INGREDIENTS:

1 16-ounce box linguine
4 gloves garlic, minced
6 tablespoons butter, softened
1 can minced clams (with juice)
3 teaspoons parsley
1/3 cup Parmesan cheese

To make:
1. Cook linguine according to package directions.
2. Mince 2 cloves garlic. Mix garlic, 2 tablespoons butter, 2 teaspoons parsley and juice from the can of clams (save clams) in a skillet and simmer over low heat.
3. Mince the remaining 2 cloves of garlic. Soften 4 tablespoons butter and mash with garlic, 1 teaspoon parsley and Parmesan cheese to make a paste.
4. 3 minutes before pasta is done, throw clams in the skillet with the simmering juice, and cook until clams are heated through. Do not

let sauce boil, and only cook for 3 minutes. If you overcook the clams, they will get rubbery.

5. Mix cooked, drained pasta with cheese paste.
6. Pour clam sauce over noodles. Serve hot.

Jazz It Up: Add cooked baby shrimp. Use tricolor pasta for a colorful plate.

Dress It Down: Go easy on the garlic.

Change It Up: Use marina sauce, and add clams to it.

We Go Good Together: Tossed salad, warm dinner rolls

SUMMER LOVIN': HAVING A BLAST

The sounds and smells of summertime shout "Come on out and play." Grilled dinners, no-cook meals and skillet suppers offer you the chance to get out of the kitchen fast, so you can soak up the sun and enjoy the slower pace during the dog days of summer.

SUMMER FARMER'S MARKET

Enjoy summer's best fruits and vegetables during their peak season while paying super-low prices for them. The sweet taste of fruits and the crisp crunch of vegetables can liven up a plain meal. Use these seasonal choices as side dishes and snacks, too.

<u>Fruits</u>
Apricots*
Avocados
Bananas
Blueberries
Cantaloupes
Casabas*
Crenshaws*
Cherries*
Figs*
Grapes
Honeydews
Kiwis
Lemons
Limes
Mangoes

Nectarines
Oranges*
Papayas
Peaches
Persimmons*
Pineapples
Plums
Strawberries
Tangelos

<u>Vegetables</u>
Asparagus*
Beans (green, lima, wax)
Beets
Cabbage

Carrots
Celery
Corn*
Cucumbers*
Eggplant*
Lettuce
Okra
Onions
Peas*
Peppers (chile, sweet)
Potatoes
Radishes*
Squash (summer)
Tomatoes

* Designates fruits and vegetables that have a shorter peak than the others on the list.

SUMMER PLAN ONE MENUS

Day 1—Sandwich Board: Ham, Cheese and Pineapple Sammies
Day 2—Everyday Dinner: Prince Primavera
Day 3—Everyday Dinner: Don't Tell the Kids It's Zucchini Quesadillas
Day 4—Backwards Meal: Strawberry Banana Breakfast Sundaes
Day 5—Everyday Dinner: Grilled Lemonade Chicken
Day 6—Everyday Dinner: Tomsho Teen's Mexican Pile-Up
Day 7—Kids' Meal: Pizza Subs
Day 8—Must-Go: Fowl and Fruit
Day 9—Sandwich Board: Western Beef Dagwoods
Day 10—Kids' Meal: Hot Diggety Coney Island Pockets
Day 11—Slow Cook Tonight: Slice of Summer Steaks
Day 12—I Can with a Can: Zap-It Crabbies
Day 13—No-Cook Night: Steak Salad
Day 14—Company's Coming: Pasta and Shrimp, Greek Style

THE SHOPPING LISTS

The Frantic Woman's Cupboard

SUMMER PLAN ONE STAPLES

Seasonings

Basil*
Garlic (minced, powder*)
Italian salad seasoning
McCormick Salad Supreme
Oregano
Red pepper flakes
Salt*
Seasoned salt
Pepper*

Side Dishes
Dill (dried), or your preference
Parsley

Jazz It Ups
Cayenne pepper
Chili powder

Condiments
Ketchup
Mayonnaise
Mustard (prepared)

Dressings, Oil and Sauces
Honey
Italian salad dressing
Oil (Olive)*
Salad dressing, your choice
Soy sauce
Wine (white)

Side Dishes
Oil (Vegetable)

Baking Needs
Side Dishes
Baking powder
Flour (all-purpose)

Frantic Necessities
Foil
Nonstick cooking spray

Dairy
Butter

Side Dishes
Eggs
Milk

Jazz It Ups
Butter

*Ingredients you'll need for both main and side dishes

The Frantic Woman Goes Shopping

MAIN-DISH INGREDIENTS YOU'LL NEED TO BUY

Produce: Fruits

1 pineapple (Day 1)
1 pound strawberries (Day 4)
4 bananas (Day 4)
½ pound seedless grapes (Day 8)
1 kiwi (Day 8)

Produce: Veggies

1 small bunch parsley (Day 2)
2 small yellow onions (Days 2, 3)
3 zucchini (Days 2, 3)
9 (7 medium-size and 2 large) tomatoes (Days 2, 6, 11, 13, 14)
2 green peppers (Days 3, 6)
1 8-ounce carton snowcap mushrooms, sliced (Day 9)
1 small bunch green onions (Day 9)
1 12-ounce bag baby cut carrots (Day 11)
2 medium-size summer squash (Days 11, 13)
1 16-ounce package ready-to-eat salad mix (Day 13)

Seasonings

1 1.25-ounce packet taco seasoning mix (Day 6)

PIT STOP: Keep It Fresh

To keep your produce as fresh as can be, think about picking up these items around Day 6: ½ pound seedless grapes, 1 kiwi, 1 bag (12 ounces) baby cut carrots, 1 carton (8 ounces) snowcap mushrooms, 1 small bunch green onions, 1 package (16-ounce) ready-to-eat salad mix, 2 summer squashes and 4 medium-size tomatoes and 2 larger ones.

Dressings, Oils and Sauces
1 24-ounce jar salsa (Days 3, 6)
1 12-ounce jar chili sauce (Day 10)

Canned Goods and Bottles
1 8-ounce can tomato sauce (Day 7)
1 2.25-ounce can black olives (Day 8)
1 7-ounce can crabmeat (Day 12)

Noodles, Pasta and Rice
1 16-ounce package bow ties (Day 2)
1 16-ounce package linguine (Day 14)

Cereal, Nuts and Such
1 15-ounce box corn flakes, or your preference (Day 4)
1 16-ounce bag Fritos (Day 6)

Bread, Chips and More
8 slices whole-wheat bread (Day 1)
8 flour tortilla (Day 3)
1 loaf Italian bread, unsliced (Day 7)
2 ounces roasted sunflower seeds, shelled (Day 8)
5 hamburger buns (Day 9)
4 pita rounds (Day 10)
6 English muffins (Day 12)

Deli

4 slices maple baked ham (Day 1)

8 slices Swiss cheese (Day 1)

5 slices cheddar cheese (Day 9)

Fish, Meat and Poultry

8 boneless, skinless chicken breasts, about 2 pounds (Days 5, 8)

2 pounds ground beef (Days 6, 9)

6 hot dogs (Day 10)

7 eye of round steaks, $\frac{1}{2}$-inch thick (Days 11, 13)

$1\frac{1}{2}$ pounds medium shrimp, peeled and deveined (Day 14)

Dairy

2 cups (8 ounces) Monterey Jack cheese, shredded (Day 3)

3 cups (12 ounces) cheddar cheese, shredded (Days 6, 10)

2 cups (8 ounces) mozzarella cheese, shredded (Day 7)

2 8-ounce containers soft cream cheese (Day 12)

$\frac{1}{2}$ pound feta cheese (Day 14)

Frozen

1 small container strawberry frozen yogurt (Day 4)

1 6-ounce can frozen lemonade (Day 5)

1 10-ounce package frozen peas (Day 8)

JAZZ IT UP INGREDIENTS YOU'LL NEED TO BUY

Produce: Fruit

Papayas, or your fruit preference (Day 8)

Produce: Veggies

2 red onions (Days 1, 10)

1 8-ounce carton baby portobello or snowcap mushrooms (Day 2)

1 head lettuce (Days 3, 6)

2 small tomatoes (Days 3, 8)

1 small bunch green onions (Day 6)
1 small bunch parsley (Day 8)

Dressings, Oils and Sauces
1 10-ounce jar relish (Day 9)
1 8-ounce jar cocktail sauce (Day 12)
Canned Goods and Bottles
1 16-ounce jar dill pickles (Day 1)
2 2.5-ounce can sliced black olives (Days 3, 7)
1 jar caramel topping (Day 4)
1 4-ounce can sliced mushrooms, or fresh (Day 7)
1 5-ounce jar green olives (Day 10)
1 6-ounce jar marinated artichoke hearts (Day 13)

Noodles, Pasta and Rice
2 cups white rice, or your preference (Day 5)
1 16-ounce box tricolor or fresh pasta (swap for regular) (Day 14)

Fish, Meat and Poultry
1 3-ounce package sliced pepperoni (Day 7)
½ pound bulk sausage (Day 7)

Dairy
4 ounces feta cheese (Day 2)
1 can whipped topping (Day 4)
1 8-ounce container sour cream (Day 6)

PIT STOP: Keep It Fresh
To keep your Jazz It Up ingredients from spoiling, buy these items toward the end of the first week: 2 papayas, 1 small bunch parsley and 1 small tomato.

WE GO GOOD TOGETHER INGREDIENTS YOU'LL NEED TO BUY

Produce: Fruit

2 melons (Days 3, 14)
Small piece watermelon (Day 6)
1 small Red Delicious apple (Day 11)
1 cantaloupe (Day 11)
1 small bunch seedless grapes (Day 11)

Produce: Veggies

Veggies, your preference (Day 1)
1 green pepper (Day 5)
1 yellow squash (Day 5)
1 zucchini (Day 5)
1 16-ounce package ready-to-serve salad (Day 7)
3 to 4 ears corn (Day 9)
6 small red potatoes (Day 10)

Bread, Chips and More

4 to 6 slices Italian bread, or your preference (Day 2)
4 to 6 muffins, your preference (Day 4)
4 to 6 breadsticks (Day 13)
1 12-ounce bag baby cut carrots (Day 12)
1 bunch celery (Day 12)
1 pint cherry tomatoes (Day 12)

Dairy

1 16-ounce container cottage cheese (Day 4)

Frozen

1 pint frozen yogurt, your preference (Day 8)

Unloading the Load

- Freeze chicken breasts in one package and mark it for Day 5, Grilled Lemonade Chicken.
- Freeze the ground beef for Day 6, Tomsho Teen's Mexican Pile-Up.
- Freeze Italian bread for Day 7, Pizza Subs.
- Freeze buns for Day 9, Western Beef Dagwoods.
- Freeze pita rounds and hot dogs for Day 10, Hot Diggety Coney Island Pockets.
- Freeze steaks for Day 11, Slice of Summer Steaks.
- Freeze muffins for Day 12, Zap-It Crabbies.
- Freeze feta cheese for Day 14, Pasta and Shrimp Greek Style.
- Freeze the mozzarella cheese for Day 7, Pizza Subs.
- Freeze ⅓ of the shredded cheddar cheese for Day 6, Tomsho Teen's Mexican Pile-Up. Freeze the other ⅔ for Day 10, Hot Diggety Coney Island Pockets. Freeze 5 slices of cheddar cheese for Day 9, Western Beef Dagwood, if you think your family will eat them.
- You might want to tuck your corn chips for Day 6, Tomsho Teen's Mexican Pile-Up, in the freezer to protect them from growling tummies in need of a snack.
- If you're jazzing up your menus and bought the recommended ingredients, freeze the sliced pepperoni and bulk sausage for Day 7, Pizza Subs.

- Freeze the breadsticks for Day 13, Steak Salad, from the We Go Good Together grocery list.
- Be sure to read the Look Ahead section in each recipe to see when you must pull items out of the freezer to put into the refrigerator to defrost.

SUMMER: PLAN ONE

➧ Day 1—Sandwich Board: ❦
Ham, Cheese and Pineapple Sammies

Fresh pineapple slices spruce up the traditional ham and cheese sandwich, making a quick but delightful summer meal on shopping day.

Dish up: 4 servings
Construction time: 10 minutes

Cooking time: 5 minutes
Paraphernalia: 12-inch skillet

INGREDIENTS:
8 slices whole-wheat bread
Butter
8 slices Swiss cheese
4 slices maple baked ham
8 slices pineapple

To make:
1. Lightly coat skillet with nonstick cooking spray. Lightly butter bread slices.
2. Place 2 slices of bread in skillet, buttered side down. Layer 1 slice of cheese, 1 slice of ham, 2 pineapple slices and another piece of cheese. Top with bread, buttered side up.
3. Cook over medium heat for about 2 to 3 minutes, until slightly toasted. Flip and cook another 2 to 3 minutes, or until cheese is melted. Do not burn the bread.
4. Place sandwiches on a plate and cover with foil to keep warm. Repeat with remaining ingredients to make 2 more sammies.

Jazz It Up: Add a slice or two of red onion or dill pickle.

Dress It Down: Switch whole-wheat bread for white, or your preference.

We Go Good Together: Sliced veggies

FRANTIC WOMAN FAMILY FUN: Picker-Upper Protein Drink

During the hot weather, it's not unusual for your energy to vanish. For a quick pick-me-up, whip up a protein drink made with the season's best. Blend 1 sliced banana, 1 cup sliced strawberries, 1 cup orange juice, 4 tablespoons honey, 8 ounces silken tofu (for protein) and 8 ice cubes for about 2 minutes, or until frothy. Pour into glasses, and enjoy a refreshing break.

◆ Day 2—Everyday Dinner: Prince Primavera ◆

Bow tie pasta tossed with summer's bounty satisfies everyone's hunger pains while answering the cook's quest for something easy.

Dish up: 4 to 6 servings

Construction time: 3 minutes

Cooking time: 15 minutes

Paraphernalia: Dutch oven, 12-inch skillet, strainer

INGREDIENTS:

1 16-ounce package bow tie pasta (⅓ set aside for Day 8, Fowl and Fruit)

1 zucchini, diced (2 additional zucchini set aside fro Day 3, Zucchini Quesadillas)

3 tablespoons olive oil

1 small onion, diced

3 tomatoes, cubed

1 tablespoon parsley, finely chopped

½ teaspoon minced garlic

To make:

1. Cook pasta according to package directions.
2. While pasta is cooking, heat olive oil in skillet.
3. Wash, peel (if preferred) and dice zucchini. Set aside ⅔ of the zucchini for Day 3, Don't Tell the Kids It's Zucchini Quesadillas. Dice onion.

4. Sauté the zucchini and onion for about 3 to 5 minutes, or until softened.
5. Wash and cube tomatoes. Wash and chop parsley.
6. Add tomatoes, garlic and parsley and cook for 5 to 7 minutes.
7. When pasta is finished, drain the water and set aside ⅓ of the bow ties for Day 8, Fowl and Fruit. Add the remaining pasta to veggie mixture.
8. Toss and serve.

Jazz It Up: Add sautéed baby portobello or snowcap mushrooms. Crumble 4 ounces of feta cheese over tossed pasta.

Dress It Down: Skip the veggies, except tomatoes.

Double It: Dice 2 extra zucchinis and store in the refrigerator for Day 3. Set aside ⅓ of pasta for Day 8.

We Go Good Together: Bread with flavored butter (See the following Basketful of Tips.)

BASKETFUL OF TIPS: No Salt Water

If you're in a hurry to get dinner on the table, skip adding salt to the pot of water when cooking pasta. Adding salt to a pot of water actually makes it take longer to boil, as salted water has a higher boiling point.

BASKETFUL OF TIPS: Flavored Butter

Soften butter in the microwave at 40 percent power for 30 seconds. Add a pinch of dried dill or another favorite herb. Mix with a fork. Spread on bread.

⇢ Day 3—Everyday Dinner: ⇠
Don't Tell the Kids It's Zucchini Quesadillas

What the kids don't know won't hurt them. So spread on the cheese, and they'll never know that what's inside the quesadilla is good for them.

Dish up: 4 servings
Construction time: 5 minutes

Cooking time: 13 minutes
Paraphernalia: 12-inch skillet, microwave-safe plates, microwave

INGREDIENTS:

2 tablespoons olive oil

1 small onion, chopped

½ teaspoon garlic powder

2 zucchini, stored from Day 2

1 green pepper, chopped 🥤 (1 additional green pepper for Day 6,
    Tomsho Teen's Mexican Pile-Up)

½ cup salsa

8 flour tortillas

2 cups (8 ounces) Monterey Jack cheese, shredded

To make:

1. Heat oil in skillet. Sauté onion and garlic for about 5 minutes on medium-high heat.
2. Wash and chop green peppers. Store 1 green pepper in the refrigerator.
3. Add zucchini and peppers. Cook 5 minutes, or until soft, stirring frequently.
4. Mix in salsa.
5. Place tortilla on microwave-safe plate. Spread zucchini mixture and cheese over tortilla. Sprinkle with cheese, and cover with another tortilla.
6. Cook in the microwave for 1 minute. Cover with foil or a lid to keep warm until serving time.
7. Repeat with remaining tortillas.
8. Cut each tortilla into quarters. Serve.

Jazz It Up: Give quesadillas a spicy flavor by adding a ½ teaspoon cayenne pepper and/or 1 teaspoon chili powder to the salsa. Top with ½ cup diced tomatoes, 1 small can of sliced black olives and/or shredded lettuce.

Dress It Down: Skip the onion and garlic.

Change It Up: Use whole-wheat tortillas for a healthier choice. Instead of microwaving, place prepared tortillas on a cookie sheet and place in the oven at 350 degrees for 5 to 7 minutes, or until cheese is melted.

Double It: Chop 1 green pepper and store it in the refrigerator for Day 6, Tomsho Teen's Mexican Pile-Up.

We Go Good Together: Melon

☀ Day 4—Backwards Meal: ☀
Strawberry Banana Breakfast Sundaes

The kids will love eating this summertime sundae as much as you'll love the easy-to-prepare dinner dish. Though it seems sinful to serve this for supper, you're actually dishing up several food groups, so relax and enjoy this quirky, no-cook meal.

Dish up: 4 servings   Cooking time: 0
Construction time: 10 minutes   Paraphernalia: Ice cream scoop

INGREDIENTS:
1 pound strawberries, sliced
4 bananas, sliced
1 pint strawberry frozen yogurt
4 cups corn flakes
Honey

To make:
1. Wash and slice strawberries. Peel and slice bananas.
2. Place 1 scoop of strawberry frozen yogurt in the middle of a bowl.
3. Sprinkle corn flakes, sliced fresh strawberries and bananas around the yogurt.
4. Drizzle honey over flakes, fruit and yogurt.

Jazz It Up: Add caramel topping over flakes, fruit and yogurt. For a sweeter variation, squirt whipped topping over the food.

Change It Up: Use your choice of cereal, such as toasted oats or one with fruit added.

We Go Good Together: Cottage cheese and muffins

Look Ahead: Pull chicken and lemonade from freezer for Day 5, Grilled Lemonade Chicken.

✦ *Day 5—Everyday Dinner: Grilled Lemonade Chicken* ✦

Here's a whole new twist on lemonade. Buy 2 cans of lemonade mix so you can serve up a chilled pitcher of this summertime thirst quencher to go with the meal.

Dish up: 4 to 6 servings

Construction time: 5 minutes

Cooking time: 20 to 25 minutes

Paraphernalia: Medium bowl, grill, basting brush

INGREDIENTS:

1 6-ounce can frozen lemonade, thawed

⅓ cup soy sauce

1 teaspoon seasoned salt

⅛ teaspoon garlic powder

4 skinless, boneless chicken breasts 🥤 (4 additional skinless, boneless chicken breasts for Day 8, Fowl and Fruit.

To make:

1. Fire up the grill.
2. Mix lemonade, soy sauce, and spices in a medium-size bowl.
3. Dip chicken in sauce to coat.
4. Place chicken on hot grill.
5. Cook for 20 minutes, basting frequently with sauce to keep the chicken from becoming dry.

Jazz It Up: Serve over buttered white rice.

Double It: Cook and freeze 4 extra boneless chicken breasts for Day 8, Fowl and Fruit.

We Go Good Together: Grilled Veggies 🌐

Look Ahead: Pull out the ground beef for Day 6, Tomsho Teen's Mexican Pile-Up. (You will be Doubling It for Day 9, Western Beef Dagwoods.) If you tucked the corn chip into the freezer, pull them out, too.

TIPS) BASKETFUL OF TIPS: Summer Grilling

My husband, Stu, seems to be the person who mans the grill any time we go to a company picnic, softball tournament or backyard party. I always tease him that he's invited to parties so he can cook. Stu offers these grill maintenance tips to keep your grill in tip-top shape.

- Condition the grill grates with nonstick cooking spray or cooking oil to prepare the surface for your next grilling session and to prevent rust. For an older grill, make sure you clean the grates first. Stu warns, "Be sure to spray the grill when it is cold. Do not spray oil on a hot grill, or you'll have the fire department in your backyard."
- Clean cast-iron grates with a stainless steel grill brush and porcelain-coated grates with a brass-bristle brush. These brushes are manufactured specifically for grills.
- Keep the grill's gas valves, the metal conduits that carry gas to the burners (known as venturis) and burners free of debris. There are special brushes to clean these areas.
- Replace lava rocks when they begin to crack or gather residue from food grease. Porcelain briquettes are easier to keep clean and radiate heat more efficiently.
- Wash the outside of your grill periodically to rid it of grease and weather residue. Be sure to dry it immediately to prevent rust.
- Take rust off the outside of the grill with a piece of fine sandpaper. Spray paint the grill with a special grill paint made to tolerate high temperatures, which can be found in the barbecue department of your home improvement center or at a fireplace store that sells summer equipment. Again, this spray paint has been manufactured specifically for grills. *Do not* use any other spray paint.
- Cover your grill when it is not in use to protect it from the elements. Be sure the grill has cooled before doing so.

FRANTIC WOMAN FAMILY FUN: Lemonade Babysitter

Call a library and reserve a copy of *The Lemonade Babysitter* by Karen Waggoner. It is delightful book you can read to the kids or the kids can read to you while sitting on the front porch or lounging on a blanket in the backyard.

PIT STOP: Pick Up Produce

Schedule a stop at your local farmer's market or grocery store on Day 5 or 6 for the following items: ½ pound seedless grapes, 1 kiwi, 1 bag (12 ounces) baby-cut carrots, 1 carton (8 ounces) snowcap mushrooms, 1 small bunch green onions, 1 package (16 ounces) ready-to-eat salad mix, 2 summer squashes and 4 medium-size tomatoes and 2 larger ones.

If you're jazzing up your entrees, purchase these ingredients: 2 papayas, 1 small bunch parsley and and 1 small tomato.

If you're making the recommended We Go Good Together dishes, you'll need to buy these items now: 1 small Red Delicious apple, 1 cantaloupe, 6 ears corn, 1 small bunch seedless grapes, 1 melon, 1 package (16-ounce) ready-to-eat salad, 6 small red potatoes, 1 12-ounce bag baby cut carrots, 1 bunch celery, and 1 pint cherry tomatoes.

✦ Day 6—Everyday Dinner: ✦ Tomsho Teen's Mexican Pile-Up

Medical transcriptionist Linda Tomsho works the grueling hours of 7:00 P.M. to 3:00 A.M. behind the computer screen. Before heading to her office, she has about 40 minutes to greet her husband as he walks in the front door, fix dinner for her family of three hungry and growing teenagers, eat and clean up. Not an easy task. Linda says this recipe is her kids' absolute favorite super-quick dinner.

Dish up: 4 to 6 servings   Cooking time: 5 minutes
Construction time: 10 minutes   Paraphernalia: 12-inch skillet

INGREDIENTS:

1 pound ground beef 🥤 (1 additional pound ground beef for Day 9, Western Beef Dagwoods)

1 green pepper, chopped, stored from Day 3

1½ cups salsa

1 1.25-ounce packet taco seasoning mix

½ cup water

1 tomato, diced

1 16-ounce bag Fritos

1 cups (4 ounces) cheddar cheese, shredded

To make:

1. Brown ground beef in skillet. Set aside the extra pound for Day 9, Western Beef Dagwoods.
2. Add peppers, salsa, seasoning mix and water. Cook 5 minutes, or until hot.
3. While meat mixture is cooking, wash and dice tomato.
4. Place a mound of Fritos on each plate.
5. Spoon beef mixture on top.
6. Sprinkle with cheese and tomatoes.

Jazz It Up: Top with shredded lettuce, chopped green onions and/or sour cream. (Simplify it: If you have an extra mouth to feed, be sure to add some toppings to extend the meal.)

Dress It Down: Skip the toppings.

Double It: Brown an extra pound of ground beef and store it in the freezer for Day 9, Western Beef Dagwoods. This pound of browned ground beef should be seasonless.

We Go Good Together: Watermelon slices

Look Ahead: If you put the Italian bread and 2 cups of mozzarella cheese in the freezer for Pizza Subs, take it out now. If you are jazzing up your entree, pull out the pepperoni slices and bulk sausage for Day 7.

✦ Day 7—Kids' Meal: Pizza Subs ✦

This family favorite is a perfect meal to fix after a stressful day at work or a relaxing day at the pool or beach.

Dish up: 4 to 6 servings   Cooking time: 7 minutes
Construction time: 10 minutes   Paraphernalia: Small bowl, baking sheet

INGREDIENTS:

1 loaf Italian bread, unsliced
2 teaspoons Italian seasoning
1 8-ounce can tomato sauce
2 cups (8 ounces) mozzarella cheese, shredded

To make:

1. Preheat oven to 350 degrees. Line baking sheet with foil, shiny side up. Slice bread in half lengthwise and place on baking sheet.
2. Stir Italian seasoning into tomato sauce.
3. Spread sauce onto each bread slice.
4. Top with shredded cheese, making sure you give equal amounts to both halves.
5. Bake for 5 to 10 minutes, or until cheese is melted. (A thicker layer of cheese will require a longer cooking time.)
6. Cut each pizza sub in half and serve.

Jazz It Up: Add sliced pepperoni, mushrooms, cooked sausage, and/or sliced black olives.

Dress It Down: Replace tomato sauce with olive oil and a sprinkle of garlic for a white pizza.

Change It Up: Add sauce to 1/2 of the loaf. Layer with 1/4 pound each of hard salami and sliced pepperoni. Add shredded cheese over meat. Top with the other bread half to make it a sandwich.

We Go Good Together: Tossed salad

Look Ahead: Take the cooked chicken and pasta out of the freezer and put it in the refrigerator for Day 8, Fowl and Fruit. Take 1 cup of frozen peas from the package and place them in the refrigerator to thaw.

POTFUL OF KNOWLDEGE:
Beware of Bulging Cans

Toss away that bulging canned good. According to the Poison Center, this is a common warning sign of infection with botulim, a bacterium whose toxin causes botulism. Don't take the chance, because botulism affects the nervous system, and the symptoms are ugly. As frantic as your life is right now, you don't need to add complications, such as double vision, inability to swallow and difficulty speaking. So stay healthy by tossing that bulging can in the recycling bin!.

✤ Day 8—Must-Go: Fowl and Fruit ✦

A little bit of this and a little bit of that create this easy meal with not much more than leftovers. And isn't it great to know that these must-go foods are going into a meal rather than into the garbage can?

Dish up: 4 servings
Construction time: 10 minutes

Cooking time: 0
Paraphernalia: Large serving bowl, strainer

INGREDIENTS:

4 boneless, skinless chicken breasts, stored from Day 5
1/3 pound pasta, stored from Day 2
1/2 cup black olives, sliced
1 kiwi, peeled and sliced
1/2 pound seedless grapes, halved
1 cup frozen peas, thawed
2 ounces sunflower seeds, shelled
1/2 cup Italian salad dressing
1 tablespoon McCormick Salad Supreme
Salt

To make:
1. Cut chicken into bite-size pieces.
2. Put pasta in strainer and run cold water through it.
3. Slice black olives if you bought whole ones. Peel and slice kiwi. Quarter each kiwi slice. Cut grapes in half. (Simplify it: If you forgot to take the peas from the freezer, thaw them in a bowl of very cold water now.)
4. Toss all the ingredients into a large serving bowl. Add Italian salad dressing and seasoning, mixing well. Add more dressing, if need be.

Jazz It Up: Add fresh parsley, diced tomatoes, papayas or other favorite fruits and vegetables.

Dress It Down: Skip the seasonings. If the kids prefer their pasta served on the side, do so.

Change It Up: Substitute your favorite dressing for Italian.

We Go Good Together: Frozen yogurt

Look Ahead: Take the cooked ground beef and cheddar cheese from the freezer and put it in the refrigerator to thaw for Day 9, Western Beef Dagwoods. Also, pull the buns out of the freezer and allow them to thaw on the countertop.

(TiPS) BASKETFUL OF TIPS: Sunflower Roast

To give plain sunflower seeds (shelled) a toasted flavor, cook them in a skillet with 1 tablespoon of olive oil and a pinch of salt for about 2 to 3 minutes. Then, toss them in your favorite recipe.

➜ Day 9—Sandwich Board: Western Beef Dagwoods ➜

Serve up a dagwood tonight—the sandwich, not the comic strip character or the similarly spelled tree.

Dish up: 5 servings   Cooking time: 20 to 25 minutes
Construction: 5 minute   Paraphernalia: 12-inch skillet, baking sheet

INGREDIENTS:

5 hamburger buns
5 slices cheddar cheese
1 pound browned ground beef, stored from Day 6
1 cup (4 ounces) mushrooms, sliced
½ teaspoon oregano
1 cup ketchup
½ cup green onions, finely chopped

To make:

1. Heat oven to 300 degrees.
2. Wash veggies. Peel and chop green onions. Slice mushrooms. Toss onions, mushrooms and meat in a skillet and cook over medium heat for about 7 to 10 minutes, or until heated through. (Simplify it: If you forgot to take the frozen meat from the freezer, thaw it in the microwave, or bang the package on the counter a few times to

loosen the meat. Then, toss it in a skillet and heat. Once the meat is heated through, add the other ingredients.)

3. Place bun bottoms on a baking sheet. Put a slice of cheese on the bottom half of each bun.
4. Spoon meat mixture onto each cheese-layered bun.
5. Add top of bun. Cover Dagwoods with a layer of foil.
6. Place in heated oven for 10 minutes. The buns will be toasty.

Jazz It Up: Add ½ cup relish.

Dress It Down: Skip heating the Dagwoods in the oven. Just scoop the hot mixture onto buns and serve.

Change It Up: Use your favorite cheese.

We Go Good Together: Corn Fritters 🌽

Look Ahead: Pull out the hot dogs and mozzarella cheese from the freezer, and store in the refrigerator to thaw for Day 10, Hot Diggety Coney Island Pockets. Pull out the pitas, too, and put them on the countertop to thaw. Also, take the steaks from the freezer and store them in the refrigerator for Day 11, Slice of Summer Steaks.

🧺 BASKETFUL OF TIPS: Frozen Dagwoods

Dagwoods are a great frozen meal to have tucked in the freezer. They are great for late-night snacks when the kids have friends over and they're looking for something to munch on. (Be aware that you should only freeze and thaw cooked meat once.) After assembling, wrap each Dagwood individually in foil. Store in freezer. When you're ready to chow down, preheat oven to 350 degrees, and place frozen Dagwoods in heated oven for about 30 minutes.

 FRANTIC WOMAN FAMILY FUN: Comic Chuckle

Grab the comics section of the newspaper, and read the family's favorite ones after dinner. If you don't have a favorite one, read several and let everyone choose a favorite. The next time you're feeling overwhelmed, lighten your day by reading the latest episode of your favorite comic strip. For now, be sure to read *Blondie* to see what antics Dagwood is up to.

❧ Day 10—Kids' Meal: ❧
Hot Diggety Coney Island Pockets

You'll be ready to feed the little ones quickly with this kid-friendly meal.

Dish up: 6 to 8 servings
Construction time: 5 minutes

Cooking time: 10 to 12 minutes
Paraphernalia: Grill, bowl, tongs

INGREDIENTS:

6 hot dogs, cubed
1 teaspoon mustard
2 tablespoons mayonnaise
1/4 cup chili sauce
2 cups (8 ounces) sharp cheddar cheese, shredded
4 pita rounds

To make:

1. Fire up the grill.
2. Mix together all ingredients, except pita rounds, in a bowl.
3. Cut pita rounds in half. Open pocket and fill with about 1/3 cup of mixture.
4. Wrap in foil with the shiny side out. Seal closed.
5. Grill foil-wrapped pockets for about 10 minutes, or until filling is hot. Be sure to turn foil packets so both sides of the pita pockets get toasted. Use tongs to turn the pockets, being careful not to rip the foil.

Jazz It Up: Add 1/2 cup diced red onions and/or 1/4 cup chopped green olives.

Dress It Down: Skip the chili sauce.

Change It Up: Cook in oven at 350 degrees for the same amount of time.

We Go Good Together: Grilled Potatoes 🌞+🥔

Look Ahead: If the morning rush has you frazzled, toss the slow-cooker Day 11, Slice of Summer Steaks, meal (except steaks) together as you're cleaning up the dinner dishes tonight. Refrigerate overnight. Then, all you'll have to do is add the steaks and plug in the slow cooker before you leave in the morning.

⇒ Day 11—Slow Cook Tonight: ⇐
Slice of Summer Steaks

Go ahead and cook without me. And that's just what this meal will do when it is teamed up with your slow cooker. Dump the ingredients in the cooker first thing in the morning, start the cooker, and head off to wherever you need to be.

Dish up: 4 servings

Construction time: 5 minutes

Cooking time: 8 to 10 hours

Paraphernalia: Slow cooker

INGREDIENTS:

3 tablespoons olive oil

2 large tomatoes, cubed 🥤 (1 extra tomato for Day 13, Steak Salad)

1 medium-size summer squash, peeled and cubed 🥤 (1 extra summer squash for Day 13)

1 12-ounce bag baby cut carrots

4 eye of round steaks, ½-inch thick (approximately 1½ pounds) 🥤 (3 additional eye of round steaks for Day 13)

½ teaspoon oregano

½ teaspoon Italian seasoning

To make:
1. Coat bottom of the cooker with olive oil.
2. Wash veggies. Core and cube tomatoes. Put half of the cubed tomato in the refrigerator for Day 13.
3. Peel and cube summer squash. Put half of the cubed squash in the refrigerator for Day 13.
4. Cut carrots in half.
5. Put steaks on the bottom of the cooker. Add oregano and Italian seasoning.
6. Cook on low for 6 to 8 hours. When finished cooking, put 3 steaks in the refrigerator for Day 13.

Jazz It Up: Add any veggies you have in the refrigerator.

Dress It Down: Cook the steaks alone.

Change It: Chop carrots. Put oil in the bottom of a larger skillet over medium heat. Add the other ingredients. Cover and cook for about 25 to 30 minutes, checking often. Be sure to turn steaks occasionally.

Double It: Cook 3 extra steaks. Cube 1 extra summer squash and 1 extra tomato for Day 13, Steak Salad.

We Go Good Together: Fruit kabobs (Place fruit on colored toothpicks.)

Look Ahead: Take the English muffins out of the freezer and put them in the refrigerator to thaw.

➤ Day 12—I Can with a Can: Zap-It Crabbies ✦

For days when you can barely make it in the front door or off the couch, even the kids can assemble this easy dinner dish, originally created years ago by my dear friend Katharine Gaspari.

Dish up: 4 to 6 servings
Construction time: 5 minutes

Cooking time: 5 to 10 minutes
Paraphernalia: Baking sheet, medium bowl, oven broiler

INGREDIENTS:

1 7-ounce can crabmeat, drained and picked over
1 stick plus 1 1/2 tablespoons butter, softened
2 8-ounce packages soft cream cheese
1/2 teaspoon garlic powder
1/2 teaspoon seasoned salt
6 English muffins, split

To make:
1. Mix the first 5 ingredients together.
2. Split English muffins.
3. Drain and pick over crabmeat. (See the Basketful of Tips on p. tk.) Spread crab mixture on muffins, and place on a baking sheet.
4. Broil for 5 to 10 minutes. (Simplify it: Turn on your oven light to keep an eye on these.)

Jazz It Up: Cut muffins in fourths, and serve with cocktail sauce for dipping.

Dress It Down: Skip the seasoned salt.

We Go Good Together: Cut up carrots, celery and cherry tomatoes.

Look Ahead: Pull out the breadsticks to thaw if you follow the We Go Good Together suggestion.

BASKETFUL OF TIPS: Do Not Close
Keep your oven door partially open when broiling. Ovens become extremely hot when broiling, and you'll end up cooking and probably burning your dinner instead of toasting the meal if you keep the door shut.

⇢ Day 13—No-Cook Night: Steak Salad ⇠

With the prepared ingredients waiting in your refrigerator, you can toss this easy meal together in less than 15 minutes.

Dish up: 4 to 6 servings

Construction time: 10 minutes

Cooking time: 0

Paraphernalia: Large serving bowl

INGREDIENTS:

3 steaks, stored from Day 11

1 16-ounce package ready-to-eat salad mix

1 summer squash, cubed and stored from Day 11

1 tomato, cubed and stored from Day 11

Salad dressing, your preference

To make:

1. Slice cold steaks into thin strips.
2. Put salad mix into a large serving bowl. Add squash and tomatoes. Top with steak strips.
3. Serve with your favorite salad dressing.

Jazz It Up: Add a jar of marinated artichoke hearts or any other salad fixings.

Change It Up: Replace salad mix with 1 head of lettuce, if the price is right.

We Go Good Together: Breadsticks

Look Ahead: Take frozen shrimp and feta cheese from the freezer, and put them in the refrigerator to thaw for tomorrow's company meal, Pasta and Shrimp, Greek Style.

FRANTIC WOMAN FAMILY FUN:
Homemade Gelatos

You don't have to spend a lot of money at a specialty ice cream parlor for a fun ice icream treat. Instead, freeze your favorite fruit juice in ice cube trays. Next, mash the cubes. In a cup, alternate layers of mashed fruit cubes with vanilla ice cream. Then, dig in.

❧ Day 14—Company's Coming: ❧
Pasta and Shrimp, Greek Style

Company's coming, and you're ready with this delicious meal, which the boss will give his or her stamp of approval.

Dish up: 4 to 6 servings
Construction time: 15 minutes

Cooking time: 15 minutes
Paraphernalia: 2 12-inch skillets, 5-quart pot, 9-by-13-inch baking dish, strainer

INGREDIENTS:

1 16-ounce package linguine
3 medium tomatoes, peeled and cubed
2 teaspoons minced garlic
5 tablespoons olive oil
1/2 cup dry white wine
1 tablespoon basil
1 tablespoon oregano
1 1/2 pounds medium shrimp, peeled and deveined
Salt and pepper, to taste
1/2 teaspoon red pepper flakes
1/2 pound (2 ounces) feta cheese, crumbled

To make:

1. Boil water for pasta and cook according to package directions.
2. Heat oven to 350 degrees.
3. Wash and cube tomatoes.
4. While pasta is cooking, sauté garlic in 2 tablespoons olive oil for 1 to 2 minutes.
5. Add tomatoes and cook 1 minute.
6. Add wine, basil, and oregano to tomato mixture. Cook 5 minutes.
7. In another skillet, heat 3 tablespoons olive oil. Add shrimp and salt and pepper, to taste. Cook about 5 minutes or until shrimp turn pink. (Do not overcook, or shrimp will be rubbery.) Sprinkle with red pepper flakes.
8. Spoon shrimp and pan juices into a baking dish. Sprinkle with feta cheese, then spoon tomato mixture over all.
9. Heat for 15 minutes in oven.
10. Serve shrimp mixture over pasta.

Jazz It Up: Serve fresh pasta or tricolor pasta.

Dress It Down: Omit shrimp.

Change It: Heat mixture in microwave at 70 percent power for 7 to 10 minutes.

We Go Good Together: Melon balls

BASKETFUL OF TIPS: Vending-Machine Meals on the Run
During the summer months, there are times when you can't make it home for a 30-minute meal. On those days, you make do with whatever you can pick up fast, including vending-machine purchases. But even these food machines hold good and bad selections. To help you choose a healthy meal from among all those little packages, the health and fitness professional Tony Sparber divides the machines into three categories and offers these tips about their contents:

- Lunch Vending Machine: Usually contains a variety of sandwiches. Stick with a turkey sandwich, and select whole-wheat bread, if possible. If you're not a big turkey fan, pick roast beef. Go easy on the condiments, including mayonnaise. Try to stay away from bologna, salami and ham. For vegetarians, choose the tuna fish, but keep in mind that tuna fish usually contains a lot of mayonnaise, which is very fatty.

- Snack Vending Machine: There's a lot less to choose from in these machines. Stay away from all chocolate candy bars, packaged pastries, cookies and potato chips. Look for pretzels, raisins, unsalted/assorted nuts, baked chips and some nutrition or protein bars. These would offer some nutritional value.

- Soda/Juice Machine: Bottled water is the best choice. If you need a little more pizzazz in your beverage selection, stay away from anything high in sugar. Apple and orange juice are high in sugar but have other vitamins and minerals that make up for it. Steer clear of regular soda and chocolate or strawberry milk.

Tony says, "Don't make vending-machine meals a daily occurrence! There just are not enough healthy choices in vending machines to incorporate into your daily nutritional habits."

SUMMER PLAN TWO MENUS

Day 1—No-cook Night: Deanna's Tortilla-wiches
Day 2—Slow Cook Tonight: Barbecued Beef over Toast
Day 3—Everyday Dinner: 'Shroom-lini
Day 4—Backwards Meal: Blueberry Pancakes
Day 5—Everyday Dinner: Polynesian Chicken
Day 6—No-Cook Night: Greek Salad
Day 7—Must-Go: BBQ Sandwiches
Day 8—Everyday Dinner: Bawk Bawk Chicken Bobs
Day 9—Everyday Dinner: Popeye and Olive Oyl's Tortellini Supper
Day 10—Kids' Meal: Wimpy's Favorite Burgers on Buns
Day 11—Slow Cook Tonight: Finger Lickin' Ribs
Day 12—I Can with a Can: One-Pan Spud Meal
Day 13—Must-Go: Tropical Tacos
Day 14—Company's Coming: Stu's Swordfish Kabobs

THE SHOPPING LISTS

The Frantic Woman's Cupboard

SUMMER PLAN TWO STAPLES

Seasonings
Basil
Chili powder
Dill*
Garlic (minced, powder)
Ginger
Onion (minced)
Oregano
Pepper
Salt

Condiments
Mustard (prepared)

Side Dishes
Honey
Salad dressing, your preference
Italian salad dressing

Jazz It Ups
Cajun seasoning
Chili powder
Crushed red pepper

Dressings, Oil and Sauces
Oil (olive, vegetable*)
Ranch salad dressing
Teriyaki sauce
Vinegar
Worcestershire sauce
Hot pepper sauce*

Jazz It Ups
Italian salad dressing

Canned Goods and Bottles
Jazz It Ups
Sweet relish
Dill pickles

Baking Needs
Baking powder
Cornstarch
Flour (all-purpose)
Sugar (brown, cane)

Frantic Necessities
Foil*
Nonstick cooking spray

Dairy
Butter* or margarine
Eggs
Milk

* Ingredients you'll need for both main and side dishes

The Frantic Woman Goes Shopping

MAIN-DISH INGREDIENTS YOU'LL NEED TO BUY

Produce: Fruits
3 small containers (about 4.4 ounces each) blueberries (Day 4)
2 lemons (Days 4, 14)
2 oranges (Day 5)
2 small pineapples (Days 5, 13)
Produce: Veggies
4 tomatoes (Days 1, 5, 6)
1 bunch celery (Day 2)
4 yellow onions (Days 2, 6, 11, 12)
3 green peppers (Days 2, 8, 13)
1 8-ounce carton snowcap mushrooms, sliced (Day 3)
1 cucumber (Day 6)
1 16-ounce package salad, ready to eat (Day 6)
1 16-ounce package spinach (Days 6, 9)
1 pint cherry tomatoes (Day 8)

Dressings, Oils and Sauces
1 16-ounce bottle barbecue sauce (Days 2, 7)
2 16-ounce bottles ketchup (Days 2, 11)
1 16-ounce bottle Greek salad dressing (Day 6)

PIT STOP: Keep It Fresh

Check the package dates on the salad and spinach before you buy it. Both of these items are on the menu near the end of the first week. You might want to make a stop at the farmer's market around Day 6 or 7 to pick up 2 green peppers, 1 small package cherry tomatoes and 1 small pineapple.

Canned Goods and Bottles

1 4-ounce can chilies, diced (Day 1)
2 16-ounce cans Italian-style tomatoes (Day 3)
1 16-ounce can Greek-style olives (Day 6)
1 14-ounce can artichoke hearts (Day 8)
1 8-ounce can sliced pineapple (Day 10)
1 10.75-ounce cream of celery soup (Day 12)
1 15-ounce can pinto beans (Day 12)

Noodles, Pasta and Rice

1 16-ounce package linguine (Day 3)

Bread, Chips and More

6 pieces bread (Day 2)
4 sandwich rolls (Day 7)
4 hamburger buns (Day 10)

Deli

¼ pound roast beef, thinly sliced (Day 1)
¼ pound turkey, thinly sliced (Day 1)

Fish, Meat and Poultry

1 6-pound sirloin tip roast (Days 2, 7)
3 pounds skinless, boneless chicken breasts (Days 5, 8)
1¼ pound ground beef (Day 10)
4 pounds pork loin back ribs or spareribs (Days 11, 13)
2 pounds swordfish (Day 14)

Dairy

1 8-ounce package cream cheese (Day 1)

8 large flour tortillas (Days 1, 13)

1 cup (4 ounces) Parmesan cheese, grated (Day 3)

1 cup (4 ounces) feta cheese (Days 6, 9)

1 8-ounce container sour cream (Day 12)

Frozen Foods

1 16-ounce package cheese tortellini, frozen (Day 9)

1 16-ounce package hash brown potatoes, frozen (Day 12)

JAZZ IT UP INGREDIENTS YOU'LL NEED TO BUY

Produce: Veggies

1 rib celery (Day 1)

1 head garlic (Day 3)

1 summer squash (Day 9)

1 head lettuce (Day 10)

1 small tomato (Day 10)

1 small green pepper (Day 12)

 PIT STOP: Keep It Fresh

If you're jazzing up your meals, buy these vegetables around Day 5 to avoid having spoiled veggies in your fridge: 1 summer squash, 1 head lettuce, 1 tomato and 1 small pepper.

Dressings, Oils and Sauces

Honey mustard sauce (Day 8)

Canned Goods and Bottles

1 2.5-ounce can sliced black olives (Day 1)

1 4-ounce can green chili peppers (Day 2)

1 8-ounce can pinto or other white beans (Day 6)

Cereal, Nuts and Such
2 ounces pecans (Day 13)

Deli
4 slices cheddar cheese (Day 7)

Frozen Foods
1 8-ounce container whipped topping (Day 4)

We Go Good Together Ingredients You'll Need to Buy

Produce: Fruit
6 peaches (Day 8)

Produce: Veggies
4 to 6 red potatoes or instant mashed potatoes (Day 2)
1 16-ounce package ready-to-eat salad (Day 3)
Green veggie, or your preference (Day 5)
2 Vidalia onions (Days 9, 10)
6 ripe tomatoes (Day 9, 12)
1 16-ounce package coleslaw mix (Day 11)
1 green pepper (Day 12)
1 bunch basil (Day 12)
2 cucumbers (Day 12)
4 to 6 ears corn (Day 13)

PIT STOP: Keep It Fresh
Hold off buying these fruits and veggies until Day 5 for the We
Go Good Together recommendations: 1 bunch basil, 1 bag (16
ounces) coleslaw mix, 4 to 6 ears corn, 2 cucumbers, 2 Vidalia onions, 6
peaches, 1 green pepper and 6 ripe tomatoes.

Dressings, Oils and Sauces
1 12-ounce jar coleslaw dressing (Day 11)
1 16-ounce bottle Greek salad dressing, or your preference (Day 9)
Caramel dip (Day 14)

Canned Goods and Bottles
1 4-ounce can black olives (Day 7)

Bread, Chips and More
1 16-ounce bag natural potato chips (Day 1)
1 4- to 6-count package pita rounds (Day 6)
4 corn muffins (Day 11)

Deli
½ pound mozzarella cheese, sliced (Day 9)

Fish, Meat and Poultry
1 pound bacon (Day 4)

Unloading the Load

- First, put the sirloin tip roast in the fridge for Day 2, Barbecued Beef over Toast.
- Next, cut half of the chicken breasts into 1-inch strips for Day 5, Polynesian Chicken, and the other half into 1-inch cubes for Day 8, Bawk Bawk Chicken Bobs. Mark each package and put them in the freezer.
- Freeze half of the feta cheese for Day 6, Greek Salad, and the other half for Day 9, Popeye and Olive Oyl's Tortellini Supper, if you fear the "mice" in your house will nibble on it.
- Freeze the sandwich rolls for Day 7, BBQ Sandwiches, and the hamburger buns for Day 10, Wimpy's Favorite Burgers on Buns.
- Freeze the beef for Day 10, Wimpy's Favorite Burgers on Buns.
- Freeze the ribs for Day 11, Finger Lickin' Ribs.

- Freeze the fish for Day 14, Stu's Swordfish Kabobs.
- If you bought cheese to jazz up Day 7, BBQ sandwiches, freeze it, too.
- For the We Go Good Together dishes, freeze the pita rounds for Day 6, Greek Salad, and the corn muffins for Day 11, Finger Lickin' Ribs.
- Freeze the mozzarella cheese for Day 9, We Go Good Together.
- Be sure to read the Look Ahead section in each recipe to see when you must pull items out of the freezer to put into the refrigerator to defrost.

SUMMER: PLAN TWO

✦ Day 1—No-Cook Night: Deanna's Tortilla-wiches ✦

Here's a recipe that's great for lunch, a make-ahead dinner, or a "Who has time to cook?" night. And this simple recipe is from my wonderful daughter, who went from "Don't ask me, I can't boil water!" to "Let me create tasty treats for mom's cookbook" when she went off to college. Of course, this couldn't have happened when she was living at home. (Psst! Having these on Day 1 will guarantee that no one will munch on the deli meats beforehand.)

Dish up: 4   Cooking time: 0
Construction time: 10 minutes   Paraphernalia: Small bowl

INGREDIENTS:
1 8-ounce package cream cheese
2 tablespoons milk
1/8 teaspoon garlic powder
1 4-ounce can diced chilies
1 tablespoon onion, minced
4 large flour tortillas
1 tomato, diced
1/4 pound roast beef, thinly sliced
1/4 pound turkey, thinly sliced

   To make:
   1. Beat together cream cheese, milk and garlic powder.
   2. Stir in chilies and onion.
   3. Lightly moisten both sides of tortilla with a little bit of water.
   4. Spread the cream cheese mixture on the tortilla.
   5. Wash, dice and sprinkle tomatoes on each tortilla.
   6. Place roast beef on half of the tortilla and turkey on the other half.
   7. Roll up and serve.

Jazz It Up: Add a favorite topping, like sliced black olives or diced celery.

Dress It Down: Skip the chilies if you're not crazy about spicy food.

Change It Up: Use cream cheese with herbs, such as dill or garlic, in place of the traditional kind. Or replace cream cheese with plain yogurt.

We Go Good Together: Natural potato chips

Look Ahead: Prepare Day 2, Barbecued Beef over Toast, tonight in your slow cooker's liner to save you from rushing around like crazy tomorrow morning. (Add the meat in the morning for food safety.) Then put the liner in the fridge until the morning.

➸ Day 2—Slow Cook Tonight: Barbecued Beef over Toast ➻

We're slow cooking earlier in the two weeks so we can have the main ingredient, barbecued beef, for several meals in the days to come. And best of all, Jan Capasso says, "This is delicious and can be frozen, too." You'll be doing just that.

Dish up: 6 servings

Cooking time: 8 to 10 hours

Construction time: 7 to 9 minutes

Paraphernalia: Slow cooker

INGREDIENTS:

6-pound sirloin tip roast 🥤 (Part of the roast will be used for Day 7, BBQ Sandwiches.)

1 celery rib, cut into 4 pieces

1 large onion, chopped

1 green pepper, chopped

1 16-ounce bottle ketchup

1½ cup water

3 tablespoons barbecue sauce

3 tablespoons vinegar

2 tablespoons chili powder

1 tablespoon salt

1 tablespoon hot pepper sauce

1 teaspoon pepper

6 pieces toast

To make:

1. Wash veggies.
2. Chop the onion and pepper. Cut the celery rib into pieces.
3. Mix all ingredients except toast in the slow cooker.
4. Plug in the slow cooker first thing in the morning. Cook for 8 to 10 hours on low.
5. When you walk in the door, remove celery pieces.
6. Put bread in toaster.
7. Shred meat with a fork. Serve ⅓ of the barbecued beef over toast. Set aside the remaining beef for Day 7, BBQ Sandwiches.

Jazz It Up: Add green chili peppers.

Dress It Down: Skip the celery, onion and pepper.

Double it: Tightly wrap the meat you set aside, and store it in freezer for Day 7, BBQ Sandwiches.

We Go Good Together: Mashed potatoes

➤ Day 3—Everyday Dinner: 'Shroom-lini ✦

This recipes fills the tummy and takes only minutes to make.

Dish up: 6 servings
Construction time: 10 minutes

Cooking time: 20 minutes
Paraphernalia: 6- or 7-quart pot, 12-inch skillet, strainer

INGREDIENTS:

1 8-ounce carton snowcap mushrooms, sliced

1 16-ounce package linguine (Part of the linguine will be used for Day 7, We Go Good Together.)

3 tablespoons olive oil

1 teaspoon garlic, minced

2 16-ounce cans Italian-style tomatoes, chopped and drained

1 cups (4 ounces) Parmesan cheese, grated

To make:

1. Wash and slice mushrooms, if need be.
2. Make pasta according to package directions.
3. Sauté mushrooms in olive oil for a few minutes until golden (not brown).
4. Add garlic and tomatoes. Simmer over medium heat for 20 minutes.
5. Set aside ⅓ of cooked pasta to be used as a We Go Good Together dish for Day 7.
6. Put remaining pasta in a serving bowl. Add sauce. Toss.
7. Top with cheese and serve.

Jazz It Up: Use fresh garlic.

Dress It Down: Skip the mushrooms.

Change It Up: Toss with ⅓ cup feta cheese rather than the Parmesan cheese.

Double It: Take the pasta you had set aside, and store it in the freezer to serve as a side dish on Day 7.

We Go Good Together: Tossed salad

POTFUL OF KNOWLEDGe: Stormy Pasta Days
Don't get frantic if your pasta is taking longer to cook than the usual 8 to 10 minutes stated on the package directions. There's not a thing wrong with your stove. Food takes longer to cook on a stormy day, because the atmospheric pressure is lower and the boiling point of water is lower than the usual 212 degrees.

✣ Day 4—Backwards Meal: Blueberry Pancakes ✣

Combine the season's best with a kid-pleasing favorite. And if anyone tries to point out that pancakes aren't supposed to be for dinner, tell them you're celebrating backwards day.

Dish up: 4 servings
Construction time: 15 minutes

Cook time: 15 to 20 minutes
Paraphernalia: Large bowl, small bowl, 12-inch skillet, baking sheet, wide spatula

INGREDIENTS:

2 cups all-purpose flour

2½ tablespoons baking powder

½ teaspoon salt

1 egg

1½ cups milk

2 tablespoons butter

3 small containers (about 4.4 ounces each) blueberries

2 tablespoons water

½ teaspoon cornstarch

2 tablespoons sugar

2 teaspoons lemon juice (from a fresh lemon)

To make:

1. Preheat oven to 250 degrees. Place baking sheet in oven to warm.

2. Combine flour, baking powder and salt in a large bowl.

3. In a separate bowl, lightly beat egg. Add milk to egg. Beat lightly. Add egg mixture to flour and mix until moistened. Melt butter in microwave for about 20 seconds. Blend melted butter into batter. Gently stir 1 small container of berries into batter.

4. Lightly coat skillet with nonstick cooking spray. Heat over medium heat until hot.

5. Drop batter, about 1/4 cup, onto hot skillet. Gently spread batter into 4-inch circles, if need be. Cook pancakes about 2 to 3 minutes per side.

6. Place finished pancakes on baking sheet in oven to keep warm (or place on a plate and cover with foil).

7. Repeat Steps 5 and 6 with remaining batter.

8. Make blueberry sauce by combining water, cornstarch, 2 small containers blueberries, and 2 tablespoons sugar in a small saucepan. Heat to boiling over medium heat and cook for about 2 minutes. (Berries will burst.) Remove from heat.

9. Squeeze 2 teaspoons juice from lemon and stir into the sauce.

10. Serve pancakes with warm blueberry sauce or warm syrup.

Jazz It Up: Add a dollop of whipped cream.

Dress It Down: Skip the blueberry sauce. Add blueberries to batter.

Change It Up: Use the boxed pancake mix of your choice, or substitute whole-wheat flour for a portion of the white flour.

We Go Good Together: Crisp bacon, of course!

Look Ahead: Take the frozen chicken for Day 5, Polynesian Chicken, out of the freezer and put it in the refrigerator to defrost.

TIPS BASKETFUL OF TIPS: Pancake Know-How

Pancakes are also known as flapjacks and silver dollars. For fluffy, delicious pancakes, follow these tips:

- Overmixing the batter makes tougher pancakes.
- Batter should not be dropped into a skillet until the skillet is hot. When a drop of water sizzles on contact with the skillet, the skillet is ready.
- Pancakes are ready to be flipped when the batter begins to set. You'll see bubbles appearing and bursting on the top. The underside will be a rich golden brown.
- Use a wide spatula to flip pancakes. This will keep them from flopping every which way.

 FRANTIC WOMAN FAMILY FUN: Blu-ana Shake

Whip up a batch of Blu-ana Shakes tonight. With fruit and low-fat milk, the shake ranks more nutritious than the ones you'd find served at the local ice cream shop. Dump 4 cups milk, 4 bananas, 2 cups fresh blueberries, 1/2 teaspoon vanilla and about 10 ice cubes into your blender, and blend on high for about 3 minutes. The mixture should be thick and creamy.

FRANTIC WOMAN FAMILY FUN: Turning Blue

On the next rainy day or a day when you need to sit for more than ten minutes, watch the original *Willie Wonka & the Chocolate Factory* movie with the family. The kids will get a kick out of seeing Violet turn blue.

❧ Day 5—Everyday Dinner: Polynesian Chicken ❧

The flavors of the islands spruce up boneless chicken. Use fresh oranges and pineapples, or if time is running short, use canned fruit instead.

Dish up: 4 servings
Construction time: 10 minutes

Cooking time: 10 minutes
Paraphernalia: Grill

INGREDIENTS:

4 skinless, boneless chicken breasts
1 cup pineapple chunks 🥤 (Part of the pineapple will be used for Day 6, We Go Good Together.)
2 sweet oranges
1 tomato

To make:

1. Fire up the grill on medium heat.
2. Cut chicken breasts into 1-inch strips, if you did not do so already.
3. Cut fresh pineapple into chunks. Set aside half of the chunks for Day 6, We Go Good Together.
4. Peel oranges. Divide into sections.
5. Wash, core and seed tomato. Chop.
6. Place ingredients in the center of a piece of foil. Fold edges together and close, making a foil packet. Make 3 more foil packets.
7. Place foil packet on grill grate. Cook for about 10 minutes, turning once. Carefully open packet to check chicken for doneness. When cooked, the chicken juices will run clear, and the center will no longer be pink.

Jazz It Up: Add 1 teaspoon chili powder.
Dress It Down: Eliminate the fruits and veggie.
Change It Up: Use 15-ounce can mandarin oranges and 1 8-ounce can pineapples. Drain juice from both. Also, have each family member make his or her own foil packet.
Double It: Refrigerate the remaining pineapple chunks for Day 6, We Go Good Together.

We Go Good Together: A green vegetable of your choice

Look Ahead: If you froze the feta cheese, take it out of the freezer and put it in the refrigerator to thaw for Day 6, Greek Salad. If you are serving pita bread on the side, defrost that, too.

🐜TiPS BASKETFUL OF TIPS: Foil Perfection

Don't let inexperience foil your foil packets. Make perfect packets by following these tips:

- Watch out for the red-hot foil packets when you're removing them from the grill. Use tongs and oven mitts to prevent burning fingers or hands.
- Use a fork to pierce the top of the foil packet right before you open it to allow steam to escape and to avoid a serious burn to the face. Let the packet stand for about 5 minutes, then fold back the foil to allow any additional steam to make its way out.
- Use a heavy-duty paper or foam plate to hold the foil packet. Eat dinner right from the foil packet. Look, mom! No dirty dishes!

PIT STOP: Pick Up Produce

Plan a trip to buy the rest of your produce now so that it is fresh for upcoming meals. You'll need 2 green peppers, 1 small package cherry tomatoes and 1 small pineapple.

If you followed the suggestion and held off buying your veggies to jazz up your meals, you'll need to buy these items now: 1 summer squash, 1 head lettuce, 1 tomato and 1 small pepper.

Also, buy these fruits and veggies for the We Go Good Together dishes: 1 bunch basil, 6 peaches, 1 package (16 ounces) coleslaw mix, 4 to 6 ears corn, 2 Vidalia onions, 2 cucumbers, 6 tomatoes and 1 green pepper.

⇥ *Day 6—No Cook Night: Greek Salad* ⬅ 🚫

Summer is the perfect time to enjoy a tasty salad. This is one of my favorites. Sometimes I wonder if I love Greek salad because of the feta cheese. Besides the wonderful flavor, it is so easy to use, since you can buy it already crumbled.

Dish up: 4 servings   Cooking time: 0
Construction time: 10 minutes   Paraphernalia: Large serving bowl

INGREDIENTS:

1 16-ounce package ready-to-eat salad
2 cups spinach, cut up
2 tomatoes, diced
1 cucumber, peeled and diced
1 onion, peeled and sliced
1/2 cup feta cheese
1/2 cup Greek-style olives, pitted and sliced
1/2 cup Greek salad dressing

To make:

1. Wash veggies.
2. Dice cucumber and tomato. Cut up spinach. Slice onion and olives.
3. Combine all ingredients in a larger serving bowl. Mix well, until dressing has thoroughly coated the salad fixings.

Jazz It Up: Add a can of white beans, like pinto. Don't forget to drain and rinse them.

Dress It Down: Eliminate the tomatoes and cucumbers to save slicing time.

Change It Up: You can use Italian or Caesar salad dressing if you have that on hand or if your family prefers them.

We Go Good Together: Pita bread. Pineapple chunks stored from Day 5. As always, pull out any leftovers from previous meals.

Look Ahead: Be sure to close the spinach bag tightly so the spinach stays fresh for Day 9, Popeye and Olive Oyl's Supper. Store the remaining olives to serve with pasta. Pull out the package of frozen slow-cooker beef stored from Day 2, Barbecued Beef over Toast, the frozen pasta stored from Day 3 and the sandwich rolls and put them in the refrigerator to thaw for tomorrow's meal. If you are jazzing up the sandwiches with cheese, pull the cheddar from the freezer to thaw.

POTFUL OF KNOWLEDGE: Color-Coded Salad

Add color to your salad while loading up on these healthy benefits:

- Green: Arugula, broccoli, kale, peppers, spinach and zucchini help build strong bones and teeth while lowering the risk of birth defects and some cancers.
- Yellow and Orange: Carrots, corn, squash and peppers can help keep your heart, eyes and immune system healthy.
- Red and Purple: Beets, eggplant, peppers and tomatoes can lower blood pressure and the risk of certain types of cancer.
- White: Cauliflower, chives, garlic, mushrooms and onions can decrease cholesterol and stimulate the immune system.

❋ Day 7—Must-Go: BBQ Sandwiches ❋

Another meal that's made from Double It ingredients awaits your family. Within minutes, you and the gang will be sitting down to a home-cooked meal without the trouble of cooking from scratch.

Dish up: 4 servings   Cooking time: 10 minutes
Construction time: 5 minutes   Paraphernalia: 3-quart pan

INGREDIENTS:

1 ½ Barbecued Beef, stored from Day 2
1 cup barbecue sauce, remaining from Day 2
4 sandwich rolls
Condiments of your choice

To make:
1. Combine beef and sauce in a pan and cook over medium heat for about 7 to 10 minutes, or until heated through.
2. Divide the beef among the four rolls. Serve.

Jazz It Up: Mix 2 teaspoons of relish into the beef. Add 1 teaspoon hot pepper sauce. Add a slice of cheddar on top of the beef.

We Go Good Together: Pasta (stored from Day 3) and black olives with Italian salad dressing.

Look Ahead: Pull out the chicken cubes you cut up on shopping day from the freezer and tuck them into the refrigerator for Day 8, Bawk Bawk Chicken Bobs.

➻ *Day 8: Everyday Dinner:* ➻
Bawk Bawk Chicken Bobs

Kabobs are a great way to cook veggies and meat all at once and a fun way to enjoy dinner. And with a silly name like Bawk Bawk Chicken Bobs, no one will mind when you're eating them with your fingers.

Dish up: 4 to 6 servings

Construction time: 10 minutes

Cooking time: 20 minutes

Paraphernalia: Grill, skewers, platter

INGREDIENTS:

1½ pounds boneless, skinless chicken breasts, cut into cubes

1 14-ounce can artichoke hearts, drained

1 pint cherry tomatoes

1 green pepper, cut into chunks

¾ cup ranch salad dressing

Olive oil

To make:

1. Fire up the grill on medium heat.
2. Cut chicken into cubes if you did not do so already.
3. Wash veggies.
4. Cut green pepper into chunks.
5. With double-prong skewers, stab chicken, pepper, tomato, artichoke hearts. Repeat once more per skewer.
6. Brush kabobs with oil. Place on hot grill grate and cook for about 15–20 minutes, or until chicken is no longer pink. Be sure to turn skewers several times and to baste with dressing for tastier Bobs.

Jazz It Up: Dip Bobs in honey mustard sauce.

Dress It Down: Skip the artichoke hearts if you're watching your pennies.

Change It Up: You can cook this in a 350-degree oven for about the same amount of time. Keep an eye on the Bobs. You can substitute veggies for the chicken.

We Go Good Together: Grilled Peaches

Look Ahead: If you've tucked the feta cheese in the freezer for Day 9, Popeye and Olive Oyl's Tortellini Supper, pull it out now Thaw the mozzarella cheese if you are making the We Go Good Together suggestion.

BASKETFUL OF TIPS: Don't Get Skewered

- Double-prong skewers will keep the Bawk Bawk Chicken Bobs from turning on their own and cooking unevenly. If you do not have double-prong skewers, use two skewers for each Bawk Bawk Chicken Bob.
- Be sure to soak wooden skewers ʃin warm water for at least 15 minutes, preferably 30, before grilling, or you might have unexpected company—the fire department.

FRANTIC WOMAN FAMILY FUN: Bawk-Bawk-Goose

Gather the kids to play a game of Bawk-Bawk-Goose while the Bawk Bawk Bobs are cooking. Okay, it's really Duck-Duck-Goose, but who's keeping track?

❖ Day 9—Everyday Dinner: ❖
Popeye and Olive Oyl's Tortellini Supper

Whatever you do, don't mention s-p-i-n-a-c-h to the kids. That word brings an immediate "Mom, I don't like that!" whine from the kids.

Dish up: 5 servings　　　　　Cooking time: 10 minutes
Construction time: 5 minutes　　Paraphernalia: Dutch oven, strainer

INGREDIENTS:

1 16-ounce package cheese tortellini

2 cups spinach, cut up

1/2 cup feta cheese

1 cup milk

1/4 teaspoon minced garlic

To make:

1. Cook tortellini according to package directions. Drain.
2. Wash and cut spinach into smaller pieces, and steam it for about 5 minutes, or until wilted. Drain.
3. Add milk, cheese, garlic and tortellini to spinach. Cook for about 3 to 5 minutes, stirring often.

Jazz It Up: Add 1 cup sautéed summer squash.

Dress It Down: Serve the tortellini without Popeye's power ingredient—spinach.

Change It Up: Use 1 10-ounce package frozen spinach, chopped and thawed. Heat spinach until water evaporates. Continue with Step 3.

We Go Good Together: Marinated tomatoes and Mozzarella Slices.

Look Ahead: Pull out the ground beef and buns for tomorrow's Wimpy's Favorite Burgers on Buns and the ribs for Day 11, Finger Lickin' Ribs, slow-cooker meal.

FRANTIC WOMAN FAMILY FUN:
Real Moms Watch Cartoons

Just for fun, borrow or rent a Popeye video for the evening. The kids might enjoy a retro evening of cartoons that were popular before video game systems invaded our country back in 1976.

☀ Day 10—Kids' Meal: ☀
Wimpy's Favorite Burgers on Buns

Light the grill, then play a game of hopscotch or catch until the grill gets hot. Once the grill is hot, toss on the burgers, and enjoy the warm summer breeze while waiting for dinner to sizzle.

Dish up: 4 or 5 servings

Construction time: 5 minutes

Cooking time: 10 minutes

Paraphernalia: Grill, spatula

INGREDIENTS:

1 1/4 pounds ground beef

1/2 teaspoon black pepper

4 hamburger buns

1 8-ounce can pineapples, sliced

To make:

1. Fire up the grill.
2. Divide the meat into 4 equal portions (or 5 for smaller burgers). Shape ground beef into patties. Sprinkle pepper on both sides of patties.
3. Place patties on hot grill grate.
4. Cook for about 10 minutes, turning patties over once.
5. Place buns, cut side down, on rack for 1 to 2 minutes to toast.
6. Place burger on bottom half of the bun, add 1 pineapple slice to each burger, and top with other half of the bun.
7. If desired, serve with favorite condiments.

Jazz It Up: Add 1 teaspoon Cajun seasoning to raw beef to add a little zip to the burgers. Grill the pineapples for 1 minute. Add lettuce, tomatoes and pickles.

Dress It Down: Skip the pepper.

Change It Up: Use ground turkey instead of ground beef.

We Go Good Together: Grilled onions. Slice onions, and place them inside a piece of foil. Add 1 teaspoon butter. Fold sides together to close pocket tight. Grill for about 5 minutes, turning foil packet once.

Look Ahead: Make sure your roast is thawed for tomorrow's dinner. In fact, throw everything in the removable crock liner (or a bowl if your slow cooker does not have a removable pot) tonight, except the meat, and put it in the refrigerator. Then, all you'll have to do is add the meat, place the liner in the cooker, and plug it in tomorrow morning. Also, thaw the corn muffins if you are serving them.

BASKETFUL OF TIPS: Wimpy's Perfect Burger

To make a mouthwatering, juicy burger, handle the ground beef as little as possible when shaping the meat into patties. If you want your burger to be a hockey puck, keep playing with the meat. forming the patties isn't a task to give to the kids, because they'll want to shape each patty perfectly.

✦ Day 11—Slow Cook Tonight: Finger Lickin' Ribs ✦

As soon as you whip off the work clothes and don the summer shorts, enjoy your own rib fest. And if you want to create the atmosphere of a real rib fest, blast some country music on the stereo.

Dish up: 8 servings
Construction time: 7 minutes

Cooking time: 8 to 10 hours
Paraphernalia: Medium bowl, slow cooker

INGREDIENTS:
4 pounds pork loin back ribs or pork spareribs
(Part of the ribs will be used for Day 13, Tropical Tacos.)
1 teaspoon salt
1/2 teaspoon black pepper
1 teaspoon garlic powder
1 large onion, sliced
1/4 cup brown sugar, firmly packed
1/4 cup prepared mustard
1 16-ounce bottle ketchup
2 tablespoon butter or margarine, melted
2 tablespoon Worcestershire sauce
1 tablespoon hot pepper sauce
1/2 teaspoon chili powder

To make:

1. Coat inside of slow cooker with nonstick cooking spray.
2. Season ribs with salt, pepper and garlic. Cut into 2 or 3-rib portions. Peel and slice onions. Place ribs and onions in slow cooker.
3. Combine the remaining ingredients in a bowl. Pour over ribs.
4. Cover and cook on low heat for 8 to 10 hours. If time is limited, cook on high heat for 4 to 7 hours or until ribs can be pulled apart with a fork. Set aside half of the ribs for Day 13.

Jazz It Up: Add more spice to the sauce by adding 1 teaspoon crushed red pepper.

Dress It Down: Skip the onions if time is limited.

Change It Up: Use bottled barbecue sauce.

Double it: Pull the meat off the ribs you set aside for Day 13 and put it in the refrigerator.

We Go Good Together: Coleslaw and corn muffins

Look Ahead: Pull out 2 cups hash brown potatoes from the freezer, and store it in the refrigerator for tomorrow.

＊ Day 12—I Can with a Can: One-Pan Spud Meal ＊

A bad day at the office, PMS or even Murphy's Law won't stop you from pulling off this brainless but belly-filling dinner.

Dish up: 4 servings

Construction time: 10 minutes

Cooking time: 15 to 20 minutes

Paraphernalia: 12-inch skillet

INGREDIENTS:

1 15-ounce can pinto beans, drained and rinsed

1/4 cup onion, diced

2 cups frozen diced hash brown potatoes, thawed

1 10.75-ounce can cream of celery soup

1/4 cup milk

3 tablespoons prepared mustard

1/2 teaspoon dried basil

1/2 teaspoon dill

1/2 cup sour cream

To make:

1. Drain and rinse beans.
2. Peel and dice onion.
3. Combine potatoes, soup, milk, mustard and seasonings in skillet over medium heat.
4. Cook until mixture comes to a boil, stirring often. Reduce heat.
5. Cover and simmer for 10 minutes.
6. Stir in beans and sour cream. Cook until heated through, about 5 to 7 minutes.

Jazz It Up: Add ¼ cup green peppers.

Dress It Down: Skip the onions.

Change It Up: Use packaged hash brown potatoes with diced onions and peppers already in it.

We Go Good Together: Marinated seasonal veggies

(TiPS) BASKETFUL OF TIPS: Must-go Hash Browns Brunch
For a weekend brunch, allow the rest of the hash brown potatoes to thaw and fry them up in a skillet with butter. Beat eggs with milk and pour the mixture into the skillet. Scramble the potatoes and eggs together. When finished cooking, serve.

✦ Day 13—Must-Go: Tropical Tacos ✦

Liven up ordinary tacos with the taste of Maui. With the sun shining, load up a tray with tacos and drinks, and head outdoors. Bring along the CD player and some fun CDs to make the evening more festive.

Dish up: 4 servings
Construction time: 10 minutes

Cooking time: 10 minutes
Paraphernalia: 12-inch skillet

INGREDIENTS:

2 cups pineapple chunks 🥤 (Part of the pineapple will be used for Day 14, We Go Good Together.)

½ green pepper, chopped

1 tablespoon vegetable oil

Pork, stored from Day 11
1 tablespoon teriyaki sauce
1 teaspoon ginger
1 teaspoon garlic powder
4 flour tortillas

To make:

1. Cut pineapple into smaller chunks. You'll need 2 cups for this recipe. (Save the remaining pieces for Day 14.)
2. Wash and chop pepper.
3. Add oil and pepper to skillet. Cook for about 3 minutes.
4. Stir in pork and teriyaki sauce. Cook for about 5 minutes.
5. Add pineapples and cook for another 7 to 10 minutes, or until heated through. Serve on tortillas.

Jazz It Up: Add ¼ teaspoon hot pepper sauce for a spicier flavor, or add ¼ cup pecans.

Dress It Down: Skip the green peppers and dry seasonings. You'll have pork and pineapples.

Change It Up: Use 1 16-ounce can pineapple chunks instead of fresh.

Double it: Be sure to put the remaining pineapple chunks into the refrigerator for Day 14, We Go Good Together.

We Go Good Together: Corn on the cob

Look Ahead: Take the swordfish out of the freezer and put it in the refrigerator to thaw.

TiPS BASKETFUL OF TIPS: Sweeter than Sweet

Remember the old cliché "Good things come in small packages"?

Well, that's especially true in pineapples, because the smaller the pineapple, the sweeter the taste. On a pineapple plantation tour a few years ago, the guide stated that the same sugar content is in each pineapple, regardless of its size. In a bigger pineapple, the sugar has to cover a larger volume. In a smaller piece of fruit, the sugar has less territory to cover, which gives the pineapple a sweet, juicy taste. So if you're thinking you're getting your money's worth from a bigger one, think again.

FRANTIC WOMAN'S FAMILY FUN: Paper Skirts

This is the frantic woman's rendition of the Hawaiian grass skirt. It's cheap. It's easy. It keeps the kids busy. Give each of the kids a brown paper grocery-store bag. Have them cut off the bottom of the bag, making a tube. Next, have them lay the bag on a flat surface and cut 1-inch strips from one end, leaving a 3-inch band at the top. (Be sure they don't cut the strips all the way to the top.) Have them cut on the fold, making one long piece. You can fit the bag to the child by cutting away the excess. With a hole punch, make a hole in the center of the band on each end. Use a piece of string, yarn, ribbon or shoelace to make a tie to hold the skirt up. The kids can hula all the way to the dinner table.

⇢ Day 14—Company's Coming: ⇠ Stu's Swordfish Kabobs 🐟

My husband loves swordfish; it's a favorite entree for him to order when we go out. This delicious meal offers a chance to combine good food and good company with the comforts of home.

Dish up: 6 to 8 servings
Construction time: 15 minutes

Cooking time: 6 to 8 minutes
Paraphernalia: Grill, skewers, small bowl

INGREDIENTS:
2 pounds swordfish, cut up
1 cup olive oil
2 teaspoons garlic powder
1 teaspoon oregano
1 tablespoon lemon juice

To make:
1. Heat grill.
2. Combine oil, garlic, oregano, and lemon juice in a small bowl.
3. Cut swordfish into 1½-inch cubes.
4. Add swordfish to oil mixture. Turn to coat both sides. Cover. Marinate in the refrigerator for 15 minutes.

5. Thread 3 swordfish cubes onto double-prong skewers, or use 2 skewers per kabob. (Again, this keeps the fish from twisting and turning to ensure even cooking.) Cook for about 3 to 4 minutes on each side and serve.

Jazz It Up: A little Cajun seasoning is a quick way to add sizzle to the taste.

Dress It Down: This is so simple, you don't have to skip anything.

We Go Good Together: Serve caramel dip with the fresh pineapple chunks stored from Day 13.

Part Three

Weekly and Daily Specials

[blank]

Celebrations, holidays, vacations and overnight company are parts of a frantic woman's life. At times like this, a typical family meal won't do. And whatever good intentions you have to find new menu ideas, you don't have the time to sift through recipe boxes or cookbooks or click through various Web sites to find what you need. To help you through these frantic times that could make your days even more chaotic, here are weekly and daily menus to help smooth the preparations for these special occasions.

TURKEY WEEK

Turkey is part of the traditional meal served on Thanksgiving, but many families think nothing of preparing another one for the other winter holidays, too. And turkey dinners have gone from a once-a-year tradition to any time of the year with the new poultry options available. So, whatever time of the year it happens to be, use this plan to make a week's worth of dinner meals the frantic way. Psst! If having turkey night after night elicits a groan from the kids, substitute canned chicken or ham, or substitute a favorite deli meat or fresh vegetables.

Turkey Week Menus

Day 1—Old Tradition: Thank Goodness for Turkey
Day 2—Soup's On: Turkey Soup
Day 3—Sandwich Board: Open-face Turkey Sammies
Day 4—Kids' Meal: Turkey Calzones

Day 5—Retro Meal: Turkey and Noodles
Day 6—Sandwich Board: Kids' Klub
Day 7—I Can with a Can: Turkey and Rice

THE SHOPPING LISTS

The Frantic Woman's Cupboard

TURKEY WEEK STAPLES

Seasonings

French-fried onion rings
Salt
Pepper

Side Dishes
Allspice
Ginger

Dressings, Oil and Sauces

Strawberry preserves

Side Dishes
Maple syrup

Baking Needs

Sugar (light brown)

Side Dishes
Artificial Sweetner

Bread, Chips and More

Bread

Jazz It Ups
Bread crumbs

Frantic Necessities
Foil
Nonstick cooking spray

Dairy
Butter*
Eggs*

Side Dishes
Milk (skim)
Orange juice

* Ingredients you'll need for both main and side dishes

The Frantic Woman Goes Shopping

MAIN-DISH INGREDIENTS YOU'LL NEED TO BUY

Produce: Veggies
2 medium yellow onions (Day 1)
1 small bunch alfalfa sprouts (Day 6)

Canned Goods and Bottles
1 16-ounce can jellied cranberry sauce (Day 1)
1 14.5-ounce can chicken broth (Day 2)
3 10.75-ounce cans turkey gravy (Days 3, 5)
1 4-ounce can mushrooms (Day 4)
1 10.75-ounce can cream of mushroom soup (Day 7)
1 8-ounce can peas (Day 7)

Noodles, Pasta and Rice
2 16-ounce bags wide egg noodles (Days 2, 5)
2 instant rice boil-in-bags (4 servings) (Day 7)

Bread, Chip and More
4 slices bread, your preference (Day 3)
8 slices whole-wheat bread (Day 6)

Deli
4 slices Colby cheese (Day 6)

Fish, Meat and Poultry
1 12- to 14 pound whole turkey (Day 1)

Dairy
1 8-ounce tube refrigerated crescent rolls (Day 4)
1 cup (4 ounces) Monterey Jack cheese, shredded (Day 4)
2 ounces cream cheese (Day 6)

JAZZ IT UP INGREDIENTS YOU'LL NEED TO BUY

Produce: Veggies
1 bunch celery (Days 2, 7)
2 yellow onions (Days 2, 6, 7)
1 8-ounce carton mushrooms, sliced (Days 3, 7)
1 head lettuce (Day 6)
1 tomato (Day 6)
1 green pepper (Day 7)

Dressings, Oils and Sauces

Turkey glaze, your preference (replaces recommended recipe) (Day 1)

Canned Goods and Bottles
1 16-ounce can sliced carrots (Day 2)

Frozen
1 16-ounce package mixed vegetables (Day 5)

WE GO GOOD TOGETHER INGREDIENTS YOU'LL NEED TO BUY

Produce: Veggies

1 bunch celery (Days 1, 4)

3 yellow onions (Day 1)

1 12-ounce bag baby carrots (Day 4)

Canned Goods and Bottles

2 26-ounce cans yams (Day 1)

1 15-ounce can chicken broth (Day 1)

1 15-ounce can pumpkin pie filling (Day 5)

1 26-ounce can whole corn (Day 7)

1 26-ounce can creamed corn (Day 7)

Baking Needs

1 3-ounce box butterscotch instant sugar-free pudding mix (Day 5)

1 16-ounce box all-purpose baking mix (Day 7)

Bread, Chips and More

3 loaves white bread or 3 packages bread cubes (Day 1)

1 16-ounce bag potato chips (Day 6)

Dairy

1 tube refrigerated biscuits (Day 2)

1 8-ounce container sour cream (Day 7)

Frozen

1 8-ounce container light whipped topping (Day 5)

Unloading the Load

- This week's unloading task will be a cinch. Freeze the whole-wheat bread to keep it fresh for Day 6, Kids' Klub.

- Also, think about freezing the Monterey Jack cheese for Day 4, Turkey Calzones and the Colby for Day 6, Kids' Klub to keep that fresh (and from disappearing).
- Freeze the potato chips for Day 6, We Go Good Together to minimize the possibility of one of the kids munching on them.

(TIPS) BASKETFUL OF TIPS: Time-saving Turkey Talk
No time to spare? Never fear. Here are a few time-saving tips from Norma Farrell, Consumer Education Specialist of Public Relations for the National Turkey Federation.

- It takes less cooking time to roast two smaller birds than it does to roast one large one. Two 12-pound birds will roast in approximately 3 hours, compared to one 24-pound bird that requires 5 hours.
- Imagine putting your turkey straight from the freezer into the oven without doing a darn thing to get it ready. There are new birds on the market that are prebasted, frozen whole birds with the giblets removed. The prebasted turkey goes straight from the freezer to the oven with no defrosting required, eliminating consumers' worries about proper defrosting and handling of raw turkey. (PS: I tried one of these products by Jennie-O when my son had a number of friends over for dinner. It was easy and delicious. So, if prepping a turkey frazzles your nerves, check out these new birds.)
- The new premarinated fresh turkey tenderloins are an alternative for smaller families that prefer white meat. This tenderloin maintains moistness and cooks in a fraction of the time of a whole turkey.
- And last, there are turkey roasts and bone-in breasts that include the added convenience of gravy packs.

Whew! That's a lot of turkey options for today's busy women. Thanks, Norma!

➳ Day 1—Old Tradition: Thank Goodness for Turkey ➳

There are many ways to cook a bird, and trying to decide which recipe to include in this book was almost impossible. Over the years, I have never cooked a turkey the same way twice. So, I went to the experts at the National Turkey Federation and found a scrumptious recipe that seems to fit the American tradition. I like this one because of its simplicity.

Dish up: 15 to 18 servings

Construction time: 10 to 15 minutes

Cooking time: 3 to 4 hours, plus 15 minutes resting time

Paraphernalia: Shallow roasting pan, wire roasting rack, kitchen string, meat thermometer, 12-inch skillet

INGREDIENTS:

1 12- to 14-pound whole turkey, thawed 🧊 (Parts of this turkey will be used throughout the week.)

Salt and pepper, to taste

2 tablespoons butter

2 medium onions, chopped

1 16-ounce can jellied cranberry sauce

⅓ cup light brown sugar

To make:

1. Preheat oven to 325 degrees. Coat wire roasting rack with non-stick cooking spray.
2. Remove giblets (discard liver), neck and any visible fat from turkey. Reserve these parts to make gravy, if you'd like, or toss them. Rinse turkey with cold running water and drain well. Dry with paper towels.
3. Salt and pepper the inside and outside of the turkey.
4. Tie legs together with kitchen string. Twist wing tips behind the back.
5. Place wire rack inside roasting pan. Put turkey, breast side up, on wire rack. Stick food thermometer in the deepest part of the thigh or breast, but do not touch the bone. Cover loosely with foil.
6. Cook in oven for about 2½ hours, basting occasionally with pan juices.
7. Around the 2-hour mark, melt butter in skillet over medium heat.
8. Peel and chop onions. Add onions to melted butter, and cook for about 15 minutes, or until very soft, stirring occasionally. (Simplify it: If onions begin to brown, lower the heat.)
9. Stir in cranberry sauce and sugar; bring mixture to a boil. Reduce heat to low. Simmer for about 10 minutes, stirring occasionally.

10. Remove foil, and pour glaze over bird. Cook for another 30 to 75 minutes, or until the thermometer registers 170 degrees in the breast or 180 degrees in the thigh.
11. Remove turkey from oven. Allow it to rest for 10 to 15 minutes before carving.
12. Carve enough slices for tonight's dinner, then follow the instructions in Double It for the remainder of the turkey.

Jazz It Up: Add your own favorite glaze instead.

Change It Up: Fill the bird's cavity with stuffing. About ¾ cup of stuffing per pound works best. To be safe, don't pack in a lot of stuffing. The temperature of the stuffing should reach 165°F. Or simply use onion and lemon wedges in the cavity to add flavor.

Double It:

- Day 2, Turkey Soup, takes advantage of the carcass, so store the carcass until tomorrow, or allow it to simmer while you're cleaning up the kitchen.

Divide the remaining turkey into 5 portions as follows:

- 2 portions should be about 1½ cups each for Day 5, Turkey and Noodles and Day 7, Turkey and Rice. Store these in freezer bags or containers, and mark with the designated days. Then, put them in the freezer.
- 2 other portions should contain 4 nice-size slices each for Day 4, Turkey Calzones, and Day 6, Kid's Klub. Again, wrap these in freezer bags and mark them for the appropriate days.
- The last portion for Day 3, Open-face Turkey Sammies, will contain the rest. Store it in a container, and put it in the refrigerator. (If you have more than enough remaining in the last portion, divvy up some of it to add to the other packages.)

We Go Good Together: Johanna's Stuffing, and Candied Yams. 🌐

POTFUL OF KNOWLEDGE: How much is enough?
Trying to figure out what size bird will feed your crowd can be daunting. I always buy one bigger than I need, because I love having the extras to make meals for the week ahead. The National Turkey Federation suggests buying 1 pound of uncooked turkey per person from an 8- to 12-pound bird. If you buy the bigger birds, you'll get more for your money, as larger turkeys have a larger ratio of meat to bones, so ¾ pound per person will work. See, I knew there was a reason I bought a bigger bird all along.

BASKETFUL OF TIPS: Store and Hide
This is the frantic woman's version of the Hide and Seek game. That game might be fun for the kids; this game is essential to moms.

- Store and hide the leftover turkey immediately, so your family members won't be tempted to nibble on it. That would mean a trip to the grocery store.
- You can get really good at this game by storing your turkey in containers marked "gizzards" or "liver."
- Be sure to follow the Double It directions and freeze some of the turkey pieces for meals that will be made later in the week.

✦ Day 2—Soup's On: Turkey Soup ✦

Deanne Thomas learned this recipe from her mother-in-law a number of years ago. Though her mother-in-law makes it with homemade dumplings, busy mom Deanne makes it with noodles. The turkey carcass adds flavor to this soup, and the slow boil easily removes any turkey slivers that are hanging on.

Dish up: 4 servings
Construction time: 5 minutes

Cooking time: 30 to 40 minutes
Paraphernalia: Roasting pan, 3-quart pot

INGREDIENTS:

1 turkey carcass stored from Day 1

1 16-ounce bag wide egg noodles

1 14.5-ounce can chicken broth

1 cup gravy stored from Day 1

Salt and pepper, to taste

To make:

1. Put the turkey carcass in a roaster on the stovetop. Fill roasting pan half full with water.

2. Bring to a slow boil over medium heat. Boil for about 30 minutes. Depending on the size of the pan, you might have to stretch it across two burners.

3. While turkey carcass is cooking, make noodles according to package directions.

4. Take any turkey pieces off carcass that haven't fallen off. Cut any larger sections of turkey into bite-size pieces. Remove carcass from pan.

5. Add any leftover gravy to pan. (If you don't have any leftover gravy, no problem.) Add chicken broth. Add cooked noodles to pan. Add Salt and pepper, to taste. Stir and serve.

Jazz It Up: Add sautéed diced onions, celery or 1 can carrots.

Change It Up: Make homemade dumplings instead of noodles, or substitute rice or orzo for the noodles.

We Go Good Together: Leftover rolls or refrigerated biscuits

TIPS BASKETFUL OF TIPS: From Window to Table

Kitchen consultant Janice Kucczler pulled lacey draperies from her storage closet to use as a tablecloth for Thanksgiving dinner one year. Not one person knew her beautiful table covering had once graced her dining room window.

⇢ Day 3—Sandwich Board: ⇠ Open-face Turkey Sammies

Your gravy and stuffing expire today. Two days have passed since that fabulous bird was cooked. Those leftovers sitting in your fridge must be eaten today or tossed in the trash, according to Turkey Federation.

Dish up: 4 servings

Construction time: 5 minutes

Cooking time: 10 to 15 minutes

Paraphernalia: 3-quart pot, baking dish, toaster

INGREDIENTS:

Stuffing, stored from Day 1

4 slices turkey, stored from Day 1

Gravy, stored from Day 1

1 10.75-ounce can turkey gravy, if needed

4 slices bread

To make:

1. Preheat oven to 350 degrees.
2. Place stuffing in a piece of foil with the dull side in, and seal closed. Place in oven for about 15 minutes, or until heated through.
3. Lay turkey slices on baking sheet. Place in heated oven for about 10 minutes, or until hot.
4. Add canned gravy to leftover gravy, and heat it all in a pot over medium heat until hot.
5. Toast bread. Put in oven to keep warm until turkey and gravy are heated through.
6. Lay 1 piece of toast on each plate. Add turkey slices next. Top with gravy. Serve stuffing on the side.

Jazz It Up: Add sliced mushrooms to the gravy.

Change It Up: Heat turkey, gravy, and stuffing in the microwave. Heat each item separately, then assemble and heat for 1 minute or so.

We Go Good Together: Serve any remaining side dishes from your turkey dinner.

Look Ahead: Pull out the container marked Day 4, Turkey Calzones, from the freezer, and put it in the refrigerator to thaw. Pull out the Monterey Jack cheese if you froze it.

FRANTIC WOMAN FAMILY FUN: Hide the Thimble (or Lid)

One of my favorite children's books is *Little House on the Prairie* by Laura Ingalls Wilder. Hide the Thimble is a game that Laura and Mary played during the cold winters on the Kansas prairie. All you'll need is a thimble. (Simplify it: If you do not have a thimble, hide the lid from a spice bottle. Be sure the lid is free of any spice particles.) Decide who will hide the thimble first. All other players must close their eyes and count to ten, while the person with the thimble finds a good spot to hide it. It can be hidden under stuff, but the hiding area, one room or two, shouldn't be one with lots of breakables. After counting to ten, the players look for the thimble, while the thimble hider counts to fifty. The first one to find the thimble gets to hide it next. If no one finds the thimble within the 50 seconds, the thimble hider gets a second turn.

✦ Day 4—Kids' Meal: Turkey Calzones ✦

Here's a great grab-and-go meal that you can prepare beforehand and reheat when the kids walk in the door. And you have the chance to catch up on some other tasks, change out of your work clothes into something comfortable, or brew a cup of tea while the calzones are baking in the oven.

Dish up: 4 servings   Cooking time: 20 to 25 minutes
Construction time: 5 to 7 minutes   Paraphernalia: Baking sheet, small bowl

INGREDIENTS:

1 egg, beaten
1 8-ounce tube refrigerated crescent rolls
4 slices turkey, stored from Day 1
1 cup Monterey Jack cheese, shredded
1 4-ounce can mushrooms, sliced

To make:

1. Heat oven to 375 degrees. Coat baking sheet with nonstick cooking spray.
2. Crack egg into a small bowl and beat.
3. On baking sheet, separate crescent roll dough into 4 rectangles. Press perforations to seal and form 4 6- by 5-inch rectangles.
4. Lay 1 turkey slice on each rectangle, leaving a 1/2-inch edge. Top with cheese and mushrooms.
5. Fold dough in half, forming a square. Pinch edges together to seal. Baste edges with egg.
6. Bake for 20 to 25 minutes, or until crust is golden.

Jazz It Up: Dip calzone in beaten egg, then coat with bread crumbs.

Dress It Down: Skip the mushrooms.

We Go Good Together: Carrot and celery sticks

Look Ahead: Pull the leftover turkey marked Day 5, Turkey and Noodles, from the freezer, and put it in the refrigerator to defrost.

POTFUL OF KNOWLEDGE: The Turkey Choice
Turkey has 8 percent more protein and less fat than beef or chicken, making it a great choice for those watching their diets and/or cutting back on their carbs.

✤ Day 5—Retro Meal: Turkey and Noodles ✦

This simple meal reminds me of my grandmother's home cooking—chunks of turkey simmered in gravy and poured over hot buttered noodles. Back then, everything was smothered in butter.

Dish up: 4 to 6 servings

Construction time: 5 minutes

Cooking time: 10 minutes

Paraphernalia: 3-quart pot, 5-quart pot, strainer

INGREDIENTS:

1½ cups cooked turkey, stored from Day 1

2 10.75-ounce cans turkey gravy

1 16-ounce package wide egg noodles

To make:

1. Dump turkey and canned gravy into smaller pot. Heat over low-medium heat.
2. Cook noodles according to package directions.
3. Turn up the heat on the turkey and gravy just before noodles are finished cooking, so gravy mixture is steaming hot.
4. When noodles are cooked, drain and add butter.
5. Serve gravy and turkey mixture over noodles.

Jazz It Up: Add cooked veggies to gravy mixture.

Change It Up: If all the leftover turkey has made its way into your family's bellies, use 2 cans of chicken instead. You can replace the noodles with rice.

We Go Good Together: Pumpkin Pudding 🌀+🥄

Look Ahead: Pull the freezer bag filled with leftover turkey marked Day 6, Kids' Klub, and tuck it into the refrigerator to thaw. Take out the whole-wheat bread, Colby cheese and potato chips, too.

⇢ Day 6—Sandwich Board: Kids' Klub ⇠

Here's a knockoff of the traditional club sandwich with a sweet addition. The Sammie has a fresh layer of veggie added to it, too. And what the kids can't see won't hurt them. This is another great grab-and-go meal.

Dish up: 4 servings   Cooking time: 0
Construction time: 10 minutes   Paraphernalia: Toaster

INGREDIENTS:

8 slices whole-wheat bread

4 tablespoons cream cheese

4 tablespoons strawberry preserves

Alfalfa sprouts

4 slices turkey, stored from Day 1

4 slices Colby cheese

To make:

1. Toast bread.
2. Spread cream cheese on 4 slices of toast.
3. Spread a thin layer of strawberry preserves on the cream cheese.
4. Add sprouts on top of the preserves.
5. Next, layer turkey and cheese.
6. Top each with a piece of toast.
7. Put 4 toothpicks in each sandwich. Put each sandwich on a plate. Cut into quarters. Serve.

Jazz It Up: Add lettuce, tomatoes and/or onions.

Dress It Down: Skip any ingredients the kids might not like.

Change It Up: Use bagels, potato buns or any other bread preference. Eliminate the meat and double the cheese to make it a meatless meal.

We Go Good Together: Potato chips

Look Ahead: Pull the container marked Day 7, Turkey and Rice, out of the freezer, and put it in the refrigerator to thaw.

✦ Day 7—I Can with a Can: Turkey and Rice ✦

Here is another easy-to-prepare meal made with the last of the turkey left-overs. As mentioned earlier, canned chicken can be substituted for turkey, if your leftovers have disappeared.

Dish up: 4 to 6 servings

Construction time: 10 minutes

Cooking time: 10 minutes

Paraphernalia: 3-quart pot, 2-quart microwave-safe baking dish, microwave

INGREDIENTS:

2 instant rice boil-in-bags (4 servings)
1 1/2 cups turkey, chopped, stored from Day 1
1 10.75-ounce can cream of mushroom soup
1/2 cup milk
1/4 cup french-fried onion rings
1 8-ounce can peas

To make:

1. Make rice according to package directions.
2. Combine rice and remaining ingredients in a microwave-safe baking dish.
3. Heat in microwave for 10 minutes.

Jazz It Up: Add sliced mushrooms, peppers, celery and onions before zapping it.

Dress It Down: Use minced onions instead of french-fried onion rings.

Change It Up: Use canned chicken. Bake in the oven at 350 degrees for about 20 to 25 minutes.

We Go Good Together: Baked Corn

HAM WEEK

Ham is traditionally served in the spring around holiday time. Many people serve it throughout the year for parties, too. Ham, like turkey, can be prepared in a variety of ways and can be jazzed up to satisfy those family members who prefer their meals with additional flavor. Follow the simple instructions in Day 1, Double it, to store your ham leftovers for the rest of the week. If ham becomes scarce midweek or you're sick of it, you can substitute canned chicken or tuna and still cook according to the plan.

Ham Week Menus

Day 1—Old Tradition: Baked Ham with Fruit
Day 2—Everyday Dinner: Potato Hamcakes
Day 3—I Can with a Can: Ham and Rice
Day 4—Everyday Dinner: Ham Skillet Dish
Day 5—Everyday Dinner: Ham-a-dillas
Day 6—Everyday Dinner: Cheesy Ham and Noodle Bake
Day 7—Kids' Meal: Green Eggs and Ham

THE SHOPPING LISTS

The Frantic Woman's Cupboard

HAM WEEK STAPLES

Seasonings
Cloves (whole)
Cheddar french-fried onion rings
Mustard (dry)

Side Dishes
Pepper (black)
Salt
Tarragon

Jazz It Ups
Mustard (dry)

Condiments

Side Dishes
Light mayonnaise
Salad dressing, your preference
Jelly, your preference

Dressings, Oil and Sauces
Maple syrup
Oil (vegetable)

Baking Needs
Sugar (brown)

Side Dishes
Sugar (cane)

Jazz It Ups
Sugar (brown)

Bread, Chips and More

Side Dishes
Bread, your preference

Frantic Necessities
Nonstick Cooking Spray

Dairy
Butter*
Eggs
Milk
Orange juice

* Ingredients you'll need for both main and side dishes

The Frantic Woman Goes Shopping

MAIN-DISH INGREDIENTS YOU'LL NEED TO BUY

Produce: Veggies

    6 to 7 green onions (Day 2)
    1 small yellow onion (Day 4)
    2 green peppers (Days 4, 5)
    1 head lettuce (Day 5)
    1 tomato (Day 5)
    1 10-ounce package spinach (Day 7)

PIT STOP: Keep It Fresh

Check the sell-by date on the package of spinach to make sure it will not expire before you need it.

Dressings, Oils and Sauces

    1 16-ounce jar salsa (Day 5)

Canned Goods and Bottles

    1 8-ounce can pineapple slices (Day 1)
    1 4-ounce can mushrooms, sliced (Day 3)
    1 10.75-ounce can cream of mushroom soup (Day 3)
    1 10.75-ounce can low-fat, low-sodium cream of mushroom soup (Day 6)

Noodles, Pasta and Rice

    1 13.3-ounce box instant mashed potatoes (Day 2)
    2 instant rice boil-in-bags (4 servings) (Day 3)
    1 16-ounce package pasta shapes (rotini or shells) (Day 6)

Bread, Chips and More

    6 flour or whole-wheat tortillas (Day 5)

Fish, Meat and Poultry

1 12- to 14-pound ham (Day 1)

Dairy

1 cup (4 ounces) cheddar cheese, shredded (Days 2, 6)
1 cup (4 ounces) Monterey Jack cheese, shredded (Day 5)
1 cup sour cream (Day 5)

Frozen

1 16-ounce package frozen pierogies (Day 4)

JAZZ IT UP INGREDIENTS YOU'LL NEED TO BUY

Produce: Veggies

1 hot pepper (Day 5)
1 small head broccoli (Day 6)
1 zucchini (Day 6)

Canned Goods and Bottles

1 16-ounce can applesauce (Day 2)
1 2.5-ounce can black olives (Day 3)
1 10-ounce jar roasted peppers (Day 3)

Cereal, Nuts and Such

1 2-ounce bag sliced almonds (Day 4)

Dairy

1 8-ounce container sour cream (Day 2)

Frozen Foods

1 10-ounce box peas (Day 6)

We Go Good Together Ingredients You'll Need to Buy

Produce: Fruit

1 lemon (Day 2)

2 bananas (Day 3)

1 pineapple (Day 3)

2 tangelos (Day 3)

Produce: Veggies

4 to 5 carrots (Day 1)

6 to 8 Idaho baking potatoes (Day 1)

1 small yellow onion (Day 1)

1 bunch asparagus (Day 2)

1 8-ounce carton snowcap mushrooms (Day 2)

1 16-ounce bag coleslaw mix (Day 5)

1 16-ounce package ready-to-eat salad (Day 6)

Canned Goods and Bottles

1 16-ounce can applesauce (Day 4)

1 8-ounce jar Miracle Whip (Day 5)

Dairy

1 quart chocolate milk (Day 7)

Unloading the Load

- Unpacking the groceries will be a cinch. Freeze the Monterey Jack cheese for Day 5, Ham-a-dillas.
- Freeze half of the cheddar cheese for Day 6, Cheesy Ham and Noodle Bake.
- Keep the veggies, including any you bought for Jazz It Ups, in the refrigerator's crisper, so they stay fresh longer.
- Cover the chocolate milk or tuck it in a second refrigerator, if you have one, so no one drinks it beforehand.

POTFUL OF KNOWLEDGE: Ham Help

There are many varieties of ham. Finding the one that is best to serve at the dinner table could throw a busy woman into a tizzy. To keep you from becoming frazzled over what ham to purchase, Hormel offers the following tips:

- Determine the type and quality of ham you want by considering your serving intentions. You will want to select a ham and water product for sandwiches. However, for a nice holiday dinner, you'll want to serve a ham with natural juices, as this is a better-quality ham.
- Before you buy the ham, determine the number of people you'll be serving to figure out how many pounds to buy. Use these guidelines: A bone-in ham yields ⅓ to ½ pound per serving. A partially boned ham yields about ⅓ to ½ pound per serving. And a boneless ham yields ¼ to ⅓ pound per serving.
- The terms on the label can be confusing, but use this explanation for the various types of hams available at your supermarket. Lean ham contains less than 10 grams of fat and 4.5 grams or less of saturated fat. Extra lean ham contains less than 5 grams of fat and less than 2 grams of saturated fat. Hickory wood must have been used in the smoking process for hickory-smoked hams. For honey-cured hams, honey is at least half of or the only sweetening ingredient used in the curing process. For sugar-cured products, cane or beet sugar is at least half of the sweetening ingredient used in the curing process. Just like the honey-cured ham, the amount of sweetening ingredient used must be sufficient to affect the flavor or appearance of the ham.
- Country hams, considered southern comfort food, are a bit saltier. If you have never tasted one of these southern hams and would like more information, visit www.countryham.org.

✦ Day 1—Old Tradition: Baked Ham with Fruit ✦

Spring has sprung, and ham is on the menu in many homes. Buy one a bit bigger than you need for the holiday dinner so you can have enough leftovers for a week's worth of meals.

Dish up: 10 to 12 servings
Construction time: 10 minutes

Cooking time: See package directions
Paraphernalia: Large roasting pan, toothpicks, basting brush

INGREDIENTS:

1 12- to 14-pound ham 🛒 (This one ham will be the foundation for your upcoming meals.)

1 cup orange juice

1 cup brown sugar

¼ cup maple syrup

2 teaspoons dry mustard

15 to 18 whole cloves

3 tablespoons pineapple juice

Pineapple slices

To make:

1. Preheat oven to 350 degrees.
2. Place ham in roasting pan and place in oven.
3. Bake ham for half of the baking time. (Check package directions for length of baking time.) Baste with orange juice occasionally. Do not baste with the ham's own cooking juices because they are too salty.
4. While ham is cooking, combine brown sugar, maple syrup, mustard and pineapple juice to make a glaze.
5. Remove ham from oven. Score with knife. (Run knife across the ham in a crisscross formation.) Add cloves to ham where the crisscrosses meets. Place pineapples slices on ham with toothpicks.
6. Baste every 15 minutes until ham has finished baking. Remove from oven, and let stand for 15 minutes before carving.
7. Carve enough ham for tonight's meal, and set aside the remaining ham. Follow the Double It suggestions below to prepare for your upcoming menus.

Jazz It Up: Add 1 teaspoon dry mustard and 1 cup brown sugar to the orange juice for a more flavorful basting sauce.

We Go Good Together: Barb's Golden Potatoes 🌐+🥔

Double It:

- Slice 4 pieces of ham for Day 4, Ham Skillet Dish, and 6 pieces for Day 7, Green Eggs and Ham, and freeze them. Be sure to label the packages.

- Dice the remaining pieces of ham.
- Freeze these amounts in containers or freezer bags: 1 1/2 cups for Day 3, Ham and Rice, 1 1/2 cups for Day 5, Ham-a-dillas, and 1 1/2 cups for Day 6, Cheesy Ham and Noodle Bake.
- Store 2 cups in the refrigerator for Day 2, Potato Hamcakes.

By dicing and slicing now, you'll save a lot of time later.

POTFUL OF KNOWLEDGE: USDA Recommendation

The USDA recommends precooked ham reach an internal temperature of 140 degrees to minimize the risk of contracting trichinosis. Trichinosis causes intestinal disorders, fever, nausea, muscular pain and edema (excessive accumulation of fluid) of the face. Be sure to cook your ham long enough to keep from sending your family off to the hospital.

BASKETFUL OF TIPS: Heirloom Arrangements

Even though you are a frantic woman, you might want to dress up your holiday table. You do not have to look any further than your family heirloom (teapot, vase or decanter) that you can pair with fresh flowers for a special touch. Floral designer Connie Lovus suggests filling the heirloom with traditional flowers (roses, peonies, sweet peas). "Our ancestors depended on their own seasonal gardens for their arrangements," says Connie. "This is a heartwarming custom to resume. The heirloom arrangement brings back special memories for all."

❧ Day 2—Everyday Dinner: Potato Hamcakes ❧

Here's another way to take advantage of leftover ham. This is a spin-off of an old recipe, potato pancakes, which has been floating around for years. Though I'm sure our grandmothers would have used real mashed potatoes, cook up this recipe using instant potatoes to make your life less stressful.

Dish up: 4 to 6 servings
Construction time: 10 minutes, plus 20 minutes chilling time

Cooking time: 10 minutes
Paraphernalia: 3-quart pot, 12-inch skillet, medium bowl, wide spatula

INGREDIENTS:

2 cups instant mashed potatoes

¼ cup green onion, finely chopped

2 cups ham, finely diced, stored from Day 1

½ cup cheddar cheese, shredded

1 teaspoon vegetable oil

To make:

1. Make potatoes according to package directions. Peel and chop onions.
2. Combine potatoes, ham, cheese and onions in a medium bowl to make dough.
3. Refrigerate for 20 minutes. (Simplify it: Chilling the mixture makes it easier to handle.)
4. Remove dough from refrigerator, and form 8 patties.
5. Heat 1 teaspoon of oil in skillet. Cook patties over medium heat for about 5 minutes on each side, or until golden.

Jazz It Up: Serve with sour cream or applesauce.

Dress It Down: Skip the onions.

We Go Good Together: Arla's Asparagus

Look Ahead: Pull out the ham marked for Day 3, Ham and Rice, from the freezer and put it in the refrigerator.

✦ Day 3—I Can with a Can: Ham and Rice ✦

Here's another simple recipe that can be whipped together with ease by pairing up prepackaged goods with leftover ham. Of course, you can add plenty of pizzazz to the dish by tossing in the family's faves. If you're not sure what to add, see the tips below.

Dish up: 4 to 6 servings   Cooking time: 10 minutes

Construction time: 10 minutes   Paraphernalia: 3-quart pot, microwave-safe casserole dish, microwave

INGREDIENTS:

2 instant rice boil-in-bags, white or brown (4 servings)

1½ cups ham, diced, stored from Day 1

1 10.75-ounce can cream of mushroom soup

½ soup can milk

1 4-ounce can mushrooms, sliced

½ cup cheddar french-fried onion rings

To make:

1. Make rice according to package directions.

2. Dump rice, ham, soup, milk, mushrooms and onion rings in microwave-safe baking dish and mix together.

3. Microwave for about 8 to 10 minutes.

Jazz It Up: Add sliced black olives, roasted peppers or another desired vegetable.

Dress It Down: Skip the onion rings.

Change It Up: Bake in oven at 350 degrees for 20 minutes for non-zappers.

We Go Good Together: Fruit salad made with bananas, pineapples and tangelos

Look Ahead: Pull out the 4 slices of ham that are marked for Day 4, Skillet Dish, from the freezer and put them in the refrigerator to thaw.

Day 4—Everyday Dinner: Skillet Dish ✦

You'll have another uncomplicated dinner to make by using a package of premade pierogies. Without much time or thought, you can customize this skillet meal to your family's liking.

Dish up: 4 to 5 servings   Cooking time: 7 minutes
Construction time: 10 minutes   Paraphernalia: 3-quart pot, 12-inch skillet

INGREDIENTS:

1 box pierogies

1 green pepper, sliced 🧊 (Dice an additional green pepper for Day 5, Ham-a-dillas.)

1 small yellow onion, sliced
4 slices ham, cut into 1-inch strips, stored from Day 1
3 tablespoons butter

To make:
1. Boil pierogies according to package directions.
2. Wash pepper. Slice onion and pepper and cut ham into strips.
3. Melt butter in skillet. Sauté onions, peppers and ham. Add pierogies. Pan fry for 3 to 4 minutes, or until heated through.

Jazz It Up: Add sliced almonds.
Dress It Down: Skip the onions and peppers.
We Go Good Together: Applesauce
Double it: Pull out the other green pepper and dice it for Day 5, Ham-a-dillas.
Look Ahead: Take out the ham and Monterey Jack cheese marked for Day 5, Ham-a-dillas and put thems in the refrigerator to defrost.

➤ Day 5—Everyday Dinner: Ham-a-dillas ◄

Offer your gang a favorite restaurant menu item easily with these Ham-a-dillas. You can have dinner ready within 10 minutes which should sound wonderful to the frantic woman's ears after a hectic day of trying to accomplish everything on the to-do list.

Dish up: 4 to 6 servings
Construction time: 5 minutes

Cooking time: 5 minutes
Paraphernalia: Microwave-safe plate, microwave, skillet

INGREDIENTS:
1 cup tomatoes, diced
1 green pepper, diced and stored from Day 4
1 cup Monterey Jack cheese, shredded
1½ cups ham, diced and stored from Day 1
6 flour or whole-wheat tortillas
Lettuce
Salsa
Sour cream

To make:

1. Wash and dice tomato. Dice green pepper if you did not do so on Day 4.
2. Coat skillet with nonstick cooking spray. Sauté peppers in skillet over medium heat.
3. Sprinkle cheese, ham, peppers and tomatoes on half of each tortilla.
4. Fold the tortilla over so the ends meet.
5. Place on a microwave-safe plate and microwave on high for 35 to 45 seconds, or until cheese is melted. Repeat with remaining filled tortillas.
6. Serve with lettuce, salsa and sour cream.

Jazz It Up: Add slices of hot peppers for those who like the burn.

Dress It Down: Skip the tomatoes and peppers.

Change It Up: Cook in a 350-degree oven for about 5 minutes, or until cheese has melted.

We Go Good Together: Barb's One, Two, Three coleslaw 🌐➕🍴

Look Ahead: Take out the container of ham and the cheddar cheese marked Day 7, Green Eggs and Ham, from the freezer. Put them in the refrigerator to thaw.

❧ Day 6—Everyday Dinner: ❧
Cheesy Ham and Noodle Bake

Working full-time at her day job and starting her new Web site, Movieloversclubhouse.com, causes the dinner hour to be crunch time for Linda Tomsho, mother of three teenagers. Making a baked ham on Sunday and stretching it into a week's worth of meals offers Linda the extra time she needs to concentrate on her site.

Dish up: 5 to 6 servings
Construction time: 10 minutes

Cooking time: 25 to 30 minutes
Paraphernalia: 3-quart pot, 2-quart baking dish, strainer

INGREDIENTS:

1 16-ounce package pasta shapes (rotini, shells)

1 1/2 cups ham, cubed, stored from Day 1

1 10.75-ounce can low-fat, low-sodium cream of mushroom soup

2/3 cup milk

1/2 cup cheddar cheese, shredded

To make:
1. Preheat oven to 375 degrees.
2. Cook pasta according to package directions. Cube ham, if not already done.
3. Mix soup and milk in a 2-quart baking dish. Add ham, cheese and pasta. Mix together.
4. Bake for 25 to 30 minutes. Check after 20 minutes.

Jazz It Up: Add 1 cup cooked peas, broccoli or zucchini before baking.
Dress It Down: Replace pasta with noodles.
We Go Good Together: Tossed salad

⇸ Day 7—Kids' Meal/Backwards Meal: ⇷
Green Eggs and Ham

This meal is sure to raise eyebrows at the table. Tell everyone that the Cat in the Hat shared the recipe with you. Only you will know it came from the frantic woman. Shhh! It's our secret.

Dish up: 4 to 6 servings   Cooking time: 10 minutes
Construction time: 5 to 7 minutes Paraphernalia: Medium-size bowl,
                                    2 12-inch skillets, microwave

INGREDIENTS:

1/2 cup fresh or frozen spinach, chopped

6 eggs

3 tablespoons milk

6 slices ham, stored from Day 1

To make:

1. Wash and dry fresh spinach. Chop into very small pieces. (For frozen spinach, cook according to package directions.)
2. Coat skillets with nonstick cooking spray. Heat ham in one skillet over medium heat.
3. Sauté spinach in other skillet over medium heat for 5 minutes, or until wilted.
4. Crack eggs into bowl. Add milk to eggs and beat together.
5. Add beaten eggs to skillet with spinach. Scramble for about 5 to 6 minutes, or until cooked through.
6. Serve hot with ham slices on the side.

Dress It Down: Eliminate the spinach, and add a few drops of green food coloring instead.

We Go Good Together: Toast with jelly and chocolate milk

FRANTIC WOMAN FAMILY FUN:
The Real Green Eggs and Ham

Green Eggs and Ham by Dr. Seuss is a childhood favorite for most kids, including mine. The outlandish story brings a smile to the face of youngsters. Though adults might have a different take on it, read it through the eyes of a child.

AND YOU'RE STAYING *HOW* LONG? COLDER CLIMATE WEEK

The colder weather welcomes Jack Frost, winter holidays and New Year's Eve. Many times, it also welcomes overnight guests. So, how do you keep your guests comfortable during one of the craziest times of the year? Start by offering great meals that will warm their tummies, and finish with conversation and friendship that will touch their hearts. Psst! These recipes will serve generous helpings for 8 to 10 people.

AND YOU'RE STAYING *HOW* LONG? COLDER CLIMATE MENUS

Day 1—Slow Cook Tonight: Turkey in a Pot
Day 2—Everyday Dinner: Diane's Kielbasa Dish
Day 3—Old Tradition: Noodle Stroganoff
Day 4—Everyday Dinner: Rice Krispies Baked Chicken
Day 5—Must-Go: Turkey Fajitas
Day 6—Slow Cook Tonight: Stuffed Pepper Soup
Day 7—Backwards Meal: Ham & Cheese Strata

THE SHOPPING LISTS

The Frantic Woman's Cupboard

AND YOU'RE STAYING HOW LONG? COLDER CLIMATE STAPLES

Seasonings

Basil
Beef bouillon cubes
Garlic (powder)
Parsley
Pepper (black, lemon)
Salt

Jazz It Ups
Garlic (powder)
Crushed red pepper

Dressings, Oil and Sauces
Vinegar

Baking Needs
Flour (all-purpose)
Sugar (brown)

Bread, Chips and More
Bread

Frantic Necessities
Nonstick Cooking Spray
Foil

Dairy
Butter
Eggs
Milk

The Frantic Woman Goes Shopping

MAIN-DISH INGREDIENTS YOU'LL NEED TO BUY

Produce: Veggies
1 bunch celery (Day 1)
4 medium red onions (Days 1, 3, 5)
1 head garlic (Day 3)
5 green peppers (Days 5, 6)

Seasonings
1 1.25-ounce package fajita seasoning (Day 5)

Dressings, Oils and Sauces

1 16-ounce jar salsa (Day 5)

Canned Goods and Bottles

1 15-ounce can chicken broth (Day 1)

2 46-ounce cans sauerkraut (Day 2)

2 6-ounce cans tomato paste (Day 3)

2 10-ounce cans beef consommé (Day 3)

1 26-ounce can tomato sauce (Day 6)

1 26-ounce can crushed tomatoes (Day 6)

Noodles, Pasta and Rice

1 16-ounce bag wide egg noodles (Day 3)

1 15-ounce box boil-in-bag instant rice (Day 6)

Cereal, Nuts and Such

1 10-ounce box Rice Krispies (Day 4)

Bread, Chips and More

10 whole-wheat tortillas, or your preference (Day 5)

Deli

1½ to 2 pounds ham (Day 7)

Fish, Meat and Poultry

1 5- to 6-pound turkey breast (Day 1)

2 pounds ring kielbasa (Day 2)

4 pounds lean ground beef (Days 3, 6)

12 skinless, boneless split chicken breasts, about 3 pounds (Day 4)

Dairy

1 12-ounce container sour cream (Days 3, 5)

Spray butter (Day 7)

1½ cups (6 ounces) cheddar cheese, shredded (Day 7)

Jazz It Up Ingredients You'll Need to Buy

Produce: Fruit
2 Jonathan apples (Day 2)

Produce: Veggies
1 8-ounce carton snowcap mushrooms (Day 3)
1 hot pepper (Day 5)
1 small head broccoli (Day 7)
1 small yellow onion (Day 7)

Dairy
1 12-ounce container guacamole (Day 5)

Seasonings
1 envelope dry onion soup mix (Day 1)

We Go Good Together Ingredients You'll Need to Buy

Produce: Fruit
Fruit, your preference (Day 7)

Produce: Veggies
4 to 5 baking potatoes (Day 1)
2 cucumbers (Days 2, 5)
2 tomatoes (Days 2. 5)
1 6-ounce bag radishes (Days 2, 5)
2 16-ounce packages ready-to-eat salad mix (Days 2, 5)
1 small head broccoli (Day 3)
1 12-ounce bag baby cut carrots (Day 3)

Canned Goods and Bottles
1 10.75-ounce can turkey or chicken gravy (Day 1)
1 bottle salad dressing, your preference (Days 2, 5)

Bread, Chips and More
Muffins and/or rolls, your preference (Day 6)

Frozen
1 32-ounce bag french fries (Day 4)

Unloading the Load

- As you unload the groceries, store the kielbasa for Day 2, Diane's Kielbasa Dish, in the fridge.
- Tuck the chicken breasts for Day 4, Rice Krispies Baked Chicken, in the freezer.
- Put the ground beef for Day 3, Noodles Stroganoff, and Day 6, Stuffed Pepper Soup, in the freezer. You can put this in one package, as you will cook all of it on Day 3.
- Dice the ham for Day 7, Ham & Cheese Strata, wrap it, and put it in the freezer.
- Tuck the tortillas for Day 5, Turkey Fajitas, in there, too.
- Be sure to stow your green peppers in the crisper to keep them fresh until you need them.
- Freeze the muffins and/or rolls you bought for Day 6, We Go Good Together.

AND YOU'RE STAYING *HOW* LONG? COLDER CLIMATE MENUS

✦ Day 1—Slow Cook Tonight: Turkey in a Pot ✦

This meal satisfies those with large appetites as well as those watching their calories. It also satisfies your need for a stress-free meal. Besides the fact that this recipe feeds a bunch, you won't have to worry if your overnight guests are an hour or so late.

Dish up: 8 to 10 servings   Cooking time: 8 to 10 hours
Construction time: 5 to 10 minutes   Paraphernalia: Slow cooker, paper towels

INGREDIENTS:

1 medium red onion, chopped

1 celery rib, chopped

1 5- to 6-pound turkey breast, thawed 🥫 (Part of the turkey will be used for Day 5, Turkey Fajitas.)

¼ cup butter, melted

1 teaspoon lemon pepper

1½ cups chicken broth

Salt and pepper, to taste

To make:

1. Coat slow-cooker liner with nonstick cooking spray.
2. Peel and chop onions. Wash and chop celery.
3. Wash turkey breast. Pat dry with paper towels. Place celery and onion inside turkey cavity. Place turkey in cooker.
4. Melt butter in the microwave. Pour butter over turkey.
5. Sprinkle with seasoning. Pour broth around turkey.
6. Cover and cook on low for 8 to 10 hours or on high for 6 hours. Remove turkey from cooker, and let it rest for 10 to 15 minutes before carving.
7. Carve enough for tonight's dinner, then wrap the leftovers for Day 5, Turkey Fajitas.

Jazz It Up: Add 1 envelope of dry onion soup mix.

Dress It Down: Skip the seasoning.

Change It Up: You can cook the turkey in the oven instead of the slow cooker. Follow the directions on the package.

Double It: Wrap the leftover turkey immediately after it cools, and store it in the freezer for Day 5.

We Go Good Together: Baked potatoes and gravy

Look Ahead: Pull out the ingredients for tomorrow's meal, and don't feel shy about asking your houseguest to help you slice the kielbasa. Toss everything together tonight, and tomorrow all you'll need to do is put it in the oven to cook.

BASKETFUL OF TIPS: Pay Back Invitations

Plan an informal gathering at the same time Aunt Mildred comes knocking at your door. Invite the relatives to see the out-of-towner. A buffet lunch or dinner will pay back any invitations you might owe. With your clean house, this is the perfect opportunity to knock off two must-dos.

FRANTIC WOMAN FAMILY FUN: Kids' Basket of Fun

Keep a large basket filled with favorite DVDs, art supplies (stencils, colored pencils, sketch pads and so forth), handheld games, miniature cars and dolls in your main living area. Not only will this keep the younger guests from getting restless, but it will save you from pulling out toys and putting them back away, again.

❧ *Day 2—Everyday Dinner: Diane's Kielbasa Dish* ❧

Beauty consultant Diane Disk shared this recipe with me a few years ago at one of our Women's Business Network meetings. There we sat at 8:30 in the morning, stomachs growling, as she passed out instructions. This is a slow-cook dish that can be prepared ahead of time. So, if you work during the day, have it ready to go the night before. Then, all you have to do is ask one of the guests to pop the pan in oven at the designated time, and it will be ready to serve when you walk in the door.

Dish up: 8 to 10 servings   Cooking time: 2 hours
Construction time: 7 minutes   Paraphernalia: Large baking dish

INGREDIENTS:

2 46-ounce cans sauerkraut
2/3 cup brown sugar
2 pounds ring kielbasa, cut up

To make:

1. Preheat oven to 250 degrees.
2. Place sauerkraut in bottom of baking dish.
3. Sprinkle brown sugar over sauerkraut.
4. Cut kielbasa into bite-size pieces, and arrange on top of sauer-kraut/sugar mixture.
5. Bake for 2 hours. Be sure to turn kielbasa halfway through the cooking time.
6. Serve hot.

Jazz It Up: Add apple slices.

We Go Good Together: Tossed salad

Look Ahead: Take ground beef from freezer and put it in the refrigerator for Day 3, Noodle Stroganoff, and Day 6, Stuffed Pepper Soup. You'll be cooking all of it.

BASKETFUL OF TIPS: Indoor Campout

If you have more guests than beds, create a campout atmosphere in one area of the house for all the kids to have a sleepover.

- This spot can be the never-used living room (stash the breakables), the largest bedroom or a great room.
- Borrow sleeping bags for each one of the kids if you do not have enough to go around.
- Be sure to borrow the sleeping bags ahead of time, and tuck them away until the day guests arrive. Sleeping bags are much easier to roll out and roll back up than a bunch of sheets, blankets and comforters.

✦ Day 3—Old Tradition: Noodles Stroganoff ✦

This recipe will have your guests thinking you've slaved over a sizzling stove all day. Andrea Verona likes to cook up Noodles Stroganoff when her sister visits from out of state.

Dish up: 8 to 10 servings   Cooking time: 10 minutes
Construction time: 15 minutes   Paraphernalia: Dutch oven, 12-inch skillet

INGREDIENTS:

1 cup onion, chopped

2 garlic cloves, crushed

4 tablespoons butter

2 pounds lean ground beef 🍲 (2 additional pounds for Day 6, Stuffed
   Pepper Soup)

1 16-ounce bag wide egg noodles

4 tablespoons flour

$\frac{1}{2}$ teaspoon pepper

2 10-ounce cans beef consommé

2 tablespoons vinegar

2 6-ounce cans tomato paste

2 cups sour cream

4 teaspoons parsley

To make:

1. Peel and chop onion and crush garlic.
2. Melt butter in Dutch oven over medium heat.
3. Add onion and garlic and cook over medium heat for about 5 minutes.
4. Add 2 pounds of ground beef and cook for about 7 to 10 minutes, or until browned.
5. Cook the additional 2 pounds of ground beef in a skillet for Day 6, Stuffed Pepper Soup. Once cooked, cool and store in the freezer. Be sure to label the package.
6. Make noodles according to package directions.
7. Sprinkle flour and pepper over meat.
8. Stir in consommé, vinegar and tomato paste.
9. Simmer, uncovered, for about 10 minutes, stirring occasionally.
10. Remove from heat. Stir in sour cream. Heat through. Sprinkle parsley over meat mixture.
11. Serve Stroganoff over noodles.

Jazz It Up: Add fresh or canned sliced mushrooms.

Dress It Down: Use dried herbs in place of fresh. Use 2 teaspoons minced garlic and 2 teaspoons parsley flakes.

Double it: Cook 2 additional pounds ground beef for Day 6, Stuffed Pepper Soup. Freeze it until Day 5.

We Go Good Together: Broccoli and carrots

Look Ahead: Take the chicken out of the freezer and put it in the refrigerator to thaw for Day 5, Rice Krispies Baked Chicken.

TiPS BASKETFUL OF TIPS: Gab-Session Snack

When friends are visiting, you can easily stay up until way passed midnight gabbing, and the hungries might attack even though you made a hearty meal. Make a batch of homemade salsa to serve with tortilla chips to satisfy the munchies. Don't fret, it's easy. This is Karla Strite's tradition when her sister Lori and family come to visit her. Dice 2 medium onions, 2 hot peppers and 1 green pepper. In a bowl, combine peppers and onions with 2 large cans diced tomatoes, 3 garlic cloves, 1 teaspoon salt, 1 teaspoon chili powder, 1 teaspoon cumin, 1 tablespoon sugar and 1 tablespoon vinegar. Mix well. Enjoy!

⇒ Day 4—Everyday Dinner: ⇐
Rice Krispies Baked Chicken

Overnight guests are frequent in Ann Stankiewicz's house. Whether it is a relative from out-of-town or grandsons who live just minutes away, there's always someone staying at Ann's. This is a perfect dish to prepare for out of town guests; you can put it together in 10 minutes and forget about it for an hour or so while you chat with your company.

Dish up: 8 to 10 servings
Construction time: 10 minutes

Cooking time: 1 hour
Paraphernalia: Baking sheet, 1-quart saucepan, plastic zippered bag

INGREDIENTS:

6 tablespoons butter, melted
3 cups Rice Krispies cereal, crushed
12 skinless, boneless split chicken breasts (about 3 pounds)
Salt and pepper, to taste

To make:

1. Preheat oven to 375 degrees. Line baking sheet with foil.
2. Melt butter in saucepan.
3. Put cereal in a plastic zippered bag and seal closed. Crush with a rolling pin.
4. Dip chicken in melted butter, then put into bag. Seal closed and shake well to coat chicken. (Simplify it: Put in several pieces of chicken at a time.)
5. Place coated chicken on baking sheet. Add salt and pepper, to taste.
6. Using a fork, lightly drizzle some of the melted butter over chicken.
7. Bake for 1 hour. (Simplify it: There's no need to turn the pieces during baking.)

Change It Up: You can substitute any variety of chicken parts (i.e., wings, thighs, drumsticks) you want, suggests Ann.

We Go Good Together: French fries

Look Ahead: Pull the turkey marked Day 5, Turkey Fajitas, and the tortillas out of the freezer, and put them in the refrigerator to thaw. Be sure to mark the packages so no one eats their contents.

BASKETFUL OF TIPS: Quick Sorbet

For a quick and inexpensive dessert, make your own sorbet. Freeze a large can of peaches packed in light syrup. When frozen, open the can and scoop out the peaches with a spoon, and put them into the blender. Blend the mixture for 1 to 2 minutes, and before you know it, you've got sorbet. You can make sorbet with any other canned fruit or frozen strawberries.

✦ Day 5—Must-Go: Turkey Fajitas ✦

Today, you will prepare your turkey leftovers as a favorite item listed on many restaurants' menus. At any restaurant, dinner patrons would fix their own fajitas. At your house, your guests will do the same, making this an uncomplicated meal to serve.

Dish up: 8 to 10 servings
Construction time: 5 minutes
Cooking time: 10 to 15 minutes
Paraphernalia: 12-inch skillet, baking sheet

INGREDIENTS:

2 small onions, chopped

4 green peppers, chopped 🍵 (1 additional green pepper for Day 6,
    Stuffed Pepper Soup)

Turkey, stored from Day 1

10 whole-wheat tortillas

2 teaspoons from fajita seasoning packet

Salsa

Sour cream

To make:

1. Preheat oven to 250 degrees.
2. Peel and chop onions.
3. Wash and chop peppers. Chop 1 additional pepper and store it in the refrigerator for Day 6, Stuffed Pepper Soup.
4. Cut turkey into smaller strips.
5. Put tortillas on a baking sheet and put them in the oven to warm.
6. Coat skillet with nonstick cooking spray. Sauté onions and peppers for about 3 to 4 minutes over medium heat.
7. Add turkey and seasoning to skillet. Stir-fry for about 5 to 7 minutes, or until heated through.
8. Put warmed turkey mixture into a bowl and cover with foil to keep warm. Pull warmed tortillas from oven and put in a shallow serving dish. Cover with lid or foil.
9. Serve turkey mixture with warmed tortillas, salsa and sour cream. Allow everyone to build his or her own fajita.

Jazz It Up: Add more pizzazz to the mixture by adding 1/4 teaspoon garlic powder or crushed red pepper. Serve with guacamole and/or hot peppers on the side.

Dress It Down: Skip the seasoning.

We Go Good Together: Tossed salad

Double It: Finely chop 1 additional green pepper for Day 6, Stuffed Pepper Soup. Wrap it and store it in the refrigerator.

Look Ahead: Pull the cooked ground beef out of the freezer for Day 6, Stuffed Pepper Soup. If you have a removable crock liner, prepare tomorrow's meal tonight, before you start the dinner dishes. (You can add the meat, as it

has already been cooked and won't contaminate the other foods.) Put it in the refrigerator overnight. Tomorrow, all you'll need to do is pop the crock liner into the slow cooker and plug it in. (Simplify it: You can crumble the frozen cooked beef into the other ingredients. It will thaw overnight.) Pull outthe muffins and rolls if you are following the We Go Good Together suggestion.

POTFUL OF KNOWLEDGE:
Company's Good for Your Health

The next time a relative calls to say she's coming to stay, don't grumble. In fact, rejoice. Recent research has linked social isolation with increased stress and greater risk of health complications, ranging from the common cold to heart disease and even some cancers. So, bring on the houseguests, and appreciate the benefits of socialization.

❧ Day 6—Slow Cook Tonight: Stuffed Pepper Soup ❧

"All about easy" is Dawn Check's motto. Dawn holds down two jobs, one as the public relations director for her local school district and the other as a church pastor. On top of that busy schedule, she is raising three children, two with special needs. Dawn describes herself as a cooking fool, and here's one of her favorite recipes.

Dish up: 8 to 10 servings, plus leftovers   Cooking time: 4 to 10 hours
Construction time: 15 minutes before   Paraphernalia: Slow cooker
    and 10 minutes later

INGREDIENTS:
2 pounds ground beef, stored from Day 3
2 cups rice, cooked
1 green pepper, chopped finely, stored from Day 5
1 26-ounce can tomato sauce
1 26-ounce can crushed tomatoes
2 beef bouillon cubes
1 teaspoon garlic powder
1 teaspoon basil
Salt and pepper, to taste

To make:

1. Brown ground beef in a skillet over medium heat if you have not already done so.
2. Cook rice according to package directions.
3. Finely chop the green pepper if you have not already done so.
4. Combine all of the ingredients in the slow cooker, and allow mixture to cook on low for at least 4 hours. However, you can leave it all day.
5. When it's done, the mixture will bes quite thick. Take 3 or 4 large spoonfuls of soup out, and put them into a pan on the stove. Add some water. Dawn starts with 2 cups. Taste to see if you need a dash of salt and/or pepper. Cook over medium heat, stirring often until it is heated through, about 5 to 7 minutes.
6. Add this thinned-out soup to the thick crock mixture, stirring until mixture is smooth and turns to soup.

We Go Good Together: An assortment of muffins and rolls

Look Ahead: Prepare Day 7, Ham & Cheese Strata, tonight, and put it in the refrigerator. Then tomorrow, all you'll need is 30 minutes to bake it in the oven.

✦ Day 7—Backwards Meal: Ham & Cheese Strata ✦

Cooking for company is a cinch for Laurie Rizzo, who has her own home-based desktop publishing company and is the mother of two young children. She figures if she can please her husband, a director of dietary, she can please anyone. The best part of this dish is you can be as creative as you wish with it.

Dish up: 8 to 10 servings
Construction time: 10 minutes
   plus overnight chilling time

Cooking time: 30 minutes
Paraphernalia: 9- by 13-inch baking
   dish, small bowl

INGREDIENTS:

6 slices bread, your preference

Spray butter

3 to 4 cups baked ham, diced (about 1 1/2 pounds deli ham)

1 1/2 cups cheddar cheese, shredded

6 eggs

2 cups milk

1/2 teaspoon salt

To prep the night before:

1. Coat baking dish with nonstick cooking spray.
2. Place bread in the dish.
3. Spray bread with butter.
4. Dice ham if you have not done so already. Sprinkle ham over bread.

Sprinkle cheese over ham.

Beat eggs, milk and salt together. Pour egg mixture into baking dish.

Cover and chill overnight.

To bake:

1. Preheat oven to 350 degrees.
2. Take baking dish from refrigerator and bake for 30 minutes.
3. Cut into squares and serve.

Jazz It Up: Add 2 cups cooked broccoli and/or 1/2 cup diced onions.

Dress It Down: Skip the ham and add cooked spinach to make it a meatless meal.

Change It Up: Change the ham to bacon or sausage.

We Go Good Together: Sliced seasonal fruit

AND YOU'RE STAYING *HOW* LONG? WARMER CLIMATE WEEK

Air travel and car trips seem to occur more often in the warmer weather, and your house might be the destination for relatives and friends when they're deciding where to spend their next week off. Don't panic. Here's a week's worth of menus that will serve 8 to 10 people that focus on simple, lighter fare that cooks up just right for this time of the year.

And You're Staying *How* Long?
Warmer Climate Menus

Day 1—Sandwich Board: Baked Sandwiches
Day 2—Soup's On: Sue's Ault-i-mate Easy Veggie Soup
Day 3—No-cook Night: Tuna Salsa Wraps
Day 4—Everyday Dinner: Honey Nut Chicken
Day 5—Everyday Dinner: Pasta Mix-Up
Day 6—Seafood Fest: Seafood Bake
Day 7—Kids' Meal: Pizza with a Zip

THE SHOPPING LISTS

The Frantic Woman's Cupboard

AND YOU'RE STAYING HOW LONG? WARMER CLIMATE STAPLES

Seasonings
Beef bouillon cubes
Chives
Garlic (powder)
Salt

Condiments
Mustard (prepared)

Dressings, Oil and Sauces
Mayonnaise
Light mayonnaise
Oil (olive, vegetable)

Side Dishes
Italian salad dressing

Baking Needs
Flour (all-purpose)
Sugar (cane)

Bread, Chips and More
Bread crumbs (Italian seasoned)

Frantic Necessities
Nonstick cooking spray
Foil

Dairy
Eggs
Milk

The Frantic Woman Goes Shopping

MAIN-DISH INGREDIENTS YOU'LL NEED TO BUY

Produce: Veggies
2 small onions (Days 1, 2)
1 medium onion (Day 7)
1 10-ounce bag carrots, shredded/matchstick (Day 3)
1 head lettuce (Day 3)
1 green pepper (Day 7)

Dressings, Oils and Sauces

1 12-ounce jar chili sauce (Day 1)

1 16-ounce mild jar salsa (Days 3, 7)

2 32-ounce jars spaghetti sauce (Day 5)

1 8-ounce jar pizza sauce (Day 7)

Canned Goods and Bottles

2 64-ounce cans tomato juice (Day 2)

2 7-ounce pouches chunk light or albacore tuna (Day 3)

2 12-ounce jars marinated artichoke hearts (Day 6)

Noodles, Pasta and Rice

1 16-ounce package mostaccioli (pasta) (Day 5)

Cereal, Nuts and Such

6 ounces nuts (Day 4)

Bread, Chips and More

12 hamburger buns (Day 1)

12 whole-wheat tortillas, or your preference (Day 3)

Deli

2 pounds chipped ham (Day 1)

12 slices cheddar cheese (Day 1)

1 cup (4 ounces) Parmesan cheese, grated (Days 5, 6)

½ cup (2 ounces) Romano cheese, grated (Day 7)

Fish, Meat and Poultry

3 pounds lean ground beef (Days 2, 5)

10 skinless, boneless chicken breasts (Day 4)

1 pound fresh or frozen shrimp, peeled and deveined (Day 6)

1 pound fresh or frozen sea scallops (Day 6)

Dairy

½ cup (2 ounces) cheddar cheese, shredded (Day 3)

6 cups (24 ounces) mozzarella cheese, shredded (Days 5, 6, 7)

2 10-ounce tubes refrigerated pizza crusts (Day 7)

Frozen

4 16-ounce packages frozen mixed soup vegetables (Day 2)

Jazz It Up Ingredients You'll Need to Buy

Produce: Veggies

2 red potatoes (Day 2)

1 bunch green onions, or your topping preference (Day 3)

1 8-ounce carton snowcap mushrooms (Day 5)

1 zucchini (Day 5)

Seasoning

McCormick Grill Mates Barbecue Seasoning (Day 4)

Canned Goods and Bottles

1 2.5-ounce can black olives (Day 5)

Deli

¼ pound sliced pepperoni (Day 7)

Fish, Meat and Poultry

1 pound bulk sausage (Day 7)

We Go Good Together Ingredients You'll Need to Buy

Produce: Fruit

Fruit, your preference (Day 7)

Produce: Veggies

Veggies, your preference (Day 3)

3 cucumbers (Day 4)

3 tomatoes (Day 4)

1 16-ounce package ready-to-eat Caesar salad (Day 5)

Deli

2 pounds pasta salad (or make your own) (Day 1)

Bread, Chips and More

Breadsticks, muffins, and/or rolls, your preference (Day 2)

Frozen

1 loaf garlic bread (Day 6)

Frozen yogurt, your preference (Day 7)

Unloading the Load

- Unloading the bags will be easier than ever. The ground beef you can store in the refrigerator for Day 2, Sue's Ault-i-mate Easy Veggie Soup, and Day 5, Pasta Mix-Up.
- Freeze the chicken breasts for Day 4, Honey Nut Chicken.
- Freeze half of the Parmesan cheese for Day 5, Pasta Mix-Up and the other half for Day 7, Pizza with a Zip.
- Freeze the mozzarella into these portions: 3 cups for Day 5, Pasta Mix-Up, 1 cups for Day 7, Pizza with a Zip, 13 cup for Day 6, Seafood Bake.
- Freeze the Romano for Day 7, Seafood Bake.
- Freeze the pepperoni and/or sausage for Day 7, Jazz It Up.
- If your family loves bread products, store the breadstick, muffins and rolls for Day 2, We Go Good Together, out of their reach.
- Mark everything with the designated day and menu. With extra people in the house, you want to eliminate any stress you can.

AND YOU'RE STAYING *HOW* LONG? MENUS

⇢ Day 1—Sandwich Board: Baked Sandwiches ⇠

This one recipe cooks up a batch of 12 sandwiches, making it perfect for company and friends. You can prepare the sammies earlier in the day and pop them in the oven when your guests ring the doorbell. By the time the hellos are exchanged and the car is unpacked, the sandwiches will be ready to hand out. And what the gang doesn't eat tonight, you'll have as leftovers for tomorrow's lunch or to serve with the soup tomorrow night. Of course, you could always freeze a number of the sammies, too. (If you're going to freeze them, eliminate the eggs from the mixture, as eggs don't freeze well.)

Dish up: 12 servings   Cooking time: 20 to 25 minutes
Construction time: 7 to 10 minutes   Paraphernalia: Large bowl, baking sheet

INGREDIENTS:

6 eggs, room temperature

1 small onion, diced

2 pounds chipped ham

1 12-ounce jar chili sauce

3 tablespoons mayonnaise

12 hamburger buns

12 slices cheddar cheese

To make:

1. Pull eggs from the refrigerator. (Don't boil eggs straight from the refrigerator, as putting cold eggs in hot water will crack the egg.)
2. Preheat oven to 350 degrees.
3. Cook eggs in gently simmering water for 7 to 8 minutes to make hard-boiled eggs. If eggs are less than 4 days old, add 30 seconds or so.
4. While eggs are cooking, peel and dice onion.
5. Allow eggs to cool in cold water.
6. Mix all ingredients, except cheese, together.
7. Evenly divide ham mixture between buns. Top with cheese slice. Individually wrap sandwiches in foil. (I have to thank Renee Knight for this little cooking tip. I wasn't one to bake the sandwiches until I had lunch at her house. Now this is common in our house.) Bake for 30 minutes.

Dress It Down: Make ham barbecues by adding bottled barbecue sauce to the deli meat.

We Go Good Together: Pasta salad

Look Ahead: Defrost the bread products for tomorrow's side dish if you froze them.

⇀ Day 2—Soup's On: ≺
Sue's Ault-i-mate Easy Veggie Soup

Sue Ault is on duty 24/7 for two weeks out of the month as a manager of a senior apartment complex. During her two weeks off, she doesn't want to spend extra time in the kitchen. Make this soup ahead of time, so all you'll have to do is heat it up later.

Dish up: 8 to 10 servings

Cooking time: 30 minutes

Construction time: 10 minutes

Paraphernalia: Dutch oven

TiPS BASKETFUL OF TIPS: A Basketful of Breakfast

The early birds can help themselves to munchies, leaving your hands free to do what you need to do.

- Keep a basket in the kitchen filled with granola bars, individually wrapped muffins, breakfast bars, meal-replacement bars and "just-add-water" instant oatmeal packages.
- Single-serving–size juices will leave fewer dishes in your sink, too.
- A pretty basket, rubberized container or compartment tray on the counter filled with small disposable plates, bowls, silverware and napkins will also keep your sink dish-free.
- Keep a container of hand wipes in a designated spot for the quick cleaning of messy hands.

INGREDIENTS:

2 pounds lean ground beef 🥛 (1 additional pound for Day 5, Pasta Mix-Up)

4 cups water

4 beef bouillon cubes

1 small yellow onion, minced

2 64-ounce cans tomato juice

4 16-ounce package frozen mixed soup vegetables

1 teaspoon salt

1 teaspoon sugar

To make:
1. In a Dutch oven, cook meat over medium heat for about 5 to 10 minutes, or until heated through. Drain excess fat.
2. Reserve 1 pound of cooked meat for Day 5, Pasta Mix-Up. Wrap it and store in the freezer.

3. While meat is cooking, boil 4 cups of water. Dissolve beef bouillon in boiling water.

4. Peel and mince onion.

5. Add onion, tomato juice, veggies, beef bouillon broth, salt and sugar to meat. Bring to a boil. Lower heat and simmer for 25 to 30 minutes.

6. Serve hot.

Jazz It Up: Add 1 cup diced potatoes.

Dress It Down: Skip the salt if someone is watching his or her sodium intake.

Double It: Cook 1 additional pound of ground beef for Day 5, Pasta Mix-Up. Store it in the freezer until Day 4.

We Go Good Together: Make an overflowing bread basket with a selection of muffins, rolls and breadsticks.

➥ Day 3—No-Cook Night: Tuna Salsa Wraps ← 🐄

JoAnn Reid concocted this no-cook meal that's easy and delicious. This is just the thing to devour after a hot day sitting in the sun or riding around town, sightseeing. You can make the filling ahead of time and finish putting together the wraps just before mealtime.

Dish up: 12 servings   Cooking time: 0
Construction time: 6 to 8 minutes   Paraphernalia: Medium mixing bowl

INGREDIENTS:

12 whole-wheat tortillas
2 7-ounce pouches chunk light or albacore tuna
1/2 cup light mayonnaise
2 teaspoons mustard
1 cup salsa
1/2 cup carrots, shredded or matchstick
1 cup lettuce, shredded
1/2 cup (2 ounces) cheddar cheese, shredded

To make:

1. Warm tortillas according to package directions.
2. In bowl, combine tuna, mayo, mustard, salsa and carrots, mixing well.
3. Lay tuna mix in the center of each warmed tortilla. Sprinkle an equal portion of shredded lettuce and shredded cheese on top of tuna.
4. Fold the long end of the tortilla up. Then roll tightly from one side to the other.
5. Enjoy!

Jazz It Up: Add other favorite toppings, like green onions.

Dress It Down: Skip whatever ingredients your family or guests will not eat.

Change It Up: Replace mayonnaise with yogurt.

We Go Good Together: Seasonal vegetables marinated in Italian salad dressing.

Look Ahead: Take the chicken breasts out of the freezer and put them in the refrigerator to defrost for Day 4, Honey Nut Chicken.

❧ Day 4—Everyday Dinner: Honey Nut Chicken ❧

Mother of two Deanne Thomas wiggles dinner preparation into her crazy schedule. She works two part-time jobs that seem to dominate most of her waking hours. Honey Nut Chicken is one meal she makes when she wants to give herself a treat. So, treat your guests to Deanne's favorite dish.

Dish up: 8 to 10 servings
Construction time: 7 to 10 minutes

Cooking time: 12 minutes
Paraphernalia: 12-inch skillet, 1 small bowl, 2 medium bowls, baking dish, food processor (or rolling pin and plastic zippered bag)

INGREDIENTS:

3 eggs

3 tablespoons milk

1 1/2 cups favorite nuts, chopped

1 1/2 cups Italian-seasoned bread crumbs

10 skinless, boneless chicken breasts

1 1/2 cups flour

Vegetable oil

To make:

1. Preheat oven to 350 degrees.
2. Coat skillet with nonstick cooking spray.
3. Crack eggs into bowl. Add milk and beat together.
4. Chop nuts in food processor. If you don't have one, put nuts in a plastic zippered bag and crush with a rolling pin.
5. Mix nuts and bread crumbs together.
6. Dip chicken in flour. Dip chicken in egg bath and then in nut mixture.
7. Pour just enough oil in skillet to cover the bottom. Heat oil in skillet over medium heat.
8. Pan-fry chicken 2 minutes on each side. Put fried chicken in baking dish. Repeat with remaining pieces.
9. Bake in oven for 12 minutes, or until juices run clear when chicken is pricked.

Jazz It Up: Add 1 or 2 teaspoons of McCormick Grill Mates Barbecue seasoning to flavor.

Change It Up: Use a portion of whole-wheat flour in place of all-purpose flour.

We Go Good Together: Sliced cucumbers and tomatoes

Look Ahead: Take the cooked ground beef out of the freezer and put it in the refrigerator to thaw for Day 5, Pasta Mix-Up. Don't forget to take the mozzarella and Parmesan out of the freezer, too, if you tucked it in there. And since you're pulling stuff out, pull out the cheeses for Day 6, Seafood Bake.

✦ Day 5—Everyday Dinner: Pasta Mix-Up ✦

All the work in this recipe is done in the early preparation. Once Pasta Mix-Up is mixed in the baking dish, the oven does the rest, allowing you to relax and enjoy your company. If you feel the urge to whip up a side dish or two, go ahead, for you have the time. You can mix in whatever ingredients you want to jazz this up.

Dish up: 8 to 10 servings
Construction time: 10 minutes

Cooking time: 20 minutes
Paraphernalia: Dutch oven, 12-inch skillet, 9- by 13-inch baking dish, strainer

INGREDIENTS:
1 16-ounce package mostaccioli (pasta)
1 pound cooked ground beef, stored from Day 2
2 32-ounce jars spaghetti sauce
½ cup Parmesan cheese
2 cups (8 ounces) mozzarella cheese, shredded

To make:
1. Preheat oven to 375 degrees.
2. Cook pasta according to package directions for al dente.
3. Drain pasta when finished cooking.
4. Combine pasta and beef in baking dish. Add sauce, reserving 1/2 jar of sauce for later. Add Parmesan, mixing well.
5. Sprinkle mozzarella on top.
6. Bake for 20 minutes.

Jazz It Up: Add sliced black olives, mushrooms or zucchini.
Change It Up: Eliminate the beef to make it a meatless meal.
We Go Good Together: Caesar salad

✦ Day 6—Seafood Fest: Seafood Bake ✦ 🦐

This dish is one of my family's favorites. I love it because it is super easy and super quick and tastes like you've gone to a lot of trouble. Get

creative and play around with the ingredients, tweakin(
your family's liking. Psst! This is a knockoff of another (
But don't tell anyone.

Dish up: 8 to 10 servings   Cooking time: 15 minutes
Construction time: 5 minutes   Paraphernalia: 9- by 13-inch baking dish

INGREDIENTS:

1 pound fresh or frozen shrimp, peeled, deveined and thawed
1 pound fresh or frozen sea scallops, thawed
2 12-ounce jars marinated artichoke hearts
1/2 cup Parmesan cheese
1 cup (4 ounces) mozzarella cheese, shredded
2 tablespoons olive oil
1 teaspoon garlic powder
1 teaspoon chives

To make:
1. Preheat oven to 450 degrees.
2. Thaw the scallops and shrimp in cold water or milk.
3. Pour oil into baking dish.
4. Add other ingredients, except mozzarella cheese, and mix together.
5. Top with mozzarella.
6. Bake for 15 minutes.

Change It Up: If you have fresh scallops but precooked shrimp. Cook scallops on the stove top in a skillet for about 5 to 7 minutes over low-medium heat. Then, add scallops to baking dish. Decrease the baking time to 5 to 7 minutes.

We Go Good Together: Garlic or Parmesan bread

Look Ahead: Take the mozzarella and Parmesan cheese out of the freezer and put them in the refrigerator to thaw. Take out the pepperoni and/or sausage if you are jazzing up your pizza.

✦ Day 7—Kids' Meal: Pizza with a Zip ✦

Here's a casual meal that should please kids and adults alike and is perfect for the last night your company will be staying at your place. You can top it with additional ingredients or delete something you know might cause a frown.

Dish up: 8 to 10 servings
Construction time: 10 minutes

Cooking time 16 to 20 minutes
Paraphernalia: 2 round pizza pans

INGREDIENTS:

1 medium onion, chopped
1 green pepper, chopped
2 10-ounce tubes refrigerated pizza crusts
1 8-ounce jar pizza sauce
1 cup mild salsa
3 cups (12 ounces) mozzarella cheese, shredded
½ cup Romano cheese

To make:

1. Preheat oven to 425 degrees.
2. Peel and chop onion. Wash and chop green pepper.
3. Coat skillet with nonstick cooking spray. Sauté veggies in skillet over medium heat for about 3 to 4 minutes.
4. Coat pizza pans with nonstick cooking spray.
5. Unroll pizza crusts onto pans. Bake for 6 to 8 minutes, or until light golden brown.
6. Mix together pizza sauce and salsa.
7. Spread sauce on crusts. Top with mozzarella and Romano cheeses. Sprinkle sautéed veggies on top.
8. Bake for 10 to 12 minutes, or until the crust is cooked the way you like it.

Jazz It Up: Add sliced pepperoni, sausage or another favorite topping.
Dress It Down: Eliminate the salsa.
We Go Good Together: Seasonal fruit and frozen yogurt

VACAY WEEK

A vacation from the responsibilities and commitments of everyday life can turn frantic cooks into enthusiastic chefs without much difficulty. Saying good-bye to the alarm clock, workplace, ringing telephone (turn off your cell phone) and car pools can lift anyone's spirit. And it doesn't matter if your time away is at a luxury beach house or a one-room cabin. What's important is that you're away from the demands of daily life.

Vacay Week Menus

Day 1—Sandwich Board: Submarine Sandwiches
Day 2—Kids' Meal: Nacho Roundup
Day 3—Seafood Fest: Seafood Bake
Day 4—Everyday Dinner: Linguine and More
Day 5—Everyday Dinner: Hot 'n' Sweet Tofuli
Day 6—Everyday Dinner: Applesauce Chicken
Day 7—Kids' Meal: Pizza, Pizza

The Frantic Woman's Home-to-Vacay Cupboard

To save some money, bring a few meal-preparation necessities from home that could otherwise drive up your grocery bill. Here's a to-do list to keep you on track and to keep those hard-earned dollars in your purse.

Pack the following dry ingredients in plastic zippered bags and mark as such:

MAIN-DISH STAPLES

1 teaspoon chili powder (Day 2)
1 teaspoon cumin (Day 2)
2¼ teaspoons garlic powder (Days 2, 3, 4, 5)
1 teaspoon red pepper flakes (Day 5)
1 teaspoon ginger (Day 5)
1 package dry onion soup mix (Day 6)
Salt
Pepper
Nonstick cooking spray
Toothpicks

JAZZ IT UP STAPLES
    1 tablespoon cinnamon (Day 6)

WE GO GOOD TOGETHER STAPLES
    Italian salad dressing, or your preference

    Put the following ingredients into small containers with tight-fitting lids, or double-bag the ingredients separately (be sure the bags are leakproof), and store them all in a container with a tight-fitting lid for safekeeping.
    2 or 3 tablespoons honey (Day 5)
    ¾ cup olive oil (Days 3, 4)
    3 tablespoons sesame oil (Day 5)
    2 tablespoons teriyaki sauce (Day 5)

The Frantic Woman Goes Shopping

MAIN-DISH INGREDIENTS YOU'LL NEED TO BUY

Produce: Fruit
    1 large lemon (Day 4)
    2 medium Yellow Delicious or Jonathan apples (Day 6)

Produce: Veggies
    1 head lettuce (Day 1)
    1 yellow onion (Day 1)
    2 tomatoes (Day 1)
    1 large red pepper (Day 5)
    1 head broccoli (Day 5)

Dressings, Oils and Sauces
    1 16-ounce bottle Italian dressing (Day 1)
    1 16-ounce jar salsa (Day 2)
    1 15-ounce jar pizza sauce (Day 7)

Canned Goods and Bottles

1 15-ounce can black beans (Day 2)

1 16-ounce can corn (Day 2)

2 12-ounce jars marinated artichoke hearts (Day 3)

1 15-ounce can tomatoes, diced (Day 4)

1 15-ounce can great northern beans (Day 4)

1 8-ounce can bamboo shoots (Day 5)

1 15-ounce jar applesauce (Day 6)

1 8-ounce can pineapple chunks (Day 6)

1 4-ounce can sliced mushrooms (Day 7)

Noodles, Pasta and Rice

1 16-ounce package linguine (Day 4)

Bread, Chips and More

1 loaf French bread (Day 1)

1 16-ounce bag tortilla chips (Day 2)

Deli

$1/2$ pound salami (Day 1)

$1/2$ pound ham (Day 1)

$1/2$ pound Swiss cheese (Day 1)

2 ounces Romano cheese, grated (Day 3)

$1/4$ pound pepperoni slices (Day 7)

Fish, Meat and Poultry

1 pound ground beef (Day 2)

2 pounds shrimp, peeled and deveined (Day 3)

4 skinless, boneless chicken breasts, about 1 to $1/2$ pounds (Day 6)

Dairy

Butter (Days 1, 2)

2 cups (8 ounces)cheddar or Monterey Jack cheese, shredded (Day 2)

$1/2$ cup crumbled feta cheese (Day 3)

3 cup (12 ounces) finely shredded mozzarella cheese (Days 3, 7)

1-pound box firm or extra-firm tofu (Day 5)

1 10-ounce tube refrigerated pizza crust (Day 7)

JAZZ IT UP INGREDIENTS YOU'LL NEED TO BUY

Produce: Veggies

1 cucumber (Day 1)

1 tomato (Day 2)

1 lemon (Day 3)

1 small bunch basil or parsley (Day 4)

Canned Goods and Bottles

1 10-ounce jar roasted peppers (Day 4)

1 2.5-ounce can black olives, or your topping preference (Day 7)

WE GO GOOD TOGETHER INGREDIENTS YOU'LL NEED TO BUY

Produce: Fruit

Fruit, your preference (Days 1, 5)

Produce: Veggie

1 16-ounce bag ready-to-eat salad (Day 2)

4 to 6 ears corn (Day 3)

2 cucumbers (Day 3)

2 tomatoes (Day 3)

Bread, Chips and More

1 16-ounce bag potato chips (Day 1)

Deli

¼ cup (2 ounces) feta cheese (Day 3)

Frozen

1 loaf Texas toast, or your preference (Day 4)

Unloading the Load

This is the easiest unpacking you will probably ever have to do.

- Freeze the chicken breasts for Day 6, Applesauce Chicken, and the pepperoni for Day 7, Pizza, Pizza. That's it.

TiPS BASKETFUL OF TIPS: Load it Up

Don't leave home until you've called the rental agency to see what's in your home-away-from-home kitchen.

- You'll want to make sure you have the following items: Dutch oven, pizza pan, skillet, 3-quart saucepan, 9-by-13-inch baking dish, sharp knife and large serving bowl.
- If the rental does not come fully equipped, be sure to pack these necessities.
- Another idea is to buy disposable pans at the dollar store, saving cleanup time. PS: You'll need a total of four 9- by 13-inch baking dishes to get through the week's menus.

VACAY WEEK MENUS

→ Day 1—Sandwich Board: Submarine Sandwiches ←

After spending hours traveling to your destination, unloading the car, and picking up supplies for the week ahead, submarine sammies are a perfect choice for your first night at your vacation destination. And while you're putting together the sub, your other half and the kids can unload the car and unpack the suitcases. And more than likely, you'll make out on the deal.

Dish up: 6 servings   Cooking time: 0
Construction time: 7 to 10 minutes   Paraphernalia: 0

INGREDIENTS:

2 tomatoes, sliced
½ yellow onion, thinly sliced
5 lettuce leaves
1 loaf French bread
Butter
Italian salad dressing, bottled
½ pound salami
½ pound Swiss cheese
½ pound ham

To make:

1. Wash veggies. Slice onion and tomatoes.
2. Cut bread in half horizontally. (Simplify it: Dig out some of the bread on the bottom half of the loaf to make a shallow well. This will keep the slippery layers from sliding off.) Spread bottom half with a thin layer of butter to keep the bread from becoming soggy.
3. Drizzle Italian salad dressing over butter.
4. Layer lettuce, salami, tomatoes, cheese, ham, and onions.
5. Finish by adding the other half of the loaf on top. Push toothpicks into the top of the bread to secure everything in place. Cut into 6 servings.

Jazz It Up: Peel and thinly slice half a cucumber and add it to the sandwich.

Dress It Down: Skip the onions for those folks who want to avoid onion breath.

Change It Up: Exchange the suggested meat and cheese for your family's favorites or whatever is on sale, or eliminate meat altogether to make it a meatless meal.

We Go Good Together: Potato chips and sliced fruit

BASKETFUL OF TIPS: Ham Goes a Long Way

Sue Kolton and her kids vacation with two other families. Sue buys half a ham on sale and freezes it. The day they leave for the beach, she pops it into a cooler with other perishables, some frozen, some not. By the time she reaches her destination, the ham has thawed, and she puts it into the oven to bake. The ham cooks while everyone is busy unloading the vans, suitcases and coolers. Once cooked, the ham is served for dinner, and then the remainder is thinly sliced to have ready for sandwiches in the days ahead. Sue's mom uses the little slivers of meat on the bone to make ham salad by grinding them and then adding mashed gherkin pickles and mayo. And Sue's sister, Wendy, uses the bone to make split pea soup. (Note: Sue asked her butcher if this traveling and defrosting method was safe to do, and he gave her the thumbs-up.)

✢ *Day 2—Kids' Meal: Nacho Roundup* ✦

With four boys ranging from preschooler to teenager and trying to jump-start a writing career, Renae Lloyd needs meals that are quick to fix that the entire family will eat. Before you say "My kids won't eat Mexican," Renae's four-year-old has never been willing to try any type of Mexican dish, but he'll eat this one. This is an ideal meal to serve outside in the fresh air.

Dish up: 6 to 8 servings

Construction time: 10 minutes

Cooking time: 15 to 20 minutes

Paraphernalia: 12-inch skillet, 9-by-13-inch baking dish

INGREDIENTS:

Butter

4 cups tortilla chips, lightly crushed

1 pound ground beef, browned

¼ teaspoon garlic powder

1 teaspoon cumin

1 teaspoon chili powder

1 15-ounce can black beans

1 16-ounce can corn

1 16-ounce jar salsa

2 cups (8 ounces) cheddar or Monterey Jack cheese, shredded

To make:

1. Preheat oven to 400 degrees. Coat a 9- by 13-inch baking dish with nonstick cooking spray. Crush chips.
2. In skillet over medium heat, brown beef with garlic, cumin and chili powder.
3. Stir in beans, corn and salsa.
4. Spread half of the chips in the bottom of the baking dish. Add half the beef mixture and half the cheese. Repeat layers, ending with cheese.
5. Bake for 15 to 20 minutes, or until warmed through and cheese has melted.

Jazz It Up: Add diced tomatoes to the beef.

Dress It Down: Skip the cumin and chili powder.

We Go Good Together: Tossed salad

Look Ahead: If you've purchased frozen shrimp for Day 3, Seafood Bake, pull them out of the freezer and put them in the refrigerator to defrost.

FRANTIC WOMAN FAMILY FUN: Alphabet Dinner

Mealtime is so much calmer when you're away from the hustle and bustle of everyday life. So take advantage of the slower pace to enjoy a great dinner, the presence of relaxed family members and an entertaining game. To play Alphabet Dinner, one person starts with the letter A, "Today I had applesauce (or something else that starts with A) for dinner." The next person repeats, "Today I had applesauce and beans (or something else with the letter B) for dinner." The game continues through the alphabet. Of course, mom and dad can help the littler ones. Or for young children, the entire family can repeat each line, and anyone can add the next-lettered food item.

✢ Day 3—Seafood Fest: Seafood Bake ✦ 🚫

Here's a simple, yet scrumptious meal that tastes like you've slaved over a hot stove all day. Only you know you haven't. It's our secret. By the way, you can cut these ingredients in half, if you prefer fewer servings. And if you're near the beach, opt for fresh, cleaned shrimp.

Dish up: 8 to 10 servings

Construction time: 5 minutes

Cooking time: 7 to 10 minutes

Paraphernalia: 9- by 13-inch baking dish, paper towels

INGREDIENTS:

2 tablespoons olive oil

½ teaspoon garlic powder

2 pounds shrimp (peeled and deveined), thawed

2 12-ounce jars marinated artichoke hearts

½ cup (2 ounces) Romano cheese, grated

1 cup (4 ounces) mozzarella cheese, finely shredded

½ cup feta cheese, crumbled

To make:

1. Preheat oven to 450 degrees. Pour olive oil in baking dish. Add garlic powder.
2. Rinse shrimp and pat dry with paper towels.
3. Combine shrimp, artichoke hearts and Romano cheese in baking dish. Sprinkle with mozzarella and feta cheese.
4. Bake for 7 to 10 minutes for precooked shrimp, or 15 minutes if you use larger raw shrimp.

Jazz It Up: Drizzle lemon juice over casserole.

Dress It Down: Use mozzarella cheese only.

Change It Up: You can use frozen salad shrimp in a bag if fresh, cleaned shrimp is too pricey. Simply thaw the frozen shrimp in cold water or milk.

We Go Good Together: Make corn on the cob as a side dish, if available. If not, sliced tomatoes and cucumbers lightly coated with Italian salad dressing and sprinkled with feta cheese will be a great addition.

⇥ Day 4—Everyday Dinner: Linguine and More ⇤ 🐄

This dish can be on the table within 30 minutes, making it perfect for a great meal after a day of playing tourist.

Dish up: 6 to 8 servings

Construction time: 15 minutes

Cooking time: 5 minutes

Paraphernalia: Dutch oven or 5-quart pot, 3-quart pot, large serving bowl, strainer

INGREDIENTS:

1 16-ounce package linguine

1 15-ounce can great northern beans (or other white beans)

1 15-ounce can diced tomatoes

1/2 teaspoon garlic powder

1/2 cup olive oil

1/4 cup lemon juice

Salt and pepper, to taste

To make:

1. Cook pasta according to package directions.
2. In a small pot, combine beans, tomatoes, garlic, olive oil and lemon juice. Cook over medium heat for 5 to 7 minutes, mixing well.
3. Drain pasta. Combine pasta and bean/tomato mixture in a large serving bowl. Mix well.
4. Add salt and pepper, to taste. Serve.

Jazz It Up: Add 1 small can of roasted peppers and 1/4 cup fresh basil or parsley to the pasta.

Dress It Down: Skip the beans if you know the family won't eat them.

Change It Up: Add 1 can of clams, replacing beans.

We Go Good Together: Texas toast or thick slices of buttered toast

---

POTFUL OF KNOWLEDGE: Lemon Math

In lemon math, 1 large lemon equals 4 tablespoons, and 4 tablespoons equal 1/4 cup of lemon juice.

⇢ Day 5—Everyday Dinner: Hot 'n' Sweet Tofuli 🚫 ⇠

The one thing great about vacations is everyone goes with the flow. You're easily tempted to try something out of the ordinary. With that in mind, chef Greg Bacasa says you can call this anything you want so the kids will try it without screaming "Tofu, yuck!" Be sure to marinate the tofu earlier in the day, before you head off to the beach or park. Of course, you can change it up, too.

Dish up: 4 servings

Construction time: 10 minutes, plus 2 hours to marinate

Cooking time: 5 minutes

Paraphernalia: 12-inch skillet, large plastic zippered bag (or container with a lid)

INGREDIENTS:

1-pound box firm or extra firm tofu, cubed
2 tablespoons teriyaki sauce
1 teaspoon ginger
1 teaspoon garlic powder
3 tablespoons sesame oil
1 head broccoli
1 8-ounce can bamboo shoots
1 large red pepper, cut into strips
Pinch red pepper flakes
2 tablespoons honey

To make:

1. Cut tofu into ¾-inch cubes. In a plastic zippered bag or container with a fitted lid, marinate tofu for at least 2 hours in teriyaki sauce, ginger, garlic and 2 tablespoons sesame oil. Shake well to coat the tofu.

2. Cut broccoli into florets.

3. Preheat skillet. (If you have access to a wok, use it).

4. Add remaining 1 tablespoon sesame oil to pan. Stir in bamboo shoots, broccoli, red pepper and a pinch of red pepper flakes. Stir-fry for 1 minute.

5. Add in tofu with marinade. Stir-fry for about 3 minutes, or until heated through.

6. Just before serving, stir in honey. Serve hot.

Jazz It Up: Add more honey for a sweeter taste.

Dress It Down: Skip the red peppers for sensitive taste buds.

Change It Up: Cook a little longer for softer veggies.

We Go Good Together: Seasonal fruit

Look Ahead: Take the chicken out of the freezer and put it in the refrigerator to defrost.

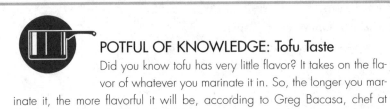

POTFUL OF KNOWLEDGE: Tofu Taste

Did you know tofu has very little flavor? It takes on the flavor of whatever you marinate it in. So, the longer you marinate it, the more flavorful it will be, according to Greg Bacasa, chef at University of Pittsburgh Medical Center's Senior Living Services.

✦ Day 6—Everyday Dinner: Applesauce Chicken ✦

This recipe, created by our daughter Deanna, reminds me of an escape weekend my husband and I enjoyed several years back to celebrate a special anniversary. Every dish on the menu was cooked with some type of fruit, adding a delicious flavor to every bite.

Dish up: 4 servings　　　　　Cooking time: 25 to 30 minutes
Construction time: 5 to 7 minutes　　Paraphernalia: 9-by-13-inch baking dish

INGREDIENTS:

2 medium Yellow Delicious or Jonathan apples, diced
4 skinless, boneless chicken breasts
1 cup applesauce
1 teaspoon dry onion soup mix
1 8-ounce can pineapple chunks

To make:

1. Preheat oven to 375 degrees. Coat baking dish with nonstick cooking spray.
2. Wash and dice apples.
3. Place chicken breasts in baking dish. Pour applesauce over chicken. Top with diced apples.
4. Sprinkle dry onion soup mix over apples. (Simplify it: Be sure not to add too much seasoning, as it can overwhelm the flavor of the entree.)
5. Drain pineapples. Scatter pineapples over apples.
6. Bake for 25 to 30 minutes, or until juices from chicken run clear.

Jazz It Up: Sprinkle cinnamon over ingredients before serving.

Dress It Down: Skip the pineapples.

Change It Up: Add sliced almonds instead of pineapples.

We Go Good Together: Finish off the rest of the applesauce.

Look Ahead: Take the pepperoni out of the freezer and put in the refrigerator to thaw.

❖ Day 7—Kids' Meal: Pizza, Pizza ❖

A vacation wouldn't be a vacation if you didn't have pizza at least one day. You can toss this together easily by taking advantage of ready-made ingredients, making this a trouble-free meal to pull together after a busy day on the beach, sightseeing or packing up to go home.

Dish up: 4 to 6 servings

Cooking time: 10 to 12 minutes

Construction time:

Paraphernalia: Pizza pan

INGREDIENTS:

1 10-ounce tube refrigerated pizza crust

1 15-ounce jar pizza sauce

2 cups (8 ounces) mozzarella cheese

1 3-ounce package pepperoni slices

1 4-ounce can sliced mushroom

To make:

1. Preheat oven to 425 dregrees or according to pizza crust package directions.
2. Coat pizza pan with nonstick cooking spray.
3. Unroll dough, and place it in the center of the pan. Press the dough to the edges with your fingers.
4. Bake 6 to 8 minutes. Remove from oven.
5. Spread pizza sauce over crust with a spoon. Sprinkle cheese over the sauce. Top with pepperoni and mushroom slices.
6. Bake for 10 to 12 minutes, or until the crust turns light brown.

Jazz It Up: Add your favorite toppings, from sliced black olives to anchovies.

Dress It Down: Use a precooked crust instead of refrigerated pizza dough.

We Go Good Together: Serve any remaining leftovers.

FRANTIC WOMAN FAMILY FUN:
Frantic Fondue with Fruit

Fondue pots were the rage back in the late 1970s and as the saying goes, *What goes around, comes around.* Fondue is trendy again. Well, you don't need a specialty pot to have a chocolate blast. Melt 8 ounces semisweet chips and ½ cup cream in a pan over medium heat until melted. While chocolate mix is melting, slice bananas, strawberries, and apples, and arrange on a serving platter. Divvy the melted chocolate amongst the family by pouring it into individual cups. (This eliminates double-dipping.) You can offer mini pretzels, dried apricots or marshmallows, too

PMS (STRESSED OUT OR BAD DAY AT THE OFFICE) WEEK

Some weeks, you wish Monday had never rolled around and you never climbed out of bed. And during those weeks, wouldn't you just love it if life operated like a DVD player, and you could skip forward past the crummy times? Unfortunately, there isn't a remote control for life. But here's a week's worth of easy menus created to help supply your body with the nutrients and vitamins it needs during this time of the month. You'll find trendy wraps and two-ingredient meals to help you get through those frantic days in life.

PMS (Stressed Out or Bad Day at the Office) Menus

Day 1—No-Cook Night: Quick and Easy Turkey Wraps
Day 2—Seafood Fest: Quick and Easy Salmon
Day 3—Light Cooking: Nutri-a-licious Salad
Day 4—Everyday Dinner: Stir-Fry Pasta
Day 5—Everyday Dinner: Two-Ingredient London Broil
Day 6—Everyday Dinner: Two-Ingredient Barbecue Chicken
Day 7—Backwards Meal: Sweet Strawberry Cakes

The Shopping Lists

THE FRANTIC WOMAN'S CUPBOARD
PMS (STRESSED OUT OR BAD DAY AT THE OFFICE) WEEK STAPLES

Seasonings
Garlic (powder)

Jazz It Ups
Crushed red pepper

Dressings, Oil and Sauces
Ranch dressing
Soy sauce

Jazz It Ups
Hot pepper sauce

Baking Needs
All-purpose baking mix or pancake mix

Frantic Necessities
Foil
Nonstick cooking spray

Dairy
Butter or margarine
Eggs*

Side Dishes
Milk*

*Ingredients you'll need for both main and side dishes

The Frantic Woman Goes Shopping

MAIN-DISH INGREDIENTS YOU'LL NEED TO BUY

Produce: Fruit
1½ pounds strawberries (Day 7)

Produce: Veggies
1 head lettuce (Day 1)
4 tomatoes (Days 1, 3)
1 8-ounce carton snowcap mushrooms (Day 2)
1 cucumber (Day 3)
1 head romaine lettuce (Day 3)

1 red onion (Day 3)
1 green pepper (Day 3)
1 red pepper (Day 3)

PIT STOP: Keep It Fresh

Consider buying your strawberries around Day 5 to keep them from spoiling before you use them.

Dressings, Oils and Sauces

1 16-ounce bottles Italian salad dressing (Days 1, 3. 5)
1 16-ounce bottle barbecue sauce (Day 6)

Canned Goods and Bottles

1 2.5-ounce can black olives, sliced (Day 3)
1 4-ounce can mushrooms, sliced (Day 4)

Noodles, Pasta and Rice

1 8-ounce box ziti (Day 4)

Cereal, Nuts and Such

1 2-ounce package sunflower seeds, shelled (Day 3)

Deli

1 pound oven-roasted turkey breast, sliced (Day 1)
½ pound Swiss cheese, sliced (Day 1)

Fish, Meat and Poultry

6 salmon fillets (about 1½ pounds) (Day 2)
1 2-pound London broil (Day 5)
1½ pounds skinless, boneless chicken breasts (Day 6)

Dairy

1 10-count package 10-inch whole-wheat tortillas (Day 1)
1 cup part-skim mozzarella cheese, shredded (Day 3)
1 can whipped topping (Day 7)

Frozen

1 10-ounce box frozen Chinese-style stir-fry veggies (Day 4)

JAZZ IT UP INGREDIENTS YOU'LL NEED TO BUY

Produce: Fruits
1 avocado (Day 1)

Canned Goods and Bottles
1 16-ounce can asparagus (Day 2)

Baking Needs
Handful of raisins (Day 3)

WE GO GOOD TOGETHER INGREDIENTS YOU'LL NEED TO BUY

Produce: Fruits
1 or 2 mangoes (Day 1)
Fruit, your preference (Day 3)
2 to 3 bananas (Day 4)
2 to 3 kiwis (Day 4)
2 to 4 plums (Day 5)
1 pineapple (Day 6)

Produce: Veggies
1 16-ounce package ready-to-eat salad (Day 5)
2 to 3 sweet potatoes (Day 5)

Canned Goods and Bottles
1 16-ounce can chickpeas (Day 6)

Noodles, Pasta and Rice
2 cups brown rice (Day 2)

Bread, Chips and More
4 to 6 breadsticks (Day 3)

Dairy

2 to 4 containers yogurt, your preference (Day 1)
1 8-ounce package (brick) cheese, your preference (Day 2)
1 16-ounce container cottage cheese (Day 3)

Frozen

1 10-ounce box brussels sprouts (Day 2)

Unloading the Load

Thankfully, this week's unloading the load is a piece of cake.

- Freeze the London broil for Day 5, Two-Ingredient London Broil.
- Freeze the chicken breasts for Day 6, Two-Ingredient Barbeque Chicken.
- Hide the can of whipped topping so the kids don't squirt it into their mouths.

PMS, STRESSED OUT OR BAD WEEK AT THE OFFICE MENUS

❧ Day 1—No Cook Night: ☙
Quick and Easy Turkey Wraps

These are the perfect dinner meal not only for shopping day, but also for when you just need a break. You can lay out the ingredients, hand everyone their own tortilla, and have them prepare their own wraps. This is a great TV dinner or grab-and-go meal. And by the way, turkey is an excellent source of iron, niacin, potassium and vitamin B_6. Swiss cheese provides the most calcium of any cheese, and wheat provides zinc.

Dish up: 4 to 6 servings
Construction time: 5 minutes

Cooking time: 0
Paraphernalia: 0

INGREDIENTS:

2 tomatoes

8 to 12 lettuce leaves

Ranch salad dressing

4 to 6 whole-wheat 10-inch tortillas, or your preference

1 pound oven-roasted turkey breast, sliced

½ pound Swiss cheese, sliced

To make:

1. Wash tomatoes and lettuce. Slice tomatoes.
2. Spread ranch salad dressing on tortilla.
3. Layer turkey, cheese, lettuce and tomato.
4. Tuck top and bottom ends up. Roll up wrap and enjoy.

Jazz It Up: Add diced avocados for more magnesium.

Change It Up: Use your favorite salad dressing instead of ranch.

We Go Good Together: Mangoes (one of the leading food sources of vitamin E) and yogurt (great for keeping away yeast infections)

POTFUL OF KNOWLEDGE: Keep PMS Away

Calcium	Studies show calcium reduces abdominal cramping and muscular contractions resulting from PMS.
Magnesium	Low zinc levels have been shown to cause symptoms of PMS.
Vitamin B$_6$	Foods high in vitamin B$_6$ may reduce depression caused by PMS. Pair foods high in B$_6$ with foods high in magnesium to reduce mood swings during your monthly cycle.
Vitamin E	Eating foods high in vitamin E can help reduce breast tenderness, depression, fatigue, headaches, insomnia and nervousness.
Zinc	Foods high in zinc may prevent PMS symptoms.

✦ *Day 2—Seafood Fest: Quick and Easy Salmon* ✦

This healthy dish tastes like you have gone to a lot of trouble to prepare it, but haven't. Turn on your favorite tunes, light a couple of candles, and pretend you're at your favorite vacation destination.

Dish up: 4 to 6 servings
Construction time: 5 minutes

Cooking time: 30 minutes
Paraphernalia: Small bowl,
9- by 13-inch baking dish

INGREDIENTS:
6 salmon fillets (about 1 1/2 pounds)
1 cup Italian salad dressing
1 cup snowcap mushrooms, sliced

To make:
1. Preheat oven to 350 degrees. Spray baking dish with nonstick cooking spray.
2. Arrange salmon fillets in a single layer in baking dish.
3. Pour salad dressing over salmon fillets.
4. Slice mushrooms and place on top of fillets.
5. Cover with foil and bake for 15 minutes. Remove foil and bake for an additional 15 minutes. Baste occasionally with liquid from baking dish.

Jazz It Up: Add a dash of crushed red pepper. Add canned asparagus to the baking dish.

We Go Good Together: Brown rice (good source of fiber), Brussels sprouts (source of vitamin C, iron and potassium), cheese cubes (calcium)

✦ *Day 3—Light Cooking: Nutri-a-licious Salad* ✦

This nearly cook-free meal is just what the doctor ordered. Studies show a balanced diet can ward off fatigue. With all you do, its no wonder you're dog-tired. This salad offers a huge dose of nutrients so you'll be eager to get up and go again. Eggs, full of protein, provide a source of energy and build and repair muscles and bones. Peppers are full of vitamins A and C. Tomatoes, another source of vitamins A and C, also contain potassium, some calcium and iron. Onions are good for the heart, and cucumbers have basically no fat, sodium or cholesterol. And cucumbers have only 7 calories per half cup. So dig in.

Dish up: 4 to 6 servings
Construction time: 10 minutes

Cooking time: 0
Paraphernalia: 2-quart pot, large serving bowl

INGREDIENTS:

4 eggs
1 head romaine lettuce, chopped
2 tomatoes, chopped
1 cucumber, chopped
1 red onion, cut in strips
1 green pepper, cut in strips
1 red pepper, cut in strips
1 4-ounce can black olives, sliced
1/4 cup sunflower seeds, shelled
1 cup part-skim mozzarella cheese, shredded
Italian salad dressing, or your preference

To make:
1. Allow eggs to sit on counter to get to room temperature. Boil eggs in gently simmering water for 7 to 8 minutes to make hard-boiled eggs.
2. Wash veggies.
3. Chop lettuce. Core and chop tomatoes. Peel and chop cucumber. Toss ingredients into large bowl.
4. Cut peppers into thin strips. Cut onion into thin strips. Add these to ingredients to the bowl. Drain olives. Add olives and sunflower seeds to the bowl.

5. Add peeled, sliced egg. Toss ingredients together to mix. Sprinkle with cheese.

6. Serve with Italian or your favorite salad dressing.

Jazz It Up: Add a handful of raisins (a concentrated source of many minerals, including iron and potassium.)

We Go Good Together: Breadsticks, cottage cheese and/or sliced fruit

Look Ahead: Pull out the London broil from the freezer, and put it in the refrigerator for Day 5, Two-Ingredient London Broil. You're thawing it a day early because you will be marinating it on Day 4 to give it a wallop of flavor.

Frantic Woman Family Fun: Husband Takes a Turn

After 30 years of eating the stuff frantic woman Karen Novak hurried to make, her husband decided to take a turn at cooking and found out he loves it. Karen's husband plans the menu, shops, chooses a video pertaining to his meal, and gets music and wine to accent it. (As an example, *The Godfather* goes with Italian food.) "Now, it's true, he isn't a frantic woman," Karen says, "but he makes this frantic woman happy."

Frantics, maybe you can persuade your spouse to follow Karen's husband's example for just one day every other week or even once a month. If your other half needs help choosing a video, check out www.movieloversclubhouse.com.

✦ Day 4—Everyday Dinner: Stir-Fry Pasta ✦

Being frantic can frazzle your nerves at times. When you are stressed out, calm your shattered nerves by eating carbohydrates. Carbohydrates produce serotonin, which gives you a calm, relaxed feeling, according to Fitnessandfreebies.com. So fill your plate with this five-ingredient pasta dish.

Dish up: 4 servings

Construction time: 15 minutes

Cooking time: 10 minutes

Paraphernalia: Dutch oven, 3-quart pot, strainer

INGREDIENTS:

1 8 ounce box ziti
1 10-ounce box frozen Chinese-style stir-fry veggies
1 4-ounce can mushrooms, sliced
2 tablespoons soy sauce
1/8 teaspoon garlic powder

To make:
1. Cook ziti according to package directions. Drain.
2. While pasta is cooking, make Chinese veggies according to package directions. Do not drain liquid when finished cooking.
3. Wash and cut mushrooms. Add mushrooms, soy sauce and garlic powder to veggies and liquid.
4. Stir in cooked ziti. Serve immediately.

Change It Up: Substitute rotini, rotelle or another pasta shape for ziti. Use fresh mushrooms instead of canned.

We Go Good Together: Bananas (one of the leading food sources of vitamin B₆), kiwi (a source of vitamin C and potassium)

Look Ahead: Pull out the London broil from the refrigerator, and marinate it according to the directions in Day 5, Two-Ingredient London Broil.

❧ Day 5—Everyday Dinner: ❧ Two-Ingredient London Broil

Beef offers the frantic woman a boost of iron. Women lose an average of 15 to 20 milligrams of iron each month through menstruation, reports the National Women's Health Information Center. Iron deficiency can cause fatigue and headaches; ailments busy women can do without. Barb Hawk's simple recipe gives you that extra dose of iron your body needs.

Dish up: 6 servings
Construction time: 5 minutes,
    plus overnight marinating time

Cooking time: 15 minutes
Paraphernalia: 9- by 13-inch baking dish

INGREDIENTS:

2-pound London broil

1 16-ounce bottle Italian salad dressing

Day before:

1. Rinse meat in cold water. Score meat diagonally on both sides to tenderize. Place meat in baking dish. Pour dressing over meat, being sure to coat both sides. Cover pan with foil, and store it in the refrigerator overnight.

On day of dinner:

2. Turn oven to broil. Broil meat for 10 minutes on one side. Flip meat over and broil for 5 minutes on other side. (It will be medium rare.)
3. Let sit for 5 minutes. Throw out the remaining marinade. Thinly slice meat and serve.

Change It Up: Replace London broil with top round steak.

We Go Good Together: Sweet potatoes (vitamin B_6), tossed salad and/or plums (full of potassium)

Look Ahead: Take the chicken breasts for Day 6, Two-Ingredient Barbecue Chicken, out of the freezer and store them in the refrigerator.

✦ Day 6—Everyday Dinner: ✦ Two-Ingredient Barbecque Chicken

This dish fills the need for a tasty dinner prepared with minimal effort. Yet it is high in protein and a good source of vitamin B_6 and zinc. So pour on the sauce, pop it in the oven, and kick your feet up until the oven timer goes off. Thanks, Andie, for the suggestion!

Dish up: 4 to 6 servings

Construction time: 5 minutes

Cooking time: 20 minutes

Paraphernalia: 9- by 13-inch baking dish

INGREDIENTS:

1 1/2 pounds skinless, boneless chicken breasts

1 16-ounce bottle barbecue sauce

To make:

1. Preheat oven to 400 degrees.
2. Line pan with foil for easier cleanup.
3. Place chicken in a single layer in baking dish.
4. Pour barbecue sauce over chicken. Be sure to cover chicken completely. You might need a pastry brush to spread the sauce.
5. Bake for 20 minutes, or until chicken is no longer pink.

Jazz It Up: Add a dash or two of hot pepper sauce to the barbecue sauce.

Change It Up: Spread chicken with mayonnaise instead of barbecue sauce.

We Go Good Together: Chickpeas (one of the leading food sources of vitamin B_6), fresh pineapples (vitamin C)

→ Day 7—Backwards Meal: → Sweet Strawberry Cakes

PMS Week has to end with something fun, and Sweet Strawberry Cakes are just that. This meal answers the craving for something sweet. However, the strawberries are packed with vitamin C and are good for your skin. The carbs in the cakes will give you a boost of energy. So indulge your sweet tooth without the guilt. Psst! For tips on making pancakes, see the Basketful of Tips in Summer Plan Two.

Dish up: 4 servings
Construction time: 5 minutes

Cook time: 15 to 20 minutes
Paraphernalia: Bowl, 12-inch skillet, baking sheet, electric mixer, wide spatula

INGREDIENTS:

2 cups all-purpose baking or pancake mix (plus ingredients, milk and eggs)
2 tablespoons butter, melted
1 can whipped topping
1½ pounds strawberries, sliced

POTFUL OF KNOWLEDGE: Good for You

Don't you just want to scream when an author writes *It's good for you* but you don't know why? Well, here are the answers to why the vitamins and minerals mentioned throughout this plan are good for you.

Vitamin/Mineral	Benefits
Calcium	Decreases risk of some cancers. Builds strong bones and teeth. Helps with proper function of heart, kidneys, muscles and nerves.
Iron	Good for blood, muscles and bones. Maintains healthy immune system.
Potassium	Helps to prevent some cancers, high blood pressure and stroke.
Vitamin A	Helps build immunity. Improves hair and skin conditions. Helps to resist infections. Plays essential role in vision.
Vitamin C	Boosts absorption of iron. Helps to prevent some cancers, high blood pressure, infections and strokes.

To make:

1. Mix baking mix or pancake mix according to package directions.
2. Lightly coat skillet with nonstick cooking spray. Heat over medium heat until hot.
3. Drop batter (about 1/4 cup) onto hot skillet. Cook pancakes about 1 to 2 minutes. Turn and cook 1 more minute.
4. Place finished pancakes on plate, and cover with foil to keep warm. Repeat with remaining batter.
5. Slice strawberries while pancakes are cooking.
6. Top pancakes with strawberries and whipped cream.

Change It Up: Top with maple syrup instead of strawberries and whipped cream. Make pancakes from scratch. See Blueberry Pancakes recipe in Summer Plan Twos.

We Go Good Together: Milk, scrambled eggs (protein)

YOU'RE HAVING A RETRO PARTY

Sometime during the year, you're bound to have a party or two. With so many trends and fads today, it's hard to plan a menu around who's eating what. Instead of trying to figure out what's in and what's not, throw a retro party, serving favorite foods that have withstood the test of time. These classic dishes are still popular today and usually disappear faster than the current trendy recipes.

In this section, you'll find an entree, side dishes and a delectable dessert to serve for your next bash. Most of these classics can be made ahead of time, keeping those last-minute anxieties at bay. For your convenience, each recipe has a menu item number beside it to correspond with the required ingredients on the shopping list.

Party Day Menu

Menu Item 1—Barbecue Beef
Menu Item 2—Pat's Haluski
Menu Item 3—Cheesy Potatoes
Menu Item 4—Broccoli Salad
Menu Item 5—Orange and Green Salad
Menu Item 6—Pistachio Heaven
Menu Item 7—Rita's Make-Ahead Mexi-Dip
Menu Item 8—Fruit Punch

THE SHOPPING LISTS

The Frantic Woman's Cupboard

YOU'RE HAVING A RETRO PARTY STAPLES

Seasonings
Garlic (powder)
Mustard (dry)
Pepper (black)
Sage (ground)

Salt
Season-All

Jazz It Ups
Bacon bits

Dressings, Oil and Sauces
Oil (canola, vegetable)
Hot pepper sauce
Vinegar (white)

Baking Needs
Sugar (brown, cane)

Frantic Necessities
Foil
Nonstick cooking spray

Dairy
Butter

The Frantic Woman Goes Shopping

INGREDIENTS YOU'LL NEED TO BUY

Produce: Fruit
1 lemon (Menu item 4)
1 orange (Menu item 8)

Produce: Veggies
2 green peppers (Menu item 1)
1 bunch celery (Menu item 1)
4 medium yellow onions (Menu items 1, 3)
1 Vidalia onion (Menu item 2)
1 medium head cabbage (Menu item 2)
2 heads broccoli (Menu item 4)

2 heads lettuce (Menu item 5)
1 small bunch parsley (Menu item 5)
1 bunch green onions (Menu item 5)

Seasonings

1 1.25-ounce package taco seasoning mix (Menu item 7)

Dressings, Oils and Sauces

1 16-ounce bottle barbecue sauce (Menu item 1)
1 16-ounce jar salsa (Menu item 7)

Canned Goods and Bottles

1 15-ounce can cream of celery soup (Menu item 3)
2 8-ounce cans mandarin oranges (Menu item 5)
2 20-ounce cans crushed pineapples (Menu item 6)

Noodles, Pasta and Rice

1 16-ounce bag egg noodles (Menu item 2)

Cereal, Nuts and Such

1 4-ounce bag slivered almonds (Menu item 5)
1 10.5-ounce bag miniature marshmallows (Menu item 6)

Beverages

1 32-ounce bottle cranberry juice (Menu item 8)
1 32-ounce bottle pineapple juice (Menu item 8)
1 2-liter bottle ginger ale (Menu item 8)

Baking Needs

2 3.25-ounce packages pistachio pudding mix (Menu item 6)

Bread, Chips and More

3 packages 8-count sandwich rolls (Menu item 1)
1 16-ounce bag tortilla chips (Menu item 7)

Fish, Meat and Poultry

1 5-pound chuck roast (Menu item 1)
1 pound ground beef (Menu item 7)

Dairy

1 8-ounce container sour cream (Menu item 3)
4 cups (16-ounces) sharp cheddar cheese, shredded (Menu items 3, 4)
1 8-ounce container plain yogurt (Menu item 4)
1 8-ounce package Velveeta cheese (Menu item 7)

Frozen

1 32-ounce bag frozen shredded potatoes (Menu item 3)
2 8-ounce containers whipped topping (Menu item 6)
1 12-ounce can frozen lemonade (Menu item 8)
1 12-ounce can frozen orange juice (Menu item 8)

JAZZ IT UP INGREDIENTS YOU'LL NEED TO BUY

Produce: Veggies

1 jalapeño pepper (Menu item 7)

Cereal, Nuts and Such

1 2-ounce bag sunflower seeds, shelled (Menu item 4)
1 2-ounce box raisins (Menu item 4)

Unloading the Load

- Hide any grocery items you think the kids might eat before the day of the party.
- Chop the onions as soon as you've finished putting away the rest of the groceries. If your bash happens to be days away, freeze the onions until you need them.
- Wash the parsley, and wrap it in a paper towel. Put it in a plastic bag.
- Cook the ground beef and freeze it if you will not be using it right away.
- If you're feeling ambitious and your party is in the next 24 hours, finish chopping and slicing your other fruits and veggies. On party day, you'll be glad you did.

PARTY DAY MENU

✦ Menu Item 1—Barbecue Beef ✦

Ann Stankiewicz's serves Barbecue Beef as the main course. What's great about this entree is once you put it together, you can go about cleaning the house without fiddling with the main course.

Dish up: 20 to 24 servings   Cooking time: 8 to 10 hours or more
Construction time: 10 minutes   Paraphernalia: Slow cooker

INGREDIENTS:

2 green peppers, chopped
3 medium yellow onions, chopped
6 celery ribs, chopped
1 5-pound chuck roast
1 cup barbecue sauce, your preference
1 tablespoon hot pepper sauce
1/2 cup white vinegar
1/2 cup water
3/4 cup brown sugar
3 packages sandwich rolls

To make:
1. Plug in slow cooker and heat on high.
2. Chop peppers, onions and celery.
3. Put roast in cooker. Add remaining ingredients, except brown sugar and buns. Cover.
4. Cook for 8 to 10 hours.
5. Take lid off cooker. Shred beef. Add brown sugar, mixing well.
6. Cook an additional 45 minutes. Serve on sandwich buns or rolls.

Dress It Down: Skip the onions and hot pepper sauce for those who prefer less sizzle in their sandwich.

Change It Up: Ann usually bakes this in the oven at 350 degrees for 6 hours. Then, she adds the brown sugar and bakes it for another 45 minutes. Afterwards, Ann puts the shredded beef in the slow cooker. I changed the cooking method to fit the frantic lifestyle.

BASKETFUL OF TIPS: Keep It Warm

If you're not serving immediately, put the cooker on low to keep it warm until the crowd is ready to chow down.

➤ *Menu Item 2—Pat's Haluski* ⬤

Family friend Pat Benzing makes a great batch of Haluski, aka cabbage and noodles. Whenever my husband and I host a party for his softball team (yes, he still plays), Pat usually brings a pan or two of Haluski, as it is a favorite dish in the Pittsburgh region. Once you've prepped every-thing, all you have to do is stir it every so often, and the roaster does the rest. PS: Have the kids do the stirring, saving you a task. PSS: If you do not have a roaster, borrow one. Ask your neighbors or friends. Someone is bound to have one to lend you for a short period of time.

Dish up: 18 to 24 servings   Cooking time: 2 hours
Construction time: 7 to 10 minutes   Paraphernalia: 8-quart electric roaster

INGREDIENTS:

1 medium head cabbage
1 medium Vidalia onion
2 sticks butter
⅓ cup canola oil
1 teaspoon salt
1 teaspoon pepper
1 teaspoon Season-All
1 teaspoon garlic powder
1 teaspoon ground sage
1 16-ounce bag egg noodles

To make:

1. Set roaster at 350 degrees.
2. Wash and cut cabbage into bite-size pieces. Peel and cut onion into bite-size pieces.

3. Melt 1 stick of butter in roaster. Add oil, cabbage and seasonings to roaster. Cook for 1½ hours, stirring every 15 minutes. (Simplify it: Give one of the kids a big wooden or plastic spoon to stir with. Have them take turns doing so.)
4. Cook noodles according to package directions. Do not overcook.
5. Add onions and cook for 30 minutes, stirring every 15 minutes.
6. Add cooked noodles. Stir everything together, mixing well.
7. As Pat says, "Dig in!" (Simplify it: You can put the roaster on low to keep the Haluski warm while serving.)

BASKETFUL OF TIPS: Simple Candle Holders

Buy several tapers and votives the next time you're at a discount store.

Then, pick up several pieces of fruit and/or vegetables (apples, oranges, lemons, limes, pumpkins or gourds) to use as candle holders. You'll need to make sure the fruits and/or vegetables will sit flat and upright. That will be the bottom. Dig out enough of the top end of each piece so you can insert the candle inside the hole snugly. Arrange several candleholders in the middle of a mirror or pretty platter, or on a variety of clear, inverted drinking glasses to put candles at varying heights. Light and enjoy the glow.

POTFUL OF KNOWLEDGE: That's a Lot of Party Stuff

Party and Paper Retailer Magazine reports 11.5 billion dollars in yearly party supply sales from independent, chain, franchise and online stores. That's a lot of money spent. So, if you have an annual party around the same time each year, think ahead. Buy seasonal or holiday-themed merchandise after the season, when it is on the clearance table.

✦ Menu item 3—Cheesy Potatoes ✦

Laurie Rizzo shared this painless recipe. Again, once you put it together, the oven does the hard part, giving you time to do something else. I've seen this potato dish at many parties, and it is always gobbled up.

Dish up: 12 to 15 servings

Cooking time: 70 minutes

Construction time: 7 to 10 minutes

Paraphernalia: 9- by 13-inch glass baking dish, large bowl

INGREDIENTS:

2 pounds frozen shredded potatoes

1 15-ounce can cream of celery soup

2 cups (8 ounces) sharp cheddar cheese, shredded

1 cup sour cream

1 yellow onion, finely chopped

To make:

1. Preheat oven to 350 degrees.
2. Combine the potatoes, soup, cheese, sour cream and onion in a large bowl. Mix together.
3. Transfer to baking dish. Bake for 70 minutes or until top is slightly golden. (Simplify it: I like to bake mine in a glass dish so I can make it earlier in the day and heat it up in the microwave later. If doing so, only bake for about 50 minutes, and then heat in microwave for 8 to 10 minutes.)
4. Serve.

Jazz It Up: Add crumbled bacon bits.

Dress It Down: Skip the onion. You can use jarred cheese sauce in place of shredded cheese.

Change It Up: Use hash brown potatoes if you can't find shredded ones or if they're pricier. You can put together the dish earlier in the day to make life a bit easier, but cut the cooking time down by 15 to 20 minutes, as the potatoes will be thawed.

FRANTIC WOMAN FAMILY FUN:
ABCs in the Kitchen

Laurie Rizzo pulls out the alphabet magnets while she's preparing Cheesy Potatoes. Her kids recite their ABCs and while putting the magnetic letters on the refrigerator. What a fun way to learn while mom is in the kitchen!

❧ *Menu item 4—Broccoli Salad* ❧

This is a family favorite and one I serve frequently at parties. It's a snap to prepare and tastes oh so good. Make it ahead of time, but don't put the dressing on until 30 minutes before serving.

Dish up: 12 to 15 servings   Cooking time: 10 minutes
Construction time: 10 minutes   Paraphernalia: Microwave

INGREDIENTS:

2 heads broccoli
2 cups (8-ounces) sharp cheddar cheese, shredded
1 cup low-fat plain yogurt
3 tablespoons fresh lemon juice
1/8 teaspoon dry mustard
Pinch garlic powder

To make:
1. Wash broccoli. Cut florets from heads of broccoli into bite-size pieces.
2. Combine florets and cheese.
3. To make dressing, combine yogurt, lemon juice, dry mustard and garlic powder, mixing well.
4. Pour dressing over broccoli mixture 30 minutes before serving. Mix to coat.

Jazz It Up: Add shelled sunflower seeds and/or raisins.
Change It Up: Use mayonnaise in place of yogurt.

❧ *Menu Item 5—Orange and Green Salad* ❧

Another uncomplicated side dish awaits you. Again, you can prepare most of Orange and Green Salad beforehand and wait until just before serving to mix it all together.

Dish up: 16 to 24 servings   Cooking time: 0
Construction time: 10 minutes   Paraphernalia: Large serving dish

INGREDIENTS:

2 heads lettuce

2 tablespoon fresh parsley, chopped

6 to 8 green onions, chopped

2 8-ounce cans mandarin oranges, drained

1 4-ounce package slivered almonds

½ teaspoon salt

4 tablespoons sugar

4 tablespoons vinegar

½ cup vegetable oil

To make:

1. Wash veggies.
2. Tear lettuce into bite-size pieces. Chop parsley and green onions.
3. Open oranges and drain juice.
4. Combine lettuce, parsley, onions, oranges and almonds in bowl.
5. To make dressing, combine salt, sugar, vinegar and vegetable oil. Blend well.
6. Pour dressing over lettuce mixture. Serve.

Jazz It Up: Add a dash of hot peppers sauce to the dressing for additional zip.

Dress It Down: Exchange 1 teaspoon dried parsley for fresh. Skip the almonds.

Change It Up: If you make this dish in advance, do not add the oranges and dressing until right before serving. This will keep the lettuce from becoming soggy.

BASKETFUL OF TIPS: Tear 'em Up

Pass that head of lettuce to the kids, and let them tear it up. And don't think your kids are too little to help (unless they're under the age of one). As reported in *The Frantic Woman's Guide to Life,* the first book I coauthored, the child chef Justin Miller started cooking at eighteen months. So, wash the kids' hands, pull up chairs, and let 'em tear it up.

❋ Menu Item 6—Pistachio Heaven ❋

"The Green Stuff" is what we call it in our house. This is one of our son and his friend's favorite desserts. It's quick and easy. All you'll need is the refrigerator after it's whipped together.

Dish up: 16 to 24 servings   Cooking time: 0
Construction time: 5 to 7 minutes   Paraphernalia: Large serving bowl

INGREDIENTS:
2 20-ounce cans crushed pineapples
2 3.25-ounce packages pistachio pudding mix
2 8-ounce containers whipped topping
2 cups miniature marshmallows

To make:
1. Open pineapple and put fruit and juice in a bowl.
2. Add pistachio mix to pineapples. Mix together. (Simplify it: Don't worry if you bought pineapple chunks instead of crushed. Just pour the fruit and juice in the blender and whirl for a few minutes to make your own crushed fruit.)
3. Add marshmallows and mix well.
4. Fold in whipped topping. Be sure to mix well.
5. Chill for at least 30 minutes before serving.

Change It Up: Replace whipped topping with a small carton of whipping cream. Use an electric mixer to whip cream for a healthier choice.

(TiPS) BASKETFUL OF TIPS: In the Party Mood
To get yourself in a party mood, inhale some peppermint, strawberries or buttered popcorn. According to a study conducted at Wheeling Jesuit University in West Virginia, these aromas can enhance your pep and motivation. So indulge your senses before your next bash.

FRANTIC WOMAN FAMILY FUN: Funny Putty

Concoct a container of funny putty for each of the kids on your guest list. And before you say, "I'll have enough to do," think about this. By giving the kids funny putty and the comic strips, you'll keep them entertained. The busier they are, the happier you will be. Bored kids make their own activities, and they might not be ones you would consider safe (for the kids or your belongings).

In a small bowl, mix together 2 tablespoons white glue and a drop of food coloring. Pour 1 tablespoon liquid starch in a second bowl. Slowly pour the glue mixture on top of the liquid starch. Allow the mixture to stand for 5 minutes or until the glue absorbs the starch. Remove the putty from the bowl and knead. The more you knead the putty, the smoother the consistency will be. Store funny putty in a plastic Easter egg, small container or zippered bag. Repeat for the number of kids attending. Psst! Give the kids the job of kneading the putty. Be sure to mark each egg, container or bag with a child's name to keep any arguments from breaking out.

⁂ Menu Item 7—Rita's Make-Ahead Mexi-Dip ⁂

Here's a quick-to-make dip from Rita Bergstein that she likes to prepare ahead of time and zaps in the microwave just before serving.

Dish up: 10 to 12 servings
Construction time: 10 minutes

Cooking time: 3 to 4 minutes
Paraphernalia: Microwave-safe baking dish, microwave

INGREDIENTS:

1 pound ground beef
1 1.25-ounce package taco seasoning mix
1 16-ounce jar salsa
1 8-ounce package Velveeta cheese
1 16-ounce bag tortilla chips

To make:
1. Cook ground beef in the skillet over medium heat until browned.
2. Drain excess fat. In baking dish, mix meat, taco seasoning and salsa.

3. Cube cheese. Top meat mixture with cheese.
4. Heat dip in microwave for about 3 to 4 minutes, or until heated through.
5. Serve with chips.

Jazz It Up: Add sliced jalapeño peppers for some sizzle.
Dress It Down: Skip the taco seasoning mix.

TiPS BASKETFUL OF TIPS:
Not All Cheese Products Are Alike
You might prefer to use a natural cheddar cheese instead of a processed cheese like Velveeta. Both will melt, but cheddar hardens more quickly than Velveeta.

❖ *Menu Item 8—Fruit Punch* ❖

Stir up a batch of punch that guests can get for themselves, saving you from fetching drinks all night. To keep the punch chilled throughout the evening, make an ice ring.

Dish up: 40 servings
Construction time: 5 to 7 minutes

Cooking time: 0
Paraphernalia: Punch bowl, ladle

INGREDIENTS:

1 32-ounce bottle cranberry juice
1 12-ounce can frozen lemonade, thawed
1 12-ounce can frozen orange juice, thawed
6 12-ounce cans cold water
1 32-ounce bottle pineapple juice
1 2-liter bottle ginger ale
1 orange, sliced, to garnish
Ice cubes

To make:

1. Mix all ingredients, except ginger ale. Allow ingredients to blend.
2. Slice orange, unpeeled.
3. Just before serving, add ginger ale, orange slices and ice cubes.

BASKETFUL OF TIPS: Fruity Ice Ring

Let the ice ring do the work of keeping the punch chilled for you so there's no need to worry about filling the ice bucket all night. To make an ice ring, pour cranberry juice in a round container or gelatin mold. Freeze. Before serving, put container or mold in warm water for 5 minutes to loosen. Pop ice ring out of container or mold and slip it into the punch.

YOU'RE HAVING A KIDS' PARTY

The celebration of your child's birthday should be a happy time. Unfortunately, all you can think about is the amount of time, energy and money involved. Each year seems to roll around faster and faster. However, keep in mind that one of these days your little one will be all grown up, and you're going to wonder where the time went? So consider your child's birthday party the chance to make memories. Don't worry about planning the food for the party—it's planned for you. And if time is limited, you have the option of choosing which entree to serve.

One last thing—each recipe is numbered, and the shopping-list ingredients correspond with the designated recipe.

PARTY DAY MENU

Menu Item 1—Lloyd's Boys' Favorite Chicken Strips
Menu Item 2—Mini Pizza Bagels
Menu Item 3—Veggies on a Frisbee
Menu Item 4—Brownie Cones
Menu Item 5—Homemade Granola
Menu Item 6—Apple-Berry Punch

THE SHOPPING LISTS

The Frantic Woman's Cupboard

YOU'RE HAVING A KIDS' PARTY STAPLES

Seasonings
Cinnamon
Garlic (powder)
Pepper
Poultry seasoning
Salt

Jazz It Ups
Cayenne pepper

Dressings, Oil and Sauces
Honey
Oil (vegetable)

Baking Needs
Flour (all-purpose)
Sugar (light brown)
Vanilla extract

Frantic Necessities
Plastic wrap or wax paper
Nonstick cooking spray

Dairy
Butter

The Frantic Woman Goes Shopping

Ingredients You'll Need to Buy

Produce: Veggies
1 head broccoli (Menu item 3)
1 8-ounce bag baby cut carrots (Menu item 3)
1 bunch celery (Menu item 3)
1 pint grape tomatoes (Menu item 3)

Dressings, Oils and Sauces
1 8-ounce can pizza sauce (Menu item 2)
1 16-ounce bottle ranch salad dressing (Menu item 3)

Cereal, Nuts and Such

12 flat-bottomed ice cream cones (Menu item 4)

1 16-ounce package chocolate crisp cereal (Menu item 5)

1 16-ounce package old-fashioned oatmeal (Menu item 5)

8 ounces walnuts (Menu item 5)

Baking Needs

1 21-ounce box brownie mix (plus ingredients: eggs, oil and water)
   (Menu item 4)

1 small container candy sprinkles (Menu item 4)

1 6-ounce package chocolate chips (Menu item 4)

1 6-ounce package flaked coconut (Menu item 5)

1 8-ounce box dried cranberries or raisins (Menu item 5)

Beverages

1 quart apple juice (Menu item 6)

1 quart cranberry juice (Menu item 6)

1 2-liter bottle ginger ale (Menu item 6)

Bread, Chips and More

1 dozen miniature bagels (Menu item 2)

Fish, Meat and Poultry

3 pounds skinless, boneless chicken breasts (Menu item 1)

Dairy

2 cups (8 ounces) mozzarella cheese, shredded (Menu item 2)

JAZZ IT UP INGREDIENTS YOU'LL NEED TO BUY

Produce: Veggies

Veggies, your choice (Menu item 3)

Baking Needs

Tropical fruit, dried (Menu item 5)

Fish, Meat and Poultry

Pizza toppings, your choice (Menu item 2)

Unloading the Load

- If the party is more than two days away, you will need to freeze your chicken for at least the first day.
- Hide groceries you feel the family might eat before you have a chance to serve them.

PARTY DAY MENU

✦ Menu Item 1—Lloyd's Boys' Favorite Chicken Strips ✦

Satisfying four hungry boys can be a feat. Renae Lloyd can cook up this main course without any complaints from her crew, ranging from age 4 to age 13. Anyone with kids knows that feeding each one the same thing and having them like it is an accomplishment. So this dish should easily curb the hunger of the kids coming to your house. Well, that is, unless they're all vegetarians.

Dish up: 8 to 12 servings

Construction time: 8 to 12 minutes

Cooking time: 12 to 15 minutes

Paraphernalia: Two 9- by 13-inch baking dish, large plastic zippered bag (or container with lid), small microwave-safe bowl, microwave

INGREDIENTS:

3 pounds skinless, boneless chicken breasts, cut into 1-inch strips

1 cup flour

2 teaspoons poultry seasoning

1 teaspoon salt

1 teaspoon garlic powder

1/2 teaspoon pepper

4 tablespoons butter, melted

To make:

1. Preheat oven to 425 degrees. Coat baking dish with nonstick cooking spray.
2. Cut chicken into 1-inch strips.
3. Combine flour, poultry seasoning, salt, garlic powder and pepper in a large plastic zippered bag. (Simplify it: If you do not have a plastic bag, a plastic container with a lid will work, too.)
4. Toss about 4 or 5 chicken strips into zippered bag. Seal closed and shake bag to coat the strips.
5. Place coated strips in baking dish. Repeat until all of the strips are coated. You might want to use two baking dishes so you can keep the chicken in a single layer to ensure even cooking. (Simplify it: Consider buying disposable baking pans to make cleanup easier.)
6. Melt butter in microwave-safe bowl in the microwave for 20 to 30 seconds. Drizzle melted butter over chicken. Bake for 12 to 15 minutes, or until juices run clear.

Jazz It Up: Add ½ teaspoon cayenne pepper for spicier strips.
Change It Up: Use whole-wheat flour for healthier strips.

FRANTIC WOMAN FAMILY FUN: Pass the Popcorn
If your party is a birthday celebration, try to play at least one game in which everyone can win something small rather than having one winner for every game. One idea would be Pass the Popcorn, a knockoff of Hot Potato. Ask the birthday child to help you make one bag (in a cellophane party-favor bag that can be tied closed or a plastic, zippered sandwich bag) of popcorn per attendee. Allow him or her to pick out her favorite music to play on party day. With this version, as each child leaves the circle, he or she gets to take the bag of popcorn. A new bag starts the next round.

❧ Menu Item 2—Mini Pizza Bagels ❧

Mini pizza bagels are a second option if time is limited. Serve these in place of the chicken strips or if you know one of the kids can't eat meat.

Of course, you could put these mini pizza bagels on the menu, too. If the attendees are teenagers, use full-size bagels instead of miniature ones.

Dish up: 12 servings

Cooking time: 5 to 6 minutes

Construction time: 5 to 10 minutes

Paraphernalia: Baking sheet

INGREDIENTS:

1 dozen miniature bagels

1 8-ounce can pizza sauce

2 cups (8 ounces) mozzarella cheese, shredded

To make:

1. Preheat oven to 425 degrees.
2. Split bagels in half.
3. Spread sauce on each bagel half.
4. Sprinkle with shredded cheese.
5. Cook for about 5 to 6 minutes.

Jazz It Up: Add toppings of choice.

TIPS BASKETFUL OF TIPS: Make-Ahead Mini Pizzas
You can prepare and bake the mini pizza bagels and then reheat them in the microwave. To reheat: Put 4 bagels on a plate and heat for 30 to 40 seconds.

✦ Menu Item 3—Veggies on a Frisbee ✦

The kids will get a kick out of seeing sliced veggies arranged on a Frisbee. Pour ranch salad sdressing into a miniature bucket to go with the veggies. Be sure the toys are new ones, and line them with wax paper or plastic wrap to keep the plastic of the toy from adding a bitter taste to the food.

Dish up: 10 to 12 servings

Cooking time: 0

Construction time: 10 minutes

Paraphernalia: Kid's toy Frisbee (or serving platter)

INGREDIENTS:

1 8-ounce bag baby cut carrots
1 bunch celery
1 head broccoli
1 pint grape tomatoes
Ranch salad dressing

To make:

1. Wash vegetables.
2. Cut the ends off each rib of celery. Cut each rib in half lengthwise and horizontally.
3. Cut the florets off the broccoli. Cut into bite-size pieces.
4. Arrange veggies on Frisbee or serving tray.

Jazz It Up: You can add sliced mushrooms, cucumbers, green peppers or any other favorite veggie.

Dress It Down: Buy precut veggies from the salad bar at your grocery store. and arrange them on the frisbee.

TIPS | BASKETFUL OF TIPS: Double-Dipping

To avoid the possibility of double-dipping, put a serving spoon in the miniature bucket containing the ranch salad dressing. The kids can scoop out some dressing onto their plates and then double-dip all they want.

❖ Menu item 4—Brownie Cones ❖

A brownie in a cone is a yummy way to end the party. The cones can be made the day before as long as you store them in an airtight container.

Dish up: 12 servings
Construction time: 10 minutes

Cooking time: 25 to 30 minutes
Paraphernalia: Muffin tin or baking sheet, small sauce pan

INGREDIENTS:

12 flat-bottom ice cream cones

1 21-ounce box brownie mix (plus ingredients: eggs, oil and water)

1 6-ounce package chocolate chips

¾ stick butter

Candy sprinkles

To make:

1. Preheat oven to 350 degrees.

2. Place cones in muffin tin. (Simplify it: A muffin tin will keep the cones upright, so you won't have to worry about them falling over.)

3. Make brownie mix according to package directions. (Be sure not to overbeat the batter to keep brownies moist. Spoon batter into cones about three-fourths of the way to the top.

4. Bake for 25 to 30 minutes, or until the tops have cracked and have risen above the cone.

5. Remove from oven and cool. (Simplify it: Remove the cones from the muffin tins. They will cool faster.)

6. While cones are cooling, melt chocolate chips and butter in a pan over medium heat. When melted, dip the tops of the cones into the chocolate. Stand cones upright and drizzle sprinkles over top.

Dress It Down: Use canned frosting instead of melting chocolate chips.

FRANTIC WOMAN FAMILY FUN:
Make Your Own Brownie Cones

Let the kids fill up their own cones before they sit down to eat their meal. By the time the meal is over, the brownie cones should be cooked and ready to be frosted. They can dip their own cones and add sprinkles, too. This is something they'll enjoy, and one less task for you to complete.

BASKETFUL OF TIPS: Crooked Cakes and More

Allow your oven to preheat for 30 minutes when baking goodies, or you might end up with crooked cakes, brownies and more. With 30 minutes of preheating time, the oven walls will have soaked up the heat, so once you open the door to slip in your pan, the correct temperature will be reached again quickly. This eliminates lopsided tops forming on baked goods. And as your mother told you, "don't peek." You're allowing precious heat to escape. One last tip: only bake one cake or tray of cupcakes at a time to allow the heat to circulate evenly in the oven.

POTFUL OF KNOWLEDGE: Story of the Cone

In 1904, at the St. Louis World's Fair, an ice cream vendor ran out of serving dishes and couldn't sell any more of his product. Ernest Hamwi, a waffle vendor next to the ice cream vender, rolled a hot waffle into the shape of a cone and offered it in place of the dish. It was an instant hit. Unfortunately, Hamwi can't take credit for the invention, even though people give him credit for popularizing cones. In 1896, Italo Marchiony, an Italian immigrant who sold ice cream from a cart on the streets of New York, invented a machine to make these delicious edible holders and was granted the patent in 1903.

✦ Menu Item 5—Homemade Granola ✦

What I find fascinating about this recipe is that Loriann Hoff Oberlin created it to enter a contest and ended up using it in two different ways in two of her books. The recipe was published in *Working at Home While the Kids Are There, Too* as a way to spend time with the kids in the kitchen and in *Writing for Quick Cash* as an example of how to write and publish recipes. Additionally, Loriann makes homemade granola and gives it as gifts to her kids' teachers and activities instructors. Now that's a lot of mileage from one recipe.

Dish up: 12 cups

Cooking time: 25 to 30 minutes, plus 30 minutes cooling time

Construction time: 5 to 7 minutes

Paraphernalia: Large bowl, 3-quart pan, baking sheet

INGREDIENTS:

1 cup walnuts

2 teaspoons cinnamon

¾ cup flaked coconut

¼ cup light brown sugar

2½ cups uncooked old-fashioned oatmeal

3 cups chocolate crisp cereal

½ cup vegetable oil

½ cup honey

1 tablespoon vanilla extract

2 cups dried cranberries or raisins

To make:

1. Preheat oven to 300 degrees. Coat baking sheet with nonstick cooking spray.
2. Mix all dry ingredients, except fruit, in a large bowl.
3. Combine oil, honey and vanilla in a small saucepan, and warm it over medium heat.
4. Add warmed liquid to dry ingredients and stir until coated.
5. Spread mixture evenly on baking sheet.
6. Bake for 25 to 30 minutes, or until granola is golden brown. Stir halfway through the baking time.
7. Cool for 30 minutes. (Simplify it: Transfer granola to another tray for cooling to keep it from sticking.)
8. Stir in dried cranberriess or raisins.
9. Store in airtight container or cleaned, empty coffee can until party time.

Jazz It Up: Add dried stropical or fall fruit in place of raisins or dried cranberries.

Change It Up: For a nutritional boost, add 2 tablespoons protein powder and/or ¼ cup nonfat dry milk.

BASKETFUL OF TIPS: Party Favors

Put a cup or so of Homemade Granola in a plastic bag and tie it closed. Put this inside a trendy plastic container or silly-looking cup. With a permanent marker, write the kids' names on the cups and give them as favors at the end of the party.

✦ Menu Item 6—Apple-Berry Punch ✦

Make Apple-Berry Punch earlier in the day and store it in two pitchers with fitted lids, if possible (or use a plastic milk jug with a lid). During the party, keep the punch pitcher on the table or nearby for easy access. You'll eliminate unnecessary trips back and forth to the refrigerator.

Dish up: 8 to 12 servings
Construction time: 5 minutes

Cooking time: 0
Paraphernalia: Large mixing bowl,
two 2-quart pitchers with fitted lids

INGREDIENTS:

1 quart apple juice
1 quart cranberry juice
1 2-liter bottle ginger ale

To make:

1. Pour the ingredients into a large mixing bowl. Stir.
2. Pour punch into 2 pitchers.

Part Four

Side Dishes

[blank]

Within these pages, you will find two additional sections, We Go Good Together and A Dish We Must Bring, full of recipes for times when you need a bit more food. The We Go Good Together section offers recipes for the side dishes listed throughout *The Frantic Woman's Guide to Feeding Family and Friends*. A Dish We The Must Bring section offers recipes to make when you must bring a dish to a function.

WE GO GOOD TOGETHER

In this section, you'll find the recipes for the side dishes marked with a 🟢 that were recommended to accompany the main courses in Part Two, Seasonal Menus. Some of these side dishes could serve as a main meal. For your convenience, the side dishes are categorized by the seasons and are in the order in which they appeared. Enjoy!

Fall

❧ *Barbecue Succotash* ❧

Succotash always reminds me of Nicky, a boy I knew in grade school. His surname was just a syllable away from succotash, and he was plagued with that nickname for as long as I can remember. I hadn't thought about Nicky for years, until Deanne Thomas gave me this recipe. Oh, those childhood memories can bring on a smile.

Dish up: 4 to 6 servings
Construction time: 5 minutes

Cooking time: 25 to 30 minutes
Paraphernalia: 12-inch skillet, 3-quart pot

INGREDIENTS:

1 20-ounce box frozen corn

½ red onion, chopped

1 red pepper, chopped

1 14-ounce can black beans

1 tablespoon virgin olive oil

Salt and pepper, to taste

¼ cup barbecue sauce

1 tablespoon chives, chopped

1 tablespoon parsley

To make:

1. Cook corn according to package directions.
2. In skillet, sauté onions and peppers in olive oil for 5 minutes.
3. Drain and rinse beans. Add beans and cooked corn to skillet. Season with salt and pepper, to taste. Heat for 5 minutes.
4. Add barbecue sauce. Heat for another 5 minutes, or until heated through.
5. Garnish with chives and parsley.
6. Serve hot or cold.

✦ Green Beans, Feta and Dill ✦

Dish up: 4 to 6 servings
Construction time: 15 minutes

Cooking time: 7 minutes
Paraphernalia: 3-quart pot, serving bowl

INGREDIENTS:

2 pounds fresh green beans

½ cup Italian salad dressing

¼ cup (1 ounce) crumbled feta cheese

¼ cup fresh dill, chopped

To make:

1. Wash and cut ends off beans. Cook beans in boiling water for 7 minutes, or until tender-crisp. Drain. Rinse with cold water.

2. Combine beans, salad dressing, cheese and dill in a serving bowl. Mix well.

3. Serve or refrigerate until you need it.

Jazz It Up: Add ¼ cup chopped onion.
Dress It Down: Use 1 or 2 teaspoons dried dill, to taste, instead of fresh.
Change It Up: Use frozen or canned green beans instead of fresh.

✦ Potato Cakes ✦

Chef Dale Reabe's family likes eating potato cakes with their mushroom steak, and this dish is another favorite of his daughter's. To save time, pull out the box of instant potato flakes.

Dish up: 4 servings
Construction time: 7 to 10 minutes

Cooking time: 6 minutes
Paraphernalia: Medium mixing bowl, 12-inch skillet, rolling pin, plastic zippered bag, paper towels

INGREDIENTS:

Instant potato flakes, enough for 4 servings
½ teaspoon mix of thyme, oregano, basil, rosemary
2 teaspoons fresh parsley, snipped
1 teaspoon yellow onion, finely chopped
¼ cup plus 2 tablespoons saltine cracker crumbs
½ cup (2 ounces) cheddar cheese, shredded
1 egg, slightly beaten
¼ teaspoon salt
1 tablespoon vegetable oil

To make:

1. Prepare potatoes mix according to package directions. Cool.

2. Combine thyme, oregano, basil and rosemary to get the mix needed. Snip parsley. Chop onion.

3. Put about 15 crackers in a plastic zippered bag, seal, and crush crackers with a rolling pin. Crush more crackers if needed.

4. Slightly beat egg.
5. Mix potatoes, cheese, cracker crumbs, egg, parsley, onion, herb mix and salt.
6. Heat oil in skillet. Drop rounded tablespoons of the potato mixture into skillet. Flatten with spatula, and fry over medium heat until light brown, about 3 minutes on each side. Drain on paper towel.

Jazz It Up: Serve with applesauce, butter or sour cream.
Change It Up: You can use whatever seasonings you prefer.

Spinach Salad

This spinach salad, created by the concierge Rosalie Lesser, has an unusual twist that adds delectable flavor to each bite.

Dish up: 4 to 6 servings
Construction time: 7 to 10 minutes
Cooking time: 0
Paraphernalia: 1 medium bowl, 1 small bowl

INGREDIENTS:
1 pound strawberries, sliced
1 16-ounce bag spinach, chopped
1 red onion, sliced
½ cup sugar
¼ cup cider vinegar
1 tablespoon poppy seeds
1½ teaspoons onion, minced
¼ teaspoon Worcestershire sauce
¼ teaspoon paprika
½ cup canola oil

To make:
1. Wash strawberries. Cut stems off and slice.
2. Wash and chop spinach. Peel and slice onion.
3. Combine strawberries, spinach and onion.

4. Combine sugar, vinegar, poppy seeds, minced onion, Worcestershire sauce, paprika and oil in a small bowl, mixing well. Pour dressing over salad.

Jazz It Up: Add crumbled blue cheese.

Winter

❧ Stir-Fried Veggies ❧

Mia Cronan manages a home-based business, owns Mainstreetmom.com, and has five children under the age of ten. Frantic? You bet! Here's one of Mia's favorite recipes, which can be a complete meal for vegetarians.

Dish up: 4 to 6 servings   Cooking time: 8 minutes
Construction time: 7 to 10 minutes   Paraphernalia: 12-inch skillet

INGREDIENTS:

2 cups carrots, sliced
1 cup onion, sliced
2 cups cauliflower or cabbage, cut up
2 cups broccoli, cut up
1 tablespoon butter
2 tablespoons vegetable oil
2 tablespoons Worcestershire sauce
2 tablespoons lemon juice
1/2 teaspoon salt, optional
Dash of pepper
2 tablespoons parsley, chopped

To make:
1. Slice carrots and onion. Cut florets from cauliflower and broccoli into bite-size pieces. Shred cabbage.
2. In skillet, heat butter, oil, lemon juice and Worcestershire sauce for 2 minutes. Add carrots and onions. Stir-fry for 3 to 4 minutes. Stir

in other veggies and stir-fry for another 2 minutes. If you prefer softer vegetables, cook them until they are the way you like them.
3. Add a dash of pepper and salt.
4. Sprinkle chopped parsley over the vegetables. Serve hot.

⤞ Fruit Parfait ⤝

Here's a fun way to serve fruit, especially if you have a little one who would prefer not to eat his or her required servings each day.

Dish up: 4 servings Cooking time: 0
Construction time: 7 to 10 minutes Paraphernalia: 4 parfait glasses, medium bowl

INGREDIENTS:
2 6-ounce containers vanilla yogurt
1 cup whipped topping
3 pears, cut into cubes
3 papayas, cut into cubes

To make:
1. Combine yogurt and whipped topping in a medium bowl, mixing well.
2. Wash, peel and cut fruit into bite-size pieces.
3. Scoop 1 large spoonful of fruit into each parfait glass. (Use wine glasses, clear juice glasses or mugs if parfait glasses are not available.) Add 1 spoonful of yogurt topping next. Add another layer of fruit and finish with a spoonful of topping.

Jazz It Up: Add grated white chocolate as a garnish.
Change It Up: Replace the suggested fruit with your own preference.

✦ Desi's Fresh Veggies ✦

Mother of four Desiree Brusco's recipe for fresh veggies looks great on the dinner table any time of the year. You might want to consider serving this during the holidays, as the colors of the vegetables complement the holiday table.

Dish up: 8 servings

Construction time: 5 to 7 minutes

Cooking time: 30 minutes

Paraphernalia: 12-inch skillet, 3-quart pot, serving bowl

INGREDIENTS:

3 plum tomatoes, diced

6 cups fresh green beans, about 2 pounds

1 8-ounce carton portobello mushrooms

1 cup olive oil

6 cloves garlic, crushed

¾ cup Parmesan cheese

To make:

1. Wash tomatoes, beans and mushrooms.
2. Slice mushrooms into bite-size chunks. Dice tomatoes. Trim beans and cut in half.
3. Cook beans in boiling water (enough water to cover beans) for 10 to 15 minutes over medium heat.
4. While beans are cooking, preheat oil in skillet. Sauté garlic for a few minutes, until lightly browned. Add mushrooms and diced tomatoes and sauté for about 15 minutes over medium heat, stirring occasionally.
5. Add green beans to skillet and simmer for 10 minutes, or until veggies are tender.
6. Remove pan from heat. Add cheese, stirring until mixed thoroughly. Pour into serving bowl.

Change It Up: Desiree skips cooking her green beans separately. She adds them during Step 5 and increases the simmering time to 20 minutes.

❧ Fried Bananas ❦

Fried bananas is a popular Chinese snack and a perfect accompaniment for with any of the Backwards Meals.

Dish up: 4 servings
Construction time: 5 to 7 minutes

Cooking time: 5 to 6 minutes
Paraphernalia: 12-inch skillet, medium bowl, paper towels

INGREDIENTS:

4 bananas
1/3 cup flour
3 tablespoons cornstarch
1/2 teaspoon salt
1/2 teaspoon baking powder
1/2 teaspoon sugar
1/3 cup water
2 cups peanut oil

To make:
1. Peel bananas. Slice diagonally into ¾-inch pieces.
2. Combine flour, cornstarch, salt, baking powder, sugar and water. Mix well.
3. Heat oil in skillet over medium heat.
4. Dip bananas into batter, then place in skillet. Fry a few pieces at a time for a few minutes on each side, or until golden brown.
5. Drain on paper towels. Serve. Can be served cold, too.

Spring

❧ Mashed Cauliflower ❦

With the low-carb diet trend, cauliflower has become very popular. Here's a takeoff of good old-fashioned mashed potatoes, without as many carbs.

Dish up: 4 to 6 servings

Cooking time: 15 minutes

Construction time: 10 minutes

Paraphernalia: Glass pie plate, mixing bowl, electric mixer, microwave

INGREDIENTS:

1 head cauliflower

¼ cup water

¼ cup plain yogurt

4 tablespoons butter

1 teaspoon garlic powder

1 teaspoon black pepper

¼ cup (1 ounce) Monterey Jack cheese, shredded

To make:

1. Wash and cut florets off cauliflower.
2. Place florets, stem down, in glass pie plate with ¼ cup water. Cover and microwave for 3 minutes on high and let sit covered, for 2 more minutes. When cooked, cauliflower will mash when you poke it with a fork. If it doesn't, cook another 2 or 3 minutes more.
3. In a large bowl, combine cauliflower, yogurt, butter, seasonings and cheese. With electric mixer, whip until desired consistency is reached.

Change It Up: You can cook the cauliflower in a traditional steamer or pan for 15 minutes. Follow the rest of the directions.

❧ Green Bean Casserole ❧

Green Bean Casserole hit its heyday in the late 1970s. It's still a standard side dish in many homes, including mine. (Psst! I use skim milk and low-fat soup without sacrificing taste.)

Dish up: 6 to 8 servings

Cooking time: 10 minutes

Construction time: 5 minutes

Paraphernalia: 2-quart microwave-safe baking dish, microwave

INGREDIENTS:

2 16-ounce cans French-style green beans

1 14.5-ounce can cream of mushroom soup

½ cup french-fried onion rings

⅓ cup milk

To make:

1. Dump beans, soup, onion rings and milk into baking dish. Stir well.

2. Cover and microwave on high for 8 to 10 minutes, stirring once or twice.

Change It Up: Cook in the oven for 20 to 25 minutes at 350 degrees instead of zapping it.

✦ Grandma's Irish Cake ✦

Grandma never looked at a cookbook in her life. (Wouldn't she find it amusing that her granddaughter is writing one?) This frustrated my aunt Mary Joyce, because she wanted to make this cake, but Grandma didn't have the ingredients or their measurements written down. So, one day my aunt watched Grandma make the cake. As Gram was about to add each ingredient, Aunt Mary made Gram wait until she measured it. A fistful of this and a fistful of that wouldn't hack it for my aunt. Thank goodness, or I wouldn't have this old-world recipe. Hugs and kisses, Aunt Mary!

Dish up: 6 to 8 servings　　　Cooking time: 1 hour

Construction time: 5 to 7 minutes　Paraphernalia: Large mixing bowl,

10½-inch cast-iron skillet

INGREDIENTS:

3½ cups all-purpose flour

3 teaspoons baking powder

1 teaspoon baking soda

¾ cup sugar

1 teaspoon salt

2 cups baking raisins

1½ cups buttermilk

2 tablespoons butter

1 egg

To make:

1. Preheat oven to 350 degrees.
2. Mix the dry ingredients first. Aunt Mary says, "Make sure you use a fresh can of baking powder and box of baking soda."
3. Add the rest of the ingredients.
4. Place in a greased and floured cast-iron skillet. Dip knife in flour and make a cross on the top of the cake from side to side.
5. Bake for 1 hour, or until toothpick inserted in the center comes out clean. Enjoy!

TIPS BASKETFUL OF TIPS: Make It Cast Iron
Some cakes turn out so much better when baked in a cast-iron skillet. Pineapple upside-down cake is another favorite that comes out moister and tastier when made in cast iron. If you don't own one already, keep your eyes peeled for one on sale. Or if garage sales are your thing, scour local ones for this old-fashioned skillet that should never become obsolete.

✦ Baked Apple Slices ✦

Over the years, I've made different variations of this dish. Originally, I baked the apples in the oven. Now I use the microwave. The choice is yours.

Dish up: 4 to 6 servings

Construction time: 7 to 10 minutes

Cooking time: 20 minutes

Paraphernalia: Microwave-safe 9- by 9-inch baking dish, microwave

INGREDIENTS:

6 Yellow Delicious or Jonathan apples

½ cup brown sugar

2 tablespoons cornstarch

1 teaspoon cinnamon

1 stick butter or margarine

To make:

1. Wash, peel, and slice apples, discarding core.
2. Place apples in dish.
3. Combine brown sugar, cornstarch and cinnamon. Sprinkle over apples. Toss to coat.
4. Cut butter into pats. Dot apples with butter.
5. Cover and microwave on high for 15 minutes, or until apples are soft, stirring every 5 minutes.

Change It Up: Cover and bake in a 350-degree oven for 20 minutes or until soft.

Summer

✤ Grilled Veggies ✤

We're going to use the grill for the side dishes, too. Change the suggested veggies to preferred ones if these are not to your liking.

Dish up: 4 to 6 servings   Cooking time: 10 to 12 minutes
Construction time: 5 to 10 minutes   Paraphernalia: Grill, grill basket

INGREDIENTS:

1 yellow squash, cubed

1 zucchini, cubed

1 green pepper, cut up

2 tablespoons olive oil

¼ teaspoon black pepper

¼ teaspoon garlic powder

To make:

1. Fire up the grill. Coat grill basket with nonstick cooking spray.
2. Wash veggies. Cube squash and zucchini.
3. Cut green pepper into 1-inch squares.
4. Toss veggies with olive oil, and sprinkle on seasonings.
5. Place veggies in grill basket and grill with lid closed for about 10 to 12 minutes, stirring occasionally.

❧ Corn Fritters ❧

Kathy Nicoletti's corn fritter recipe brings back memories of her childhood in Wilmington, Delaware, in the 1950s. Her mother always bought huge quantities of fresh vegetables at the farmer's market in July and August. This is one dish Kathy loved and has served many times to her own children. Though this is offered as a side dish, Kathy says it can be a main course when made as thick as pancakes and served with syrup or when served in addition to fresh vegetables. Beefsteak tomatoes, Kathy's mom's favorite, complement the corn fritters.

Dish up: 4 to 6 servings
Construction time: 7 to 10 minutes

Cooking time: 4 minutes
Paraphernalia: Medium mixing bowl,
12-inch skillet, wide spatula,
paper towels

INGREDIENTS:

3 to 4 ears corn
2 eggs
1 teaspoon salt
2 level teaspoons baking powder
¾ cup milk
1 cup flour
Vegetable oil

To make:

1. Cut kernels off corn.
2. Combine all ingredients, except vegetable oil, to make batter, mixing well.

3. Pour oil into skillet to a depth of about ½ inch. Heat oil over medium heat.

4. Drop a heaping tablespoon of batter into the hot oil. Fry until golden brown and bubbles appear on the surface of the fritter, about 2 minutes. Turn and fry uncooked side for another 2 minutes, or until golden brown and crispy. Be sure to adjust the heat if fritters brown too quickly.

5. Drain on paper towels.

6. Serve plain, or enjoy with maple syrup.

➤ Grilled Potatoes ◄

For potato lovers, here's a way to enjoy the great outdoors and your favorite side dish.

Dish up: 4 to 6 servings   Cooking time: 14 to 18 minutes
Construction time: 5 minutes   Paraphernalia: Grill, tongs

INGREDIENTS:
6 small red potatoes
Vegetable oil
Parsley
Basil
Garlic

To make:
1. Fire up the grill.

2. Scrub and dry potatoes. Cut into quarters. Coat with vegetable oil. Sprinkle with seasonings.

3. Place potatoes, cut side down, on hottest part of grill. (Simplify it: Use a grill basket if the slats on your grill grates are soaced wide or your spuds could land on the charcoal.) Cook for 4 to 5 minutes. Turn to other cut side and cook for 4 to 5 minutes. Move potatoes to a cooler part of the grill and cook for 5 minutes. Potatoes should be tender when pierced with a sharp knife. If not, cook 1 to 2 minutes longer.

❧ Grilled Peaches ❧

Grill up peaches for something a little off the beaten path. This is quick and easy to make when the grill is sizzling.

Dish up: 6 servings
Construction time: 2 minutes

Cooking time: 4 minutes
Paraphernalia: Grill, tongs, basting brush

INGREDIENTS:

6 peaches
2 tablespoons vegetable oil
2 tablespoons honey

To make:

1. Heat grill to high.
2. Wash and dry fruit. Cut peaches in half. Remove pit. Brush cut side of peaches with oil.
3. Place on grill, cut side down. Grill for about 2 minutes, or until golden brown. Turn over and grill the outside for 2 minutes.
4. Place grilled fruit on a platter. Drizzle honey over fruit. Serve warm.

POTFUL OF KNOWLEDGE: Brown-Bag Ripening
Don't wait for fruit to ripen. Stick it in a brown bag, and it will do its thing faster. Fruit naturally discharges ethylene gas, which causes ripening, so being trapped inside a brown bag will speed up the process. Be sure to poke about a half dozen small holes in the bag so the fruit can get some fresh air.

❧ Marinated Tomatoes and Mozzarella Slices ❧

Homegrown tomatoes and mozzarella slices make a refreshing summertime salad.

Dish up: 4 to 6 servings
Construction time: 10 minutes

Cooking time: 0
Paraphernalia: Serving bowl

INGREDIENTS:

4 ripe tomatoes, sliced

½ pound mozzarella cheese, sliced

½ small Vidalia onion, sliced

½ cup Greek salad dressing, or your preference

½ teaspoon dill

To make:

1. Wash and slice tomatoes. Slice cheese if not already sliced, then quarter. Slice onion.
2. Put tomato, cheese and onion slices in bowl. Pour salad dressing on top. Toss together to coat veggies. Sprinkle dill on top.

Change It Up: You can replace the Greek salad dressing with Italian salad dressing.

⇜ Marinated Seasonal Veggies ⇝

The fresh taste of summer's best will burst in your mouth when you take the first bite.

Dish up: 4 to 6 servings
Construction time: 10 minutes

Cooking time: 0
Paraphernalia: Serving bowl

INGREDIENTS:

2 ripe tomatoes, sliced

2 cucumbers, peeled and sliced

1 green pepper, sliced

½ cup Italian salad dressing

1 teaspoon fresh basil, optional

To make:

1. Wash veggies. Peel cucumbers. Slice veggies.
2. Put sliced veggies in a bowl. Add salad dressing to veggies, mixing together to coat.
3. Top with basil.

Turkey Week

→ *Johanna's Stuffing* ←

Stuffing is one of those side dishes many people love to eat during the fall holiday but never seem to make during other times of the year. The recipe is a tradition in Johanna Roediger's house. It's a little different, as it bakes in a casserole dish instead of inside the turkey. Therefore, you can make it any time of the year.

Dish up: 15 to 18 servings
Construction time: 10 to
    15 minutes, plus drying time

Cooking time: 1 hour
Paraphernalia: 12-inch skillet, large
    mixing bowl, 9- by 13-inch baking
    dish

INGREDIENTS:
10 ribs celery, diced
3 loaves white bread or 3 packages bread cubes
3 yellow onions, diced
1 stick butter
Salt and pepper, to taste
1 cup milk
1 15-ounce can chicken broth

To make:
1. Wash celery.
2. Dry out three loaves of bread. The night before or morning of cooking day, lay bread slices on countertop. You'll need to flip them over at some point. (Simplify it: Buy packaged bread cubes to save time.)
3. Coat baking dish with nonstick cooking spray. Finely chop celery and onions.
4. Sauté onions and celery in butter.
5. Tear bread into smaller pieces and place in mixing bowl. (Simplify it: Give the kids this task.) Salt and pepper the bread.
6. Slowly add milk a little at a time. You only want to use enough to hold the bread together. If the bread falls apart, slowly add more milk. Add sautéed ingredients. Stir all ingredients together.

7. Pour into baking dish.
8. Add broth until you can see it around the sides of the dish.
9. Bake for 1 hour, or until crusty on top.

✣ Candied Yams ✣

Fall wouldn't be the same without a dish made from the orange veggie that we seem to forget about for the rest of the year. Pick up an extra can or two while they're on sale to make later. You can prepare this dish earlier in the day and heat it up in the oven right before serving it.

Dish up: 8 servings
Construction time: 15 minutes

Cooking time: 10 minutes
Paraphernalia: 3-quart pan, 9- by 13-inch baking dish

INGREDIENTS:
2 26-ounce cans yams
3/4 cup orange juice
1/3 cup maple syrup
3 tablespoons butter
1 teaspoon ginger

To make:
1. Preheat oven to 350 degrees.
2. Heat yams in pan over medium heat and cook for about 10 minutes.
3. Add remaining ingredients to yams. Mash ingredients together with fork.
4. Transfer ingredients to baking dish and heat for about 10 minutes in the oven.

Jazz It Up: Top with ½ cup miniature marshmallows.

✣ Pumpkin Pudding ✣

Michael Roediger, coordinator of East Pittsburgh Stay-at-Home Dads, offered this recipe for a tasty pudding dessert that is low in fat and calories.

Dish up: 6 to 8 servings
Construction time: 5 to 7 minutes

Cooking time: 0
Paraphernalia: Large bowl

INGREDIENTS:

1 3-ounce box butterscotch instant sugar-free pudding mix
2 cups skim milk
1 tablespoon artificial sweetener
1 cup canned pumpkin pie filling
1 teaspoon allspice or to taste
¼ cup light whipped topping

To make:
1. Mix all the ingredients together, except whipped topping.
2. Fold in whipped topping.
3. Chill and serve. (Michael says to chill overnight for best flavor.)

⤜ Baked Corn ⤛

Here's a great dump-and-bake recipe for the turkey dinner submitted by Loretta Shelapinsky, who needs uncomplicated meals she can fix quickly after a hectic day keeping 100 senior citizens busy at her day job.

Dish up: 6 to 8 servings
Construction time: 5 minutes

Cooking time: 45 minutes
Paraphernalia: 2-quart baking dish,
2 small bowls, microwave

INGREDIENTS:

2 eggs, beaten
½ cup butter or margarine, melted
1 cup all-purpose baking mix
1 26-ounce can whole corn
1 26-ounce can creamed corn
1 cup sour cream

To make:

1. Preheat oven to 350 degrees. Coat baking dish with nonstick cooking spray.
2. Beat eggs. Melt butter in microwave by cooking for 20 to 30 seconds.
3. Mix all ingredients together.
4. Pour into baking dish and bake for 45 minutes. Test for doneness by inserting a knife in the middle. If knife comes out clean, the casserole is ready to eat.

Change It Up: Replace the all-purpose baking mix with 1 box Jiffy Corn Muffin mix.

Ham Week

✄ Barb's Golden Potatoes ✄

Barb Hawk gathered together quick and easy family recipes and compiled them in a book for her daughter as a bridal shower gift. This is one of Barb's recipes from the family cookbook. As Barb suggests, this is a great way to get the kids to eat carrots.

Dish up: 6 servings
Construction time: 7 to 10 minutes

Cooking time: 15 to 20 minutes
Paraphernalia: Dutch oven, electric mixer, large serving bowl

INGREDIENTS:
6 to 8 baking potatoes (Idaho), peeled and cubed
4 to 5 carrots, peeled and sliced
1 small onion, chopped
1 stick butter or margarine
Salt and pepper, to taste

To make:

1. Boil potatoes, carrots and onion in pot for 15 minutes to 20 minutes, or until tender.
2. Drain and rinse vegetables in hot water.
3. Add butter and seasonings to potato mixture. With electric mixer, whip for a few minutes until smooth and creamy.

Jazz It Up: Add garlic powder or lemon pepper.

Dress It Down: Skip the onion.

Change It Up: Barb's family members like their potatoes stiff. If you like your potatoes thinner, slowly add milk until they are thin enough for your liking.

❖ *Arla's Asparagus* ❖

Arla Seybert works for a builder/land development company in Pittsburgh. During the warm-weather months, her office is full of people rushing to accomplish as much as possible before the cold weather arrives. And in Pittsburgh, there are more cold, dreary days than warm, sunny ones. When Arla arrives home at night, she wants to make something uncomplicated, but flavorful. Arla has tweaked this dish so that it can be cooked for company, too.

Dish up: 4 servings

Construction time: 10 minutes

Cooking time: 7 to 10 minutes

Paraphernalia: 3-quart pot, serving platter, small bowl, paper towels

INGREDIENTS:

1 1/4 teaspoons tarragon

1 bunch fresh asparagus

1 8-ounce carton snowcap mushrooms

1/2 cup light mayonnaise

1 tablespoon fresh lemon juice

1 tablespoon plus 1 teaspoon water

To make:

1. Rub tarragon to a powder. Wash vegetables.
2. Prepare fresh asparagus by bending each stalk until the woody base snaps off.
3. Blanch asparagus in boiling water for 7 to 10 minutes until tender-crisp, or to your liking. Cool and pat dry.
4. Slice mushrooms. (Do not cook.)
5. Arrange asparagus and mushrooms on a serving dish.

6. Blend mayonnaise, tarragon, lemon juice and water to make sauce.

7. Drizzle sauce over vegetables. Refrigerate until ready to serve.

Jazz It Up: Add roasted red peppers

Dress It Down: Skip the mushrooms.

Change It Up: Use frozen asparagus and cook according to package directions.

❧ Barb's One, Two, Three Coleslaw ❧

Barb Hawk's coleslaw recipe is so simple that the kids can whip it up without any help from you. Barb uses this same dressing for potato salad and broccoli salad, too.

Dish up: 6 servings

Cooking time: 0

Construction time: 5 to 7 minutes

Paraphernalia: Large serving bowl

INGREDIENTS:

1/2 cup Miracle Whip

1/4 cup sugar

1 16-ounce package coleslaw mix

To make:

1. Mix Miracle Whip and sugar in a large bowl until sugar is dissolved.

2. Add coleslaw and toss together until coated.

3. Refrigerate until ready to serve.

A DISH WE MUST BRING

Throughout the year, there will be many times you'll need to bring a dish. It could be for a family celebration, potluck supper, banquet, fundraiser, classroom party, holiday dinner—the list of occasions goes on and on. I pulled together some of the favorites that fellow frantics have prepared. Some are favorites because they're simple, make oodles, are gobbled up quickly, or are cheap eats when money is tight. So, try one of these frantic favorites the next time you're off to a bash and must take a dish.

Appetizers and Dips

✦ Desi's Dip ✦

Desiree Brusco's dip is one of those fast and furious recipes you need when invited to a party last-minute.

Dish up: 8 to 10 servings   Cooking time: 0
Construction time: 10 minutes   Paraphernalia: Medium bowl, electric mixer, serving tray

INGREDIENTS:
1 14.25-ounce can chunk chicken
1 8-ounce package cream cheese, softened
2 tablespoons onion, finely chopped
1 16-ounce package crackers, your preference

To make:
1. Peel and finely chop onion.
2. Combine softened cream cheese and chicken. Mix with electric mixer on low for 1 or 2 minutes, or until blended together.
3. Add onions and stir by hand.
4. Put dip in small bowl. Place bowl of dip in center of a serving tray, and surround with crackers.

➤ Rita's Travel Dip ◄

Here's Rita Bergstein's five-ingredient dip, which takes 5 minutes to prep and 5 minutes to cook. Best of all, it travels better than the kids do.

Dish up: 8 to 10 servings
Construction time: 5 minutes

Cooking time: 5 to 7 minutes
Paraphernalia: Pie plate

INGREDIENTS:

1 8-ounce package cream cheese
1 can chili (with or without beans)
1 cup salsa
½ teaspoon onion powder
2 cups (8 ounces) Mexican cheese blend, shredded

To make:

1. Press cream cheese into bottom of pie plate.
2. Layer chili over cream cheese. Top with salsa.
3. Sprinkle onion powder over the ingredients, to taste.
4. Top with cheese. Rita says, "Do not use cheddar, as it gets too hard too fast."
5. Heat in the microwave until the dip gets bubbly, about 5 to 7 minutes.
6. Serve with tortilla chips.

Change It Up: Use 1 can chopped green chilies instead of salsa.

➤ Spinach Balls ◄

You can make these appetizers ahead of time and freeze them without losing any of the flavor. And these little balls pack a lot of taste in every bite. This is another recipe that was passed from one person to another. Johanna Roediger passed it down to her son Michael, who passed it along to this frantic woman.

Dish up: 20 servings
Construction time: 10 minutes

Cooking time: 20 minutes
Paraphernalia: Large mixing bowl, baking sheet

INGREDIENTS:

2 10-ounce packages frozen spinach, chopped

2 packages herb stuffing
6 eggs, beaten
1 tablespoon pepper
1 tablespoon Italian seasoning
½ teaspoon thyme
1 tablespoon garlic powder
½ cup (2 ounces) Parmesan cheese
¾ cup (3 ounces) cheddar cheese, melted

To make:
1. Preheat oven to 350 degrees.
2. Cook spinach according to package directions and drain.
3. Mix all ingredients together.
4. Shape into small balls, about 1 inch in diameter.
5. Place on baking sheet. Bake for 20 minutes.

＊ Zucchini Appetizer ＊

Diane Etherington knows how to work a room, mingling with those she knows and those she soon will. And she's not so bad in the kitchen, either, as this recipe shows.

Dish up: 10 to 12 servings Cooking time: 30 minutes
Construction time: 7 to 10 minutes Paraphernalia: 9- by 13-inch baking dish, small bowl

INGREDIENTS:
3 cups zucchini, diced
½ cup onion, diced
½ cup green pepper, diced
1 cup pepperoni (about 20 slices), diced
4 eggs, beaten
½ cup (2 ounces) Romano or Parmesan cheese, grated
½ teaspoon oregano
2 tablespoons parsley
½ teaspoon black pepper
1 cup all-purpose baking mix
½ cup oil

POTFUL OF KNOWLEDGE: A Girl's Best Friend
Eat up that broccoli, because it's a girl's best friend. Researchers found that two ½-cup servings per week may reduce your risk of breast cancer. Two cancer-fighting components, indoles that may block estrogen's role in breast cancer and sulforaphane that increase the enzymes that clear chemical carcinogens, are found in broccoli. So girlfriend, take another scoop of that broccoli casserole.

To make:

1. Preheat oven to 350 degrees. Coat baking dish with nonstick cooking spray.
2. Wash veggies. Diced zucchini, leaving skins on. Peel and dice onion. Dice green pepper and pepperoni.
3. Beat eggs in a small bowl.
4. Mix all ingredients together in baking dish.
5. Bake for 30 minutes, or until golden brown. Cut into squares and serve.

Side Dishes

⇢ Broccoli, Rice and Cheese ⇠

I love dump-and-bake recipes, and so does Loretta Shelapinsky. As an activities professional, some days she's more frazzled than she'd like to be. On those days, dump-and-bake recipes are lifesavers. And as a covered dish, the casserole looks like it was more of an effort than it really was.

Dish up: 10 to 12 servings
Construction time: 5 minutes

Cooking time: 1 hour
Paraphernalia: 9- by 13-inch baking dish, small bowl, microwave

INGREDIENTS:
1 24-ounce bag frozen broccoli, chopped
½ cup celery, chopped
½ cup yellow onion, chopped

½ cup butter, softened

1 cup instant rice

1 cup cold water

1 10.75-ounce can cream of mushroom soup

1 8-ounce jar cheese sauce

To make:

1. Preheat oven to 350 degrees.
2. Chop broccoli, celery and onion. Soften butter in the microwave for about 10 to 15 seconds.
3. Mix all ingredients together in baking dish.
4. Cover and bake for 55 minutes. Remove cover and bake for another 5 minutes.

⇒ Cannon's Crunchy Grapes ⇐

This is a favorite dish my longtime friend Linda Cannon, who seems to find herself in the middle of more madcap adventures than a television character, likes to take to family gatherings. And with five siblings, there's a constant flow of celebrations. Linda warns, "Make sure you buy seedless grapes." Once she mistakenly picked up seeded grapes. Guests thought the crunch was the pecans!

Dish up: 10 to 14 servings   Cooking time: 0

Construction time: 7 to 10 minutes,   Paraphernalia: Large bowl, medium bowl
    plus overnight chilling time

INGREDIENTS:

1½ pounds green grapes, seedless

1½ pounds purple grapes, seedless

1 cup pecans, chopped

½ cup brown sugar

1 8-ounce package cream cheese, softened

1 8-ounce container sour cream

1 tablespoon vanilla

½ cup cane sugar

Basketful of Tips: Traveling Dishes

Follow these tips for transporting your covered dishes to the shindig:

- The next time you're at the local dollar store, buy several airtight containers, disposable baking pans and plastic serving trays. This way when you take a dip, casserole or dessert to a party, you won't have to worry about getting back one of your much-loved serving pieces.
- Consider buying a package of serving utensils, too. Sometimes, you can find three or four pieces in a bag for a dollar. This will keep guests from scooping out the tossed salad with plastic forks. By taking the utensil your dish needs, you'll save your hostess from searching for one, and she'll probably return the favor when the bash is at your place.
- Wrap the dish in a heavy towel to keep it warm until you arrive. If you think the dish will cool too quickly before your arrival, save the last 10 minutes of baking time until you get there. Be sure to let the hostess know ahead of time that you'll need the oven for a few minutes.

To make:

1. Wash grapes. Chop pecans.
2. Combine grapes, brown sugar and pecans in large bowl.
3. In another bowl, mix together softened cream cheese, sour cream, vanilla and cane sugar. This is your dressing.
4. Pour dressing over grapes. Do not mix dressing into grapes. The dressing will slide down through the ingredients. Chill overnight. Before serving, mix gently.

✦ French Rice ✦

This recipe from Diane Disk can be tossed together in minutes. Then as it bakes, you have plenty of time to get dressed for the event.

Dish up: 8 to 10 servings
Construction time: 3 minutes

Cooking time: 1 hour
Paraphernalia: 9- by 13-inch baking dish

INGREDIENTS:
1 14.5-ounce can beef broth

1 14.5-ounce can French onion soup
1 4-ounce jar mushrooms, drained
1 cup white rice, washed (not instant)
1 stick margarine, cut into pats

To make:
1. Preheat oven to 350 degrees.
2. Pour all ingredients into baking dish.
3. Bake for 1 hour, or until all liquid is absorbed.

⟶ *Jilly-ental's Salad* ⟵

Business manager Jill Allan and I allowed our hearts to overrule our common sense. We each adopted a puppy within a few days of each other. (And the timing was wrong for both of us. For me, it was four weeks before this book was due on my editor's desk. For Jill, it was 2 weeks before leaving on a vacation. With this recipe, though, Jill could create her salad, participate in a dinner party, and still keep an eye on her adventurous pup.

Dish up: 24
Construction time: 10 to 15 minutes

Cooking time: 0
Paraphernalia: Large serving
    bowl, small mixing bowl

INGREDIENTS:

2 12-ounce packages coleslaw mix
2 3-ounce packages ramen noodles, beef flavored
1 bunch green onions
1 cup almonds, slivered
1 cup sunflower seeds, shelled
1 cup oil
1/2 cup vinegar
1/2 cup sugar

To make:
1. Dump coleslaw mix into large bowl. Break up uncooked ramen noodles and put into the bowl. (Do not add beef flavoring.)
2. Wash and dice green onions, including tops. Add to coleslaw mixture.
3. Add almonds and sunflower seeds.
4. Combine oil, vinegar, sugar, and beef seasoning packets from noodles in small bowl. Whisk the ingredients together. Pour over coleslaw mixture, mixing well to coat.

Change It Up: Cut the ingredients in half if you need fewer servings.

☞ Linda's Special Delivery ☜

This delicious dish shared by Linda Cannon is perfect for a potluck supper, a surprise meal for a new mom or to drop off to a friend or neighbor who is under the weather.

Dish up: 4 to 6 servings
Construction time: 10 to 15minutes

Cooking time: 25 to 30 minutes
Paraphernalia: Large bowl, small microwave-safe bowl, 3-quart pot, 9-by-13-inch baking dish, plastic zippered bag, rolling pin

INGREDIENTS:
2½ cups chicken, cubed (about 1½ pounds)
1 10.75-ounce can cream of chicken soup
2 teaspoons poppy seeds
2 cups sour cream
1 sleeve Ritz crackers
½ cup butter, melted

To make:
1. Preheat oven to 350 degrees. Coat baking dish with nonstick cooking spray.
2. Cube chicken. Cook in boiling water for about 10 minutes.

3. Combine soup, sour cream and poppy seeds in a large bowl.
4. Stir in chicken. Pour mixture into baking dish.
5. Put crackers in plastic zippered bag and crush them with the rolling pin.
6. Melt butter in a small bowl in microwave for about 20 seconds.
7. Dump crushed crackers into bowl with melted butter and mix well.
8. Pour crumb mixture on top of chicken mixture.
9. Bake for 25 to 30 minutes.

✤ Sweet Salad ✦

Here's another favorite recipe from Linda Cannon, who gives new meaning to the word frantic. With her oldest child married and two in college, she started her own business as a nanny, and she's in high demand. Working longer hours than she did at her office job, she looks for uncomplicated recipes that still taste good.

Dish up: 8 to 10 servings
Construction time: 10 to 12 minutes,
   plus 1 hour resting time

Cooking time: 5 minutes
   Paraphernalia: 2-quart pot, large
   servings bowl, medium mixing
   bowl, wax paper

INGREDIENTS:

¾ cup butter
3 ounces slivered almonds
¾ cup sugar
1 package dry Good Seasons Italian salad dressing mix, plus ingredients
1 8-ounce can mandarin oranges
1 head romaine lettuce

To make:
1. Melt butter in pot. Toss in almonds. Sprinkle sugar on top, stirring slowing. Cook about 5 minutes.
2. Scoop almonds out of pot and lay on a piece of wax paper to dry. Allow nuts to rest for 1 hour. (Almonds will be too sticky if you do not allow them to dry.)
3. Mix together dry Good Seasons mix with liquid from mandarin oranges.

4. Add the required ingredients according to the Good Seasons package directions to make salad dressing.

5. Tear lettuce into bite-size pieces and put into large bowl. Add oranges and almonds.

6. Pour dressing over lettuce fixings right before serving.

☀ Vegetarian Ramen Salad ☀

Michael Roediger, coordinator of East Pittsburgh Stay-at-Home Dads, shared this unusual side dish, which is perfect for those who prefer a vegetarian meal.

Dish up: 10 to 12 servings
Construction time: 15 minutes
    plus 2 hours chilling time

Cooking time: 10
Paraphernalia: Large serving bowl, small bowl, skillet

INGREDIENTS:

1 cup almonds, slivered
8 green onions, chopped
2 3-ounce packages ramen noodle soup, mushroom flavor
1 16-ounce bag coleslaw salad mix
⅔ cup olive oil
6 tablespoons white vinegar

To make:

1. Coat skillet with nonstick cooking spray. Cook almonds in skillet over medium heat for about 3 to 4 minutes to toast almonds. If almonds start to burn, lower the heat.

2. While almonds are toasting, chop green onions. Crumble Ramen noodles. (Set ramen noodles seasoning packets aside.)

3. Combine green onions, noodles and coleslaw mix in large bowl.

4. In separate smaller bowl, combine olive oil, vinegar and ramen seasoning packets.

5. When almonds are toasted, add to noodle and coleslaw mixture.

6. Add oil and seasoning mixture to coleslaw mixture. Toss all ingredients together. Chill for at least 2 hours so noodles become soft.

Desserts

✤ *Angel Cake* ✦

This is one of Dawn Check's favorite goodies to make for church dinners. It's easy. It's light. It's yummy!

Dish up: 8 to 10 servings
Construction time: 5 minutes

Cooking time: According to package directions.
Paraphernalia: Tube pan or loaf pan

INGREDIENTS:

1 box angel food cake mix
1 20-ounce can crushed pineapples

To make:

1. Preheat oven to 350 degrees. Coat pan with nonstick cooking spray.
2. Combine angel food cake mix and crushed pineapples. Do *not* add any of the ingredients directed on the box.
3. Put the mixture in a cake pan and bake according to package directions. Let cool.

Jazz It Up: Top with ice cream, whipped cream or whipped topping.

✤ *Ann's Coconut Cream Dessert* ✦

Ann Stankiewicz's daughter Joann loves this dessert, which her mom whips up during summer vacation at their cabin or for parties.

Dish up: 12 servings
Construction time: 10 minutes

Cooking time: 25 minutes, plus overnight freezing time
Paraphernalia: Smaller skillet, microwave-safe small bowl, medium bowl, 9- by 13-inch baking dish

INGREDIENTS:

1 cup slivered almonds, toasted

½ cup butter, melted

½ cup coconut

1 cup flour

¼ cup packed brown sugar

2 3-ounce packages coconut cream instant pudding

1 3-ounce package vanilla instant pudding

4 cups milk

1 12-ounce container whipped topping

To make:

1. Coat skillet with nonstick cooking spray. Heat almonds in skillet over medium-low heat for 3 to 4 minutes, toasting nuts.

2. Cut butter into pats. In small bowl, melt butter in microwave for 20 to 30 seconds.

3. Combine butter, coconut, almonds, flour and brown sugar. Reserve 1 cup of this crumb mixture for topping. Spread the remainder evenly in baking dish. Bake for 25 minutes at 350 degrees, stirring every 10 minutes.

4. In medium bowl, combine coconut cream pudding mix, vanilla pudding mix and milk, mixing well.

5. Add whipped topping to pudding mixture. Spread whipped pudding mixture on top of crumb crust.

6. Sprinkle the reserved uncooked crumbs on top.

7. Refrigerate overnight.

(TIPS) BASKETFUL OF TIPS: Crumb-free Cake Separation

Freeze cakes slightly before you try slicing them. The slightly frozen cake allows the knife to glide through and eliminates excess crumbling.

❧ Boston Cream Pie, Simplified ❧

Dish up: 8 to 10 servings

Construction time: 7 to 10 minutes

Cooking time: 20 to 25 minutes

Paraphernalia: Mixing bowl, electric mixer, two 8-inch round cake pans

INGREDIENTS:

1 box yellow cake mix, plus ingredients (eggs, oil and water)

1 teaspoon lemon extract

1 16-ounce can vanilla pudding, chilled

1 16-ounce can chocolate frosting, softened

Butter

Flour

To make:

1. Preheat oven to 350 degrees. Grease and flour cake pans.

2. Prepare cake mix according to package directions. Add in lemon extract.

3. Pour batter into two 8-inch round cake pans and bake according to package directions. Cool completely.

4. Split cakes in half horizontally with a serrated knife. (See Basketful of Tips below.)

5. Divide pudding in half. Spread pudding over bottom half of each cake. Place the top half of each cake over the pudding.

6. Spread frosting on the top of one cake layer. Top this frosted layer with the second cake layer. Frost the top of this second layer. (Simplify it: You can heat the can of frosting in the microwave for 30 seconds to make frosting the layers easier. Be sure to take off the lid and foil from the container.)

❧ Ann's Drumstick Dessert ❧

Drumstick Dessert is another favorite from the Stankiewicz family. It has ingredients similar to those in the delicious cones sold from ice cream trucks. This recipe needs to be made the night before the party, which saves you from a task to accomplish on party day.

Dish up: 15 servings

Construction time: 15 minutes, plus overnight freezing time

Cooking time: 0

Paraphernalia: 9- by 13-inch baking dish, 2 large bowls, plastic zippered bag, rolling pin

INGREDIENTS:

60 vanilla cookie wafers

¼ cup butter, melted

½ cup nuts, chopped

4 tablespoons peanut butter, creamy (for crust)

1 8-ounce cream cheese, softened

½ cup sugar

1 cup peanut butter, creamy (for batter)

1 teaspoon vanilla

1 16-ounce container whipped topping

Chocolate syrup

To make:

1. Coat baking dish with nonstick cooking spray.

2. Put wafers in a plastic zippered bag and crush them with a rolling pin.

3. Cut butter into pats and melt in microwave for 20 to 30 seconds or on the stove top. Mix 4 tablespoons peanut butter with melted butter in a large bowl. Add wafers and nuts and mix together to form crust. Reserve ½ cup of crust mixture to use as topping. Press remaining crust mixture into baking dish.

4. In a bowl, blend together cream cheese, sugar, 1 cup peanut butter and vanilla, mixing well. Fold in whipped topping. Pour this mixture over crust, spreading to seal all edges. Drizzle chocolate syrup in a crisscross design over top of cream cheese mixture. Sprinkle the reserved ½ cup of crust mixture on top.

5. Freeze overnight. Remove 20 minutes before serving. Cut into squares.

⇢ Grandma Stinemetz's Peach Crisp ⇠

Alice Stinemetz passed this tasty fruit dessert on to her grandson Michael Roediger, who passed it on to me.

Dish up: 6 to 8 servings　　　　Cooking time: 45 minutes

Construction time: 5 to 7 minutes　Paraphernalia: Mixing bowl, small bowl, sifter, 8- by 9-inch baking dish

INGREDIENTS:

1 egg

1 46-ounce can sliced peaches

1 cup sugar

1 cup flour

1 teaspoon baking powder

1/4 teaspoon salt

Cinnamon

Butter

To make:

1. Preheat oven to 350 degrees.
2. Put peaches in baking dish.
3. Crack egg into a small bowl and beat lightly with fork.
4. Sift together sugar, flour, baking powder and salt.
5. Mix sifted ingredients with egg until course in texture.
6. Sprinkle egg and sugar mixture evenly over peaches.
7. Sprinkle cinnamon over entire dish, to taste.
8. Dot with butter.
9. Bake for 45 minutes.

⇒ Ho Ho Cake ⇐

Caterer Gloria Czesnakowski has prepared many dishes over the years. Though Gloria has created many complicated dishes, one that seems to be a hit with many people is Ho Ho Cake. If you're a chocolate lover, this one is definitely for you.

Dish up: 12 servings

Construction time: 10 minutes

Cooking time: 35 minutes

Paraphernalia: Two mixing bowls, 15½ by 10½ by 1/8-inch jelly roll pan

INGREDIENTS:

1 double chocolate cake mix, plus ingredients (eggs, oil and water)

1/2 cup butter or margarine

2/3 cup vegetable shortening

3/4 cup sugar

5 ounces evaporated milk

1 can milk chocolate frosting

To make:

1. Preheat oven to 350 degrees.
2. Prepare cake mix according to package directions. Pour into jelly roll pan and bake according to package directions.
3. Cool cake.
4. Whip together butter, shortening, sugar and evaporated milk. Spread over cake.
5. Heat chocolate frosting in the microwave for 45 seconds. (Be sure to take off the lid and foil first.) Pour heated frosting over cake. Spread frosting to cover.
6. Refrigerate until frosting sets.

⇸ Pineapple Pudding ⇷

Anne Marchesani has many recipes that were passed down from one family member to another. But after working with senior citizens as a volunteer for 25 years, Anne has even more tips than she does recipes. Fortunately for me, Anne has shared many of them during the past seven years.

Dish up: 8 to 12 servings
Construction time: 10 minutes

Cooking time: 35 to 45 minutes
Paraphernalia: Large bowl, small microwave-safe bowl, 9- by 13-inch baking dish, microwave

INGREDIENTS:

8 slices bread, crusts removed and cubed
1 stick butter, melted
3 eggs, lightly beaten
1/2 cup milk
3/4 cup sugar
1 20-ounce can crushed pineapple in natural juice
Pinch nutmeg

To make:

1. Preheat oven to 350 degrees. Coat baking dish with nonstick cooking spray.
2. Remove crust from bread and cut into cubes. Toss in large bowl.
3. Melt butter in a small, microwave-safe bowl in the microwave for about 20 seconds.
4. Add melted butter to bread cubes.
5. In melted butter bowl, slightly beat eggs.
6. Add eggs, milk, sugar and pineapples to bread cubes, mixing well. Pour mixture into baking dish.
7. Sprinkle nutmeg on top.
8. Bake, uncovered, for about 45 minutes, or until the edges are brown. (Check after 35 minutes.)

Snacks and Munchies

→ Cookie Kisses in a Hurry ←

Need a quick cookie? Here's Dawn Check's recipe for cookies that look like homemade but aren't. Dawn uses this fast and furious recipe to make "omigod-I-forgot-the-bake-sale" cookies!

Dish up: 2 dozen cookies   Cooking time: 8 to 10 minutes
Construction time: 5 to 7 minutes   Paraphernalia: Mini-muffin pan

INGREDIENTS:
1 tube refrigerated chocolate chip cookie dough
1 bag Hershey's Kisses

To make:

1. Preheat oven to 350 degrees.
2. Slice cookie dough according to package directions. Press dough into the cups of the mini-cupcake pan.
3. Top with a Hershey's Kisses. (Be sure to unwrap the candies first!)
4. Bake 8 to 10 minutes.

☀ Cracker Cookies ☀

Even though Dawn Check is a frantic woman herself, she continually seeks out recipes, as cooking is one of her passions, just as is her role as a pastor and her church.

Dish up: 15 to 18 servings
Construction time: 10 minutes, plus chilling time

Cooking time: 7 minutes
Paraphernalia: 3-quart pan, baking sheet

INGREDIENTS:

35 saltine crackers
2 sticks butter (not margarine)
1 cup brown sugar
1 cup milk chocolate chips
1 cup semisweet chocolate chips

To make:

1. Coat baking sheet with nonstick cooking spray. Preheat oven to 350 degrees.
2. Lay saltine crackers on sheet, covering it completely with crackers.
3. In a pan, melt butter over medium-low heat. Add brown sugar to melted butter, stirring constantly. Bring to a boil.
4. Remove pan from heat and pour sugar/butter mixture over saltines, covering completely.
5. Bake for 7 minutes. Do not bake longer, because it can burn easily.
6. Remove and sprinkle chips on top. Let them sit for 1 to 2 minutes to soften. Then "ice" by spreading the chocolate over the top.
7. Dawn likes to cut her cookies with a pizza cutter while they are still hot.
8. Once cut, let the sheet cool to room temperature, then put it in the refrigerator to harden the cookies.
9. Dawn takes the baking sheet out and cuts the cookies again, then keeps them stored in the refrigerator.

Change It Up: Make a double batch so you can freeze one. Dawn likes to eat her cookies straight from the freezer.

✷ Fruit in a Bucket ✦

Serving fruit from a pail is a fun way to get the kids to eat items from this food group. Be sure to make the fruit dip recipe to go with the fruit. Serve the dip in a miniature bucket. These are easily found at your local dollar store.

Dish up: 10 to 12 servings
Construction time: 10 minutes

Cooking time: 0
Paraphernalia: Kid's toy bucket

INGREDIENTS:

1 pound strawberries
1 pound seedless grapes
1 cantaloupe
1 pineapple

To make:
1. Wash fruit.
2. Slice strawberries, disposing of stem.
3. Cut cantaloupe into chunks, slicing rind away.
4. Cut pineapple into chunks, slicing rind away.
5. Mix fruit together in the bucket. Serve with a shovel for scooping.

Jazz It Up: Add blueberries, raspberries or another favorite fruit or two.

Dress It Down: Use canned pineapple chunks instead of a fresh one. Buy precut fruit from your grocer's salad bar.

We Go Good Together: Scrumptious Fruit Dip

✷ Scrumptious Fruit Dip ✦

This dip is so scrumptious, adults have been know to eat it by the spoonful. Watch out for double-dippers.

Dish up: 10 to 12 servings
Construction time: 5 minutes

Cooking time: 0
Paraphernalia: Miniature bucket or
small bowl

INGREDIENTS:

1 8-ounce package cream cheese, softened

1 13-ounce jar Marshmallow Fluff

½ teaspoon cinnamon

¼ teaspoon nutmeg

To make:

1. Blend cream cheese and Marshmallow Fluff until creamy.
2. Blend spices into mixture.
3. Put dip in a miniature bucket or small bowl.
4. Dress It Down: Cut the amount of spices in half.

✦ Grandma Roediger's Snickerdoodles ✦

In some homes, snickerdoodles are the cookie jar staple. Frantic father Michael Roediger offers his grandmother's much-loved recipe, which makes about six sdozen. Eat some now. Put some in the cookie jar. Freeze some for later.

Dish up: 6 dozen cookies

Construction time: 10 to 15 minutes

Cooking time: 8 to 10 minutes per tray

Paraphernalia: Baking sheet,
2 mixing bowls, small bowl

INGREDIENTS:

½ cup soft shortening

½ cup butter

1½ cups cane sugar

2 eggs

2¾ cups flour

2 teaspoons cream of tartar

1 teaspoon baking soda

1 teaspoon salt

2 tablespoons sugar

2 tablespoons cinnamon

To make:
1. Preheat oven to 400 degrees.
2. Mix shortening, butter, sugar and eggs thoroughly.
3. Mix flour, cream of tartar, soda and salt in a separate bowl and stir until combined.
4. Combine flour mixture and butter mixture, mixing well.
5. Form into balls the size of walnuts.
6. Mix together sugar and cinnamon in a small bowl. Roll balls in sugar and cinnamon mixture.
7. Place dough balls 2 inches apart on ungreased baking sheet.
8. Bake 8 to 10 minutes.

↠ Holiday Mixed Nuts ↞

Eleanor Kane's simple-to-make holiday nuts are always a hit with dinner hosts and houseguests, and they make the house smell wonderful while baking.

Dish up: 2 cups

Construction time: 5 to 7 minutes

Cooking time: 30 minutes

Paraphernalia: Medium bowl, small bowl, baking sheet

INGREDIENTS:

2 cups mixed nuts (walnuts, pecans, almonds and peanuts)
1 egg white
1/4 cup sugar
1 tablespoon cinnamon

To make:
1. Preheat oven to 300 degrees.
2. Coat the nut mixture with the egg white.
3. Combine the sugar and cinnamon and sprinkle over the nuts. Mix until the nuts are evenly coated.
4. Spread on a cookie sheet and bake in oven for 30 minutes.

☞ Kiddie Kookies ☜

These no-bake cookies, aka Kindergarten Kookies, are so easy that the kids can make them with very little help from mom. And they're perfect for a classroom treat.

Dish up: 3 to 4 dozen
Construction time: 10 minutes,
   plus 1 hour chilling time

Cooking time: 3 to 5 minutes
Paraphernalia: Baking sheet,
   3-quart saucepan

INGREDIENTS:

2 cups sugar
1/4 cup cocoa
1/2 cup milk
1/2 cup butter
1 teaspoon vanilla
1/2 cup peanut butter, creamy
3 cups quick-cooking oats

To make:

1. Coat baking sheet with nonstick cooking spray.
2. Put sugar, cocoa, milk, butter, and vanilla in pan. Bring to rolling boil and cook 1 minute.
3. Remove from heat. Add peanut butter and oats. Mix well.
4. Drop from spoon onto baking sheet. (Simplify it: Use a small melon scoop instead of a spoon. Be sure to give the inside of the scoop a squirt with the nonstick cooking spray to make dropping the dough onto the baking sheet easier.)
5. Chill for 1 hour, or until firm.

☞ Pretzel Bars ☜

Here's another yummy treat shared by Lindsey Rankin. When you're feeling really frantic and you must take something with you to a get-together, these cookie bars, which need only 3 minutes in the microwave, are a great option. Keep these ingredients stocked in your pantry (store the cereal, pretzels and M&M's in the freezer) for the last-minute call for you to bring a dish.

Dish up: 15 servings

Construction time: 7 to 10 minutes

Cooking time: 3 minutes

Paraphernalia: 15- by 10-inch baking pan, large microwave-safe bowl, microwave

INGREDIENTS:

1 cup sugar

1 cup light corn syrup

½ cup peanut butter

5 cups crisp rice cereal

2 cups pretzel sticks

1 cup plain M&M's

To make:

1. Coat pan with nonstick cooking spray.

2. In bowl, combine the sugar and corn syrup. Microwave on high for 3 minutes, or until sugar has dissolved.

3. Stir in peanut butter until blended.

4. Add cereal, pretzels and M&M's. Stir until completed coated. Press into baking dish. Cut into bars.

Part Five

Extra Helpings

After a hectic day, your mind is somewhat foggy. Sometimes you need just a little bit of extra help. You'll discover that extra dose of help here, along with a variety of other tips that could ease those frenetic days in the kitchen.

COOKING GLOSSARY

In my original outline for this book, I hadn't planned on including a section explaining cooking terms. My daughter Deanna, one of my kitchen testers, called one day and asked how to brown the meat. Though a little surprised, I explained the simple process. Deanna responded, "I thought so, but if you're writing a cookbook, you need to explain that stuff. There are cooking newbies like me who need a detailed explanation." And I'm sure somewhere along the way, I had to have someone explain it to me, too.

So here you have it—an explanation of various cooking terms and ingredients (that might be uncommon) used in this book.

Bake: Cook by dry heat in an oven.
Baste: Spoon liquid (or use a brush) over meat or poultry occasionally as it cooks.
Beat: Vigorously mix by hand, or use an electric mixer.
Bouillon: A concentrated broth flavoring made in granulated or cube form and found in the spice department.
Broil: Cook with direct, extreme heat in oven.
Brown: Cook on medium-high to high heat (usually raw meat or poultry) on stove top to brown.

Chop: Cut food into small pieces about the size of peas.

Cube: Cut food into 1/2-inch or 1-inch cubes.

Dice: Cut food into tiny cubes, about 1/4-inch in size.

Dot: Scatter small amounts of an ingredient (usually butter) on top of food.

Dredge: Cover food with a coating of bread crumbs, cornstarch or flour.

Drippings: Liquids resulting from meat being cooked.

Egg bath: Beat egg and milk or water together. Dip foods into the mixture. Usually, you dredge foods after dipping them in an egg bath.

Fillet: A piece of meat or fish that does not have bones in it.

Fold: Blend beaten egg whites or whipped cream into a thicker mixture carefully, being sure not to overmix.

Fritters: Vegetables or fish covered with batter and fried, or small, dumpling-like pieces of fried bread (usually corn).

Fry: Cook in oil on stove top.

Fusilli: Small, twisty pasta.

Giblets: Poultry liver, neck and heart often found wrapped in plastic inside the cavity of the bird. Cook separately or use for making gravy.

Grease and flour: Coat pan (usually a cake pan) with shortening, then dust with flour.

Knead: Press the dough with the heel of the hand, fold it over, turn it, and repeat the process until the dough is homogenous and elastic.

Marinate: Soak foods (fish, meat, poultry or tofu) in a liquid mixture (usually with spices added) to increase the flavor and/or tenderness. Place foods in the refrigerator to marinate for the amount of time specified.

Mince: Finely cut into tiny pieces.

Orzo: Small pasta that is shaped like rice.

Parboil: Precook in boiling water.

Pare: Cut off the skin or peel.

Pastina: Tiny pieces of pasta, often used in soups.

Prosciutto: Italian spiced ham, usually thinly sliced.

Puree: Blend food until it has a thick, smooth consistency.

Rest: Allow meat or poultry to sit for 10 to 15 minutes after cooking to let the juices distribute evenly.

Roast: Cook with dry heat (usually in the oven).

Sauté: Cook food, usually in a small amount of oil, in a skillet on the stove top, stirring frequently.

Score: Make shallow cuts with a sharp knife (sometimes a fork) to make decorative lines.

Shred: Finely cut or tear into thin threads.

Sift: Allow dry ingredients to fall through a fine mesh cup called a sifter to aerate them and remove any lumps.

Simmer: Cook at low heat. Do not boil.

Sliver: Thin slice, such as slivered almonds.

Steam: Cook by steam only. Put food in a steamer pot (with holes in bottom), then place steamer pot over a pot of boiling water.

Stir-fry: Cook quickly, usually with a bit of oil, over high heat, stirring constantly.

Stock: Liquid that has been used to boil meat, poultry or vegetables. Used for making soups and other dishes.

Tofu: Food made from soybeans, with no particular flavor, that is often pressed into a cake form.

Whip: Beat food rapidly, making it light and increasing its volume.

Whisk: Briskly whip with a wire whisk. (A fork can be used as well.)

Wrap: Sandwich fixings rolled in a tortilla.

Zest: Outer part of citrus rind.

RUNDOWN ON HERBS

In your frantic pantry, you should have many, if not all, of these herbs. This summary gives a brief lists of what herbs complement what dishes. For more information about herbs, check out *Herbs for all Seasons* by Karen Patterson and *The Complete Book of Herbs* by Lesley Bremness.

Allspice: The ground dried berries of an evergreen. Used with desserts, eggs, fresh fruits, meat dishes, soups and vegetables.

Basil: Great in breads, broiled and roasted meats, dips, eggs, fish, pasta, poultry, salad and dressings, sauces, stuffing and veggies.

Caraway: Used in dips, meat loaves, pot roasts, salads, sauces, spreads, stews, stuffings and veggies.

Cayenne: Spicey and used in dips, chili, cream soups, Mexican dishes and spreads.

Chives: Has a mild flavor of onion. Add to cream cheese, fish dishes, omelets, salads, sandwiches and soups.

Cumin: A bitter, meaty flavor with an Asian tone. Use sparingly in casseroles. Great in chili.

Dill: Add in beef, breads, dips, egg dishes, lamb, poultry, salads and dressings, sauces, seafood and veggies.

Ginger: Can replace garlic in many dishes. Popular in Asian dishes. Use in breads, chicken dishes, cookies, fruits, meats, marinades, salad dressings and vegetables.

Mustard: Can add flavor to corned beef, dips, dressings, egg dishes, marinades, sauces and sauerkraut.

Nutmeg: A strong flavor used in breads, cookies, custards, egg dishes, fruit desserts, puddings, stuffed cabbage and stuffing.

Paprika: A sweet and colorful seasoning used in Hungarian cuisine. Add to creamy dishes, meat sauces and as a garnish for hors d'oeuvres.

Oregano: Great addition to casseroles, egg dishes, garlic toast, meat, tomato sauce, poultry, pies, salads, seafood, stews and vegetables.

Sage: Used in cheese, meat and vegetable dishes and in poultry and meat stuffings.

Sesame seed: A rich, nutty flavor and used roasted as an accent in dishes.

Thyme: Used in casseroles, meat loaves, meat dishes, salads and vegetables.

WINE AND FOOD GUIDE

For company and special occasions, pair up wine and food so they complement each other. Here are some basic suggestions of wines to match with different foods. If you crave more detailed information about wines, click on www.vinography.com or www.wine-lovers-page.com. Or check out *The Wine Bible* by Karen MacNeil.

- Salad: A light dry white, such as sauvignon blanc, is a good choice for salads, especially those with lemon- or vinegar-based dressings.
- Fish dishes: A dry white tastes great with fish cooked in a creamy sauce.
- Egg meals: A sparkling wine is a perfect match for meals made with eggs.
- Rich and saucy: A medium- to full-bodied white will best suit a rich, creamy sauce dish. Chardonnay is a good match. Avoid very fruity wines.
- Hot and spicy: Beer compliments spicy food better than wine.
- Fruit plates: Sweet whites or sparkling wines are a good match for fruit dishes.
- Hearty comfort foods: A full-bodied red wine, such as cabernet sauvignon, needs to be teamed up with a heavy meal.

The following chart is a quick reference, listing various kinds of wines and what foods to serve with them so they will complement each other.

WHITE WINES
- Chardonnay: Serve with chicken, fish and grilled summer foods.
- Riesling: Serve with Chinese food, roasted chicken and lightly spiced foods.
- Sauternes: Serve with rich foods like dessert, duck, pâté and Roquefort cheese.
- Sauvignon blanc: Serve with fish, poultry or shellfish.

RED WINES
- Beaujolais: Serve with meats and poultry.
- Beaujolais Nouveau: Serve with turkey.
- Bordeaux: Serve with red meats.

- Burgundy: Serve with game, red meat, pork, poultry and salmon.
- Cabernet sauvignon: Serve with hearty meats, poultry and stews.
- Chianti: Serve with hamburgers, tomato-based pasta meals, pizza and steaks.
- Merlot: Serve with hens, lamb, sausages and stews.
- Pinot noir: Serve with cheese, ham, pork, poultry, salmon and veal.

Zinfandel: Serve with hamburgers, game, lamb, steaks and veal.

SPARKLING WINE

Champagne: Serve with most foods, including desserts.

Rosé: Serve with lighter foods.

Wine Drinking Order

Here are a few practical pointers regarding what types of wine to drink in what order.

- Serve inexpensive wine before expensive. Taking a step back in quality will be very noticeable.
- Drink dry wine before sweet. A dry wine will taste acidic after a glass of sweet wine.
- Sip light wines before full-bodied ones, as the weighty wines will overpower the lighter ones.
- In wine drinking, the young comes before the old.

FOOD-STAIN REMOVAL CHART

You're in the kitchen, scrambling to serve and eat dinner before you need to leave for your child's soccer game. In your mad rush, you drop the spoon into the tomato-based sauce, which splatters all over your white top. (Of course, Murphy's Law dictates that it would be red against white.) Food accidents are bound to happen when you're hurrying, and as a frantic woman, you're *always* hurrying. (Better food accidents than broken-toe accidents, like my friend Deanne. Twice she broke her toe when she was in a hurry to get dinner on the table. The first time, she dropped a roaster holding a whole turkey on her foot. The second time, she dropped the kitchen table bench on her foot.)

Here are tips for removing common food stains. PS: Though the wash suggestions recommend hot suds, read the garment's care instructions before using hot water. PPS: If you need additional stain-removal advice, check out *The Royal Guide to Spot and Stain Removal* by Linda Cobb.

STAIN	PRETREAT TIP	WASH SUGGESTION
Chocolate	Soak in weak solution of bleach or hydrogen peroxide.	Wash in hot suds.
Coffee/Tea	Stretch fabric taut over a bowl. From 3 feet above, pour boiling water through stain.	Wash in hot suds.
Egg	Scrape off excess. Soak in cool water.	Wash in warm suds.
Peach/pear cherry/plum	Sponge with cool water. Rub lightly with glycerin. Let stand several hours. Apply a few drops of vinegar. Rinse.	Wash in warm suds.
Berries	Same as coffee stain.	Wash as usual.
Meat juices	Soak in cool water.	Wash in hot suds.
Milk/cream	Sponge with cool water or soak.	Wash in hot suds.
Mustard	Sponge with cool water. Rub with warm glycerin.	Wash in hot suds.
Soft drinks	Sponge with cool water or with a solution of equal parts alcohol and water.	Wash in hot suds.
Tomato	Sponge with cool water.	Wash in hot suds.
Ketchup	Rub with glycerin. Let stand 30 minutes.	Wash in hot suds.
Wine, red	Mix equal parts liquid dishwashing soap with hydrogen peroxide. Pour over stain. Let sit as a presoak.	Wash as usual.

RESOURCES

Here is a bonus section that will help alleviate any problems that might occur in your kitchen. First, in the Honorable Mention section, you'll find the books, newsletters, companies, organizations, movies and Web sites mentioned throughout the book, so you'll fingers don't have to do the walking through the frantic pages.

In the Additional Resources section, you'll find a plethora of URLs that can answer your questions, from the shelf life of canned goods to the freezer life of turkey products, plus a whole lot in between.

Honorable Mention

These associations, books, companies, movies, newsletters and Web sites were mentioned throughout the pages of The Frantic Woman's Guide to Feeding Family and Friends. Here they are in one place for your convenience.

Books and Newsletters
BoxCar Children Surprise Island by Gertrude Chandler Warner (Albert Whitman & Company, 1989); www.awhitmanco.com
Brave Potatoes by Toby Speed (Putnam Juvenile, 2000); www.penguin-putnam.com
Cat Poems by Dave Crawley (Wordsong/Boyds Mills Press, 2005); www.boydsmillspress.com
Common Sense Organizing by Debbie Williams (Champion Press, 2005); www.organizedtimes.com
The Complete Book of Herbs by Lesley Bremness (Studio Books, 1994); www.us.penguingroup.com
The Confident Coach's Guide to Teaching Basketball by Beverly Breton Carroll (The Lyons Press, 2003); www.globepequot.com
Elbows Off the Table, Napkin in the Lap, No Video Games During Dinner by Carol McD. Wallace (St. Martin's Griffin, 1996); www.st.martins.com
Four Sides, Eight Nights: A New Spin on Hanukkah by Rebecca Tova Ben-Zvi (Roaring Book Press, 2005); www.macmillan.com

The Frantic Woman's Guide to Life by Mary Jo Rulnick and Judith Schneider (Warner Books, 2004); www.twbg.com; www.maryjorulnick.com

Gatherings Newsletter by Beverly Breton Carroll and Alrie McNiff Daniels; PO Box 2051, Natick, MA, 01760

Green Eggs and Ham by Dr. Seuss (Random House, 1960); www.randomhouse.com

Handy Kitchen Tips by Monica Resinger (Homemaker Journal); www.HomemakerJournal.com

Herbs for all Seasons by Karen A. Patterson (ACW Press, 1999); www.acwpress.com

If You Give a Mouse a Cookie by Laura Joffe Numeroff (Laura Geringer, 1996); www.harperchildrens.com; www.lauranumeroff.com

The Kitchen Witch by Annette Blair (Berkley Sensation, 2004); www.annetteblair.com

The Lemonade Babysitter by Karen Waggoner (Joy Street. Books, 1992) www.karenwaggoner.com

Little House on the Prairie by Laura Ingalls Wilder (HarperTropy, 1953); www.harperchildrens.com

The Royal Guide to Spot and Stain Removal by Linda Cobb (Pocket, 2001); www.pocketbooks.com; www.queenofclean.com

The Wine Bible by Karen MacNeil (Workman Publishing, 2001); www.workman.com; www.winefoodandfriends.com

365 Manners Kids Should Know by Sheryl Eberly (Three Rivers Press, 2001); www.randomhouse.com

We Eat Dinner in the Bathtub by Angela Shelf Medearis (Cartwheel, 1999); www.scholastic.com; www.medearis.com

Working at Home While the Kids Are There, Too by Loriann Hoff Oberlin (Career Press, 1997); www.careerpress.com; www.loriannoberlin.com

Writing for Quick Cash by Loriann Hoff Oberlin (American Management Association, 2003); www.amanet.org; www.loriannoberlin.com

Your Own Big Bed by Rita Bergstein (Viking, 2006); www.penguinputnam.com

MOVIES

Because of Winn-Dixie (Walden Media, 2005); www.walden.com

Charlie and the Chocolate Factory and *Willy Wonka & the Chocolate Factory* (Warner Bros., 2005 and 1971 respectively); www.warnerbros.com

Harry Potter and the Sorcerer's Stone (Warner Bros., 2001); www.warnerbros.com

Houseguest (Buena Vista, 1995); www.bvimovies.com

The Sandlot (Twentieth Century Fox, 1993); www.foxmovies.com

Scooby-Doo 2 (Warner Bros., 2004); www.warnerbros.com

Shrek 2 and *Shrek* (Dreamworks, 2004 and 2001, respectively); www.shrek.com; www.dreamworks.com

COMPANIES AND ORGANIZATIONS

Alameda County Waste Management Authority & Source Reduction and Recycling Board, Alameda County, California; www.stopwaste.org

Let's Dish: Make and Take Family Meals, founders Darcy Olson and Ruth Lundquist; www.letsdish.com

Pennsylvania Resources Council, 412-488-7490; www.prc.org

WEB SITES

Allens Naturally: www.aliensnaturally.com

Community Supported Agriculture (CSA): www.sare.org/csa; www.nal.usda.gov/afsic/csa

The Cook's Thesaurus: www.foodsubs.com

Earth Friendly Products: www.ecos.com

Ecover: www.ecover.com

Farmer's Market: www.ams.usda.gov/farmersmarkets

Fitness and Freebies: www.fitnessandfreebies.com

Greeting Card Writing: www.greetingcardwriting.com

Main Street Mom: www.mainstreetmom.com

The Manners Lady: www.themannersclub.com

Mary Jo Rulnick: www.maryjorulnick.com

Movie Lovers Clubhouse: www.movieloversclubhouse.com

National Hot Dog and Sausage Council: hot-dog.org

National Turkey Federation: www.eatturkey.com
The National Women's Health Information Center: www.4woman.gov
Seventh Generation: www.seventhgeneration.com
Sun & Earth: www.sunandearth.com
Vinography: www.vinography.com
Wine Lovers' Page: www.wine-lovers-page.com
Women's Business Network: www.womensbusinessnetwork.org

Additional Resources

The following associations, organizations and Web sites are listed as additional resources for your convenience.

COOKWARE AND KITCHEN TOOLS
These sites offer cookware, kitchen and organizational tools.
Chef's Resource: www.chefsresource.com
CorningWare: www.corningware.com
International Dutch Oven Society: www.idos.org
Stacks and Stacks: www.stacksandstacks.com

COUPONS AND SAMPLE WEB SITES
These sites offer coupons for your favorite products and more. Click and print to save money at the grocery store. Also, visit the sites that offer free sample products. This is a fun task the kids will love doing for you. Samples arrive in your mailbox within a few week.

SmartSource: Smartsource.com
Valpak: Valpak.com
Value Page: Valuepage.com
Start Sampling: www.startsampling.com
Trialsize: www.trialsize.com

FOOD-RELATED WEB SITES
These food-related sites offer the latest news regarding their specific product.
American Beverage Association: www.ameribev.org
American Egg Board: www.aeb.org
Beef Industry Resource, National Cattleman's Beef Association: www.beef.org

Butterball Turkey Talk-Line; 800-Butterball; www.butterball.com

Canned Food Alliance: www.mealtime.org

Empire Kosher Poultry Customer Hotline; 800-267-4734; www.empirekosher.com

Food Products Association (formerly known as National Food Processors Association): www.fpa-food.org

Food Safety Consortium: www.uark.edu/depts/fsc

International Dairy Foods Association: www.idfa.org

National Association of College & University Food Services: www.nacufs.org

National Chicken Council: www.eatchicken.com

National Dairy Development Board: www.milkmagic.com

National Fisheries Institute: www.nfi.org

National Frozen & Refrigerated Foods Association: www.nfraweb.org

National Grocers Association: www.nationalgrocers.org

National Nutritional Foods Association: www.nnfa.org

National Pasta Association: www.ilovepasta.org

National Pork Board: www.theotherwhitemeat.com

National Turkey Federation: www.eatturkey.com

New York Apple Country: www.nyapplecountry.com

Produce for Better Health Foundation: www.5aday.org

Snack Food Association: www.sfa.org

United Fresh Fruit & Vegetable Association: www.uffva.org

USA Rice Federation: www.usarice.com

U.S. Department of Agriculture's Food Safety and Inspection Service: www.fsis.usda.gov

HEALTH-RELATED WEB SITES

American Diabetes Association: www.diabetes.org

American Heart Association: www.americanheart.org

American Obesity Association: www.obesity.org

Susan G. Komen Breast Cancer Foundation: www.komen.org

About the Author

Mary Jo Rulnick, events manager for a national nonprofit organization, has written extensively about home, family and life issues. She is the coauthor of *The Frantic Woman's Guide to Life: A Year's Worth of Hints, Tips and Tricks* (Warner Books, 2004) and a regualr feature writer for Family Digest and *Pittsurgh Parent Magazine*. As a self-taught writer and business entrepreneur, she teaches writing and business courses at her local community college and online at www.writerscollege.com.

She has been a speaker for such organizations as Viacom, Pennsylvania Governor's Conference for Women, Komen Race for a Cure, American Heart Association, and Romance Writer's of America. She speaks about balancing work and family and reaching personal goals. Rulnick has been a guest on many radio and television shows, and her books have been featured in *USA Today, Real Simple, Family Circle, Woman's Day, Allure,* and *Writer's Digest Magazine*.

Rulnick has served on the board of seven nonprofit organizations and has helped with everything from organizing a day camp to building a community playground to raising funds for a women's shelter.

She is the founder of MaryJoRulnick.com, a Web site that offers real tips for busy people. She lives in Pittsburgh, Pennsylvania, with her husband and two children.

To contact Mary Jo Rulnick, email her: MaryJo@MaryJoRulnick.com. Or write to her ar: P.O. Box 14282, Pittsburgh, PA 15239